Symbol
&
Sense

Writing Instruction
for
Middle School

Stephen R. Hawley, M.A.

READ

Read Press, New York

Symbol & Sense
Writing Instruction for Middle School

Read Press LLC
305 Madison Ave.
Suite 449
New York, NY 10165
http://www.readpress.net

ISBN-10: 0-9815025-0-4
ISBN-13: 978-0-9815025-0-2

Library of Congress Control Number: 2006935834

First Printing, December, 2006
Second Printing, March, 2007
Third Printing, August, 2007
Fourth Printing, February, 2008

Stephen R. Hawley, M.A., has been an English teacher for over fifteen years. He is the author of several novels and short stories. Hawley served in the Navy as a Russian translator and passed the Army's proficiency test for Japanese. In addition to his public school teaching experience, Hawley has worked as a consultant in Japan, where he developed and taught English courses to executives of Ricoh and Unisys. Hawley is a member of the National Council of Teachers of English, the Mystery Writers of America, and the Linguistic Society of America.

Read Press and the "READ dot" logo are trademarks belonging to
Read Press LLC

Printed in the United States of America

Acknowledgments

The author thanks and acknowledges the help of

Ronald J. Hawley, PhD
John A. Hawley, PhD
&
Margaret E. Wallace, J.D.

in the preparation of this text.

Contents

Chapter 1

Communication

People love to talk, read, write, listen, and think. All these activities have one thing in common: they are forms of communication. *Communication* is the exchange of thoughts or information. Books, TV, and magazines are all forms of communication. Talking is a form of communication, so is sign language. We communicate even when we are not speaking. A laugh communicates happiness. We might roll our eyes to communicate boredom.

Suppose you are sitting in a dark room with your eyes closed. The room is completely silent. You are alone with your thoughts. Are you communicating? Yes! You are communicating with yourself.

Try to imagine a world with no communication. Even our most basic needs would go unmet. How could we tell others we were hungry? How could we warn them of danger? How would we be able to think to ourselves?

It would be impossible to live in a world without communication. Communication is a basic human need. We all communicate with each other every day, and we communicate with ourselves every time we think.

Generally speaking, there are two forms of communication: nonverbal and verbal.

Nonverbal communication
Nonverbal communication is communication that does not require words.

For example, a smile might communicate happiness. A yawn

might communicate boredom. The sound of crying might communicate sadness.

When we hear a siren, we are listening to nonverbal communication. The siren might be warning us of danger. A fire truck might be headed our way.

Traffic lights are another form of nonverbal communication. Red lights tell us to stop; green lights tell us to go. Yellow signals caution.

One interesting form of nonverbal communication is body language. When we gesture or make a face we are using body language. Oftentimes, we can tell whether people are happy or sad simply by looking at their faces or the way they are holding their bodies. Entire books have been written about body language. A careful observer can tell much about a situation simply by looking at body language.

Of course, we use more than just body language to communicate. When we have an idea, we like to share it with others. Usually, we use words to communicate. Communication which requires words is called verbal communication.

Verbal communication

Verbal communication is communication which requires words. Reading, writing, and speaking are forms of verbal communication.

When we talk with a friend, we are using verbal communication. When we write a report we are using verbal communication. Any communication that requires words is verbal communication.

This book is a writing manual. It will focus on improving writing skills. Therefore, this book will be dealing with verbal communication.

Exercise 1-1

Number your work paper 1-5. Write short answers to the questions.
1. What is communication?
2. What kind of communication uses words?
3. What is the difference between verbal and nonverbal communication?
4. Why is body language considered nonverbal communication?
5. Would a report on Mars be considered verbal or nonverbal communication?

Thinking

Thinking is a mysterious process. We all do it everyday, but no one can really say what thinking is. One thing is certain, though, thinking is very important to writers. When we are writing, we have time to think about exactly what we want to say. We also have time to consider how other people might understand what we are writing. Clear thinking leads to clear writing.

We might believe that video tapes and photographs are just as good as writing. In fact, writing is a type of photograph. A photo captures what is seen. Writing captures what is thought.

Ambiguous communication

Ambiguous means unclear. *Ambiguous communication* is unclear communication. It is confusing. Something that is ambiguous might have more than one meaning. We can't tell what it means. Here is an ambiguous word:

Live

This word has two possible pronunciations, and two possible meanings.
*I enjoy **live** music.*
*We **live** near the school.*

When writing we must make our meaning clear the first time. Ambiguous writing is unclear. Ambiguous writing confuses the reader.

Homophones

Homophones are words which are pronounced the same way but are spelled differently and have totally different meanings. Look.
to   two   too

These words sound alike but they have different spellings and different meanings. Of course, we don't notice errors with homophones when people are speaking, but when we are writing, incorrect use of homophones can lead to ambiguous situations. Look.
There are two too many to count.

Here's another version:
There are too, too many to count.

Spelling correctly is an important part of written communication. Two common homophones are the words *its* and *it's*. The word *its* shows a form of ownership. Look.

The dog wagged its tail.

The word *it's* means *it is*. This kind of word has a special name. It is called a contraction. A *contraction* is a shortened form of a word. Notice the little mark in the middle of *it's*. The mark is called an *apostrophe*. The apostrophe serves a function in this word. It takes the place of the letter *i* in the word *is*. Look.

it's = it is

By remembering that the apostrophe is taking the place of the letter *i*, we will be able to remember that *it's* means *it is*.

Exercise 1-2
Number your work paper 1-10. Write the word that correctly completes each sentence.

> (Its - ownership) The dog scratched ***its*** ear.
> (It's - contraction) ***It is***.

1. (Its, It's) time to go home.
2. The mouse ran into (its, it's) hole.
3. (Its, It's) home destroyed by a flood, the beaver built a new dam.
4. (Its, It's) left engine in flames, the jet made a safe landing.
5. People agree that (its, it's) wrong to lie.
6. Grab the TV by (its, it's) handles.
7. The Ford lost (its, it's) transmission fluid.
8. (Its, It's) not too late to check if (its, it's) working,
9. (Its, It's) important to remember that (its, it's) important not to forget.
10. There is (its, it's) home.

Exercise 1-3
Number your work paper 1-10. Write either *it's* or *its*.

1. The Loch Ness Monster is known for _____ serpentine neck.
2. _____ snake-like shape is well known.

3. _____ an international legend.
4. Some people think _____ a plesiosaur.
5. Others think _____ a fake.
6. Loch Ness is known for _____ deep water.
7. _____ too cold to swim for long in Loch Ness.
8. _____ interesting to study _____ history.
9. Loch Ness is famous because _____ home to the Loch Ness monster.
10. _____ fame has grown over the years.

Summary

✓ Communication is a basic human need. There are two types of communication: nonverbal and verbal. Body language is a type of nonverbal communication. Writing is verbal communication.

✓ Ambiguous means unclear, and ambiguous writing confuses readers.

✓ Certain words, called homophones, are words which sound alike, but which are spelled differently and have different meanings.

✓ *It's* means *it is*.

Chapter 2

Symbols

We communicate to express our thoughts. One way we communicate is by writing. We also talk to each other. Writing and speaking are forms of verbal communication. Another form of communication, one which does not require words, is called nonverbal communication. We communicate in different ways, but we are always communicating our thoughts.

In the previous chapter we mentioned that thinking is a mysterious process. No one can really say how we think. For example, do we think in words or pictures?

As writers, it is important to consider how people think.

One way to describe the way people think is to say that people think in symbols.

What are symbols? *Symbols* are objects that represent ideas.

For example, an American flag is an object. We can touch it. We can see it. It is an object, but it is also a symbol. To millions of people the American flag represents hope and freedom. Hope and freedom are ideas. Therefore, the flag is an object that represents ideas. It is a symbol.

Words
Words are symbols, too. Let's look at the word *dog* as an example. We

all know what a dog is. The written word *dog* is not a real dog. The word *dog* is a symbol. When we read the word *dog* we form a picture of a dog in our minds. The word *dog* is a symbol. In this book, we will say that words are symbols.

Everyone recognizes the word *dog*, but if we were asked to draw a picture of a dog, we would all draw different pictures. This is because when we read, or hear, the word *dog* we all form our own idea of a dog in our own individual minds. On the other hand, if we were all presented with pictures of dogs, we would have no trouble recognizing them as dogs.

When we write the word *dog*, we communicate the idea of an actual dog to our audience. It is important to remember that everyone has their own individual mental picture of a dog. Everyone thinks differently. As writers, we share our ideas with others who think differently than we do.

As writers, our job is to make our thoughts clear to others.

We might write the word *dog* while thinking of a German shepherd, but a person who reads our writing might think of a poodle.

Always remember that everyone thinks in their own way.

We must think clearly before we can write clearly.

When we write clearly, others will understand our thoughts.

Exercise 2-1

Number your work paper 1-5. Write short answers to the following questions.

1. What is a word?
2. Name two types of communication.
3. The word *dog* is a _____ for a real dog.
4. Everyone _____ in their own way.
5. We must think clearly before we can write _____

Our audience

Our readers are our audience. Think of a theater filled with people who have come to see a movie. At the beginning of the movie, every member of the audience expects to understand the movie they are about to see. It is the same with our writing. Our audience expects to understand what we have written.

Now, suppose the movie begins. It is out of focus. There is

something wrong with the sound, and we can't exactly hear what his being said. We lose interest and leave the theater.

Just as an audience will lose interest in a movie which they can't understand, our readers will not read our writing if what we write confuses them.

Our job as writers is to communicate our thoughts clearly in writing.

We write for an audience. Our audience will judge how well we have done our job.

In this course, we will follow two simple rules for writing:

1.) We will always write for our audience.

2.) The teacher is the most important member of the audience.

Exercise 2-2

Number your work paper 1-5. Write short answers to the following questions.

1. What is communication?
2. What are the two types of communication?
3. Words are _____
4. Whom do we write for?
5. The most important member of our audience is our _____

Speaking and Writing

Writing is not the same thing as speaking. Writing is not the same as a conversation.

When speaking to others in face-to-face situations, nonverbal communication adds to the force of our words. We can make faces or roll our eyes. Waving our hands might help us make a point.

The word *converse* means to speak. It helps form the word conversation. A conversation is a talk.

A conversation with a friend or a teacher may move rapidly, leaving us little time to organize our thoughts. This may lead to ambiguous communication. Ambiguous communication is unclear communication. While conversing, we may misspeak, or say the wrong thing. We may confuse those who are listening to us.

How many times have you found yourself waving your hands around while trying to explain something you've just said? How many times have you watched someone scratch their head as you tried to make a point clear?

Luckily, during conversation, we can slow down and explain our meaning. We can clear up our ambiguous statements.

Furthermore, when we are speaking, no one is checking our spelling. Your friend might say, "The wind blew it past here." Look at how someone might write what was said. It makes no sense.

The wind blue it passed hear.

When writing we must make our meaning clear the first time. We are unable to use body language to make ourselves understood. A teacher must be able to understand our writing the first time she reads it. If our writing is confusing or ambiguous, our meaning will not be understood. Ambiguous writing is unclear and confuses the reader.

Remember, we always write for our audience. Our audience does not think in the same way that we do. We can help our audience understand our meaning by using clear words (symbols) to express ourselves.

Punctuation marks

Punctuation marks are symbols that help make our meaning clear. Look.

John saw a horse

This sentence is missing a mark of punctuation at the end. *End marks of punctuation* are punctuation marks that come at the end of a sentence. There are only three end marks of punctuation:

. (period)
? (question mark)
! (exclamation mark)

By adding the end marks to the original sentence, we can make three new sentences with different meanings. Look.

John saw a horse. (statement)
John saw a horse? (question)
John saw a horse! (exclamation)

Without an end mark, the original sentence, *John saw a horse*, is ambiguous. It is unclear because it can be read in three different ways. As writers, we must use the tools we are given, words and punctuation marks, to make our meaning clear.

In order to make sense, we must be certain to use correct words. We know that *its* and *it's* are not the same word. In fact, the word *it's* means *it is*.

Two other homophones (words which sound the same) are *there* and *their*.

The word *there* often begins sentences. It doesn't seem to have any real meaning. Look.

> **There** *is a bird in the tree.*
> **There** *are seven books on the shelf.*

The word *their* shows ownership. Look.

> **Their** *house is on Elm Street.*
> **Their** *dog is named Spot.*

Exercise 2-3

Number your work paper 1-10. Copy the sentences. Insert the proper word, either *there* or *their*.

1._____ are seven boys in the class.
2._____ dog is in the yard.
3._____ is a dog in 4. _____ yard
5._____ dog is 6._____ in 7._____
yard.
8._____ were dogs 9._____ in 10._____
yard.

Homophones are words that sound the same.

It is important that we spell homophones correctly so that our writing won't be ambiguous.

Exercise 2-4

Number your work paper 1-5. Write the correct word.

1. It was (to, too) hot to play.
2. The wind (blue, blew) through the trees.
3. Tim (passed, past) the football.
4. John likes one particular (seen, scene) in the movie.
5. It was time for the crew to (meat, meet).

In the next chapter, we will look at some basic rules for using

17

words and punctuation correctly.

Summary

- ✓ Symbols are objects used to represent ideas. Words and pictures are symbols, so are punctuation marks.
- ✓ We write for our audience, and our teacher is the most important member of our audience.
- ✓ Writing is not the same as speaking. When we converse with others, we can use body language to make our meaning clear, but we can't use body language when we write.
- ✓ As writers, our tools are words, punctuation, and clear thinking. Thinking clearly will lead to clear, unambiguous writing.
- ✓ *There* is often used to start sentences. It seems to have no real meaning.
- ✓ *Their* shows ownership.
- ✓ Homophones are words that sound the same.

Chapter 3

Conventions

Conventions are rules. When we speak, we follow the conventions for spoken English. When we write we follow the conventions for written English.

Whenever we use language, we are following rules. Let's return for a moment to the word *dog*. If we are listening to the radio and we hear someone talking about a *dog*, we can be pretty certain that a furry, four-legged creature is being discussed. We may not know exactly what type of dog is being talked about, but we have an understanding of the topic.

We are able to form this understanding because we follow conventions when we speak. One simple convention in English is that the word *dog* is used to describe a certain kind of furry, four-legged creature. The word *cat* describes another kind of creature, as do the words *mouse*, *tiger*, and *cow*.

Suppose one day little Billy wanted to play a practical joke and decided to call a *dog* a *fish*. He told his neighbor things like:

"I took my fish for a walk today."

and

"My fish chased a cat."

The neighbor was confused, to say the least. He couldn't understand what little Billy was saying.

Conventions are rules, and little Billy changed the rules without telling anyone. No wonder the neighbor was confused! He questioned little Billy about the *fish*. At last, little Billy told him it was a joke.

When we write we must follow conventions, too. In fact, we must follow conventions very carefully, because unlike little Billy, after we turn in an assignment, we probably won't be around to answer questions about what we have written. Remember, we write for our audience, and our teacher is the most important member of our audience. Consider this simple sentence that Kristen wrote:

I saw a drib.

What's a drib?

Kristen corrected her sentence to make it clear:

I saw a bird.

It's very easy to make mistakes when we are writing. Changing just one letter in just one word can make an entire sentence impossible to understand.

Here is an important point: words are symbols. The word *dog* is a symbol for the family pet. The word *dig* is a symbol for an action that might involve a shovel.

The two words are both symbols. They both have completely different meanings, although they look quite a bit alike:

dog
dig

Spelling

A word has a shape. The shape is the spelling of the word. When you think about it, words are really nothing more than tiny pieces of art work. Words are collections of lines and squiggles. The lines and squiggles are important, though, and if they are made in the wrong shape or placed in the wrong order, our audience will not understand our meaning. Look.

bat
cat
cut

Changing the order of the letters or changing the shapes of the letters changes the meaning of a word.

Exercise 3-1

Number your work paper 1-10. Each word below can be changed into a new word by simply changing one letter in the word. Decide which letter you want to change. Write the new word on your work paper.

1. Run
2. Bear
3. Best
4. Rage
5. Cane
6. Cook
7. Take
8. Time
9. Golf
10. Seem

As we read through this book we will want to pay attention to certain interesting relationships between words, sentences, and paragraphs.

Words and sentences

One interesting relationship between words and sentences is that they work in much the same way. How?

Words are made up of letters, which give the word meaning; likewise, sentences are made up of words which give the sentence meaning.

Just as changing a letter in a word can change the meaning of the word, so it is with sentences: changing just one word in a sentence can change the entire meaning of the sentence. Look.

John saw a fish.
John was a fish.

When writing in English we must pay attention to the spelling of individual words. We must also pay attention to the order of the words in the sentence.

By shifting just a couple of words in a sentence a whole new sentence with a completely different meaning can be constructed. Look.

John ate the fish.
The fish ate John.

When writing in English, the order of the words is very important. Here are two more conventions about writing sentences:

First, a sentence must express a complete thought. Look.

(*incorrect*) *While walking next to the river.*

(*correct*)   *While walking next to the river, John saw a fish.*

Second, a sentence must begin with a capital letter, and it must end with an end mark of punctuation. By convention there are only three end marks of punctuation.

. *(period)*
? *(question mark)*
! *(exclamation mark)*

The end marks help give the sentence its meaning. Remember our example from the previous chapter:

John saw a horse. (statement)
John saw a horse? (question)
John saw a horse! (exclamation)

Exercise 3-2

Number your work paper 1-10. Rearrange the words in the sentences to create sentences with new meanings. Write the new sentences on your work paper.

Example: John beat Mary at chess.

Answer: Mary beat John at chess.

1. The blue sky turned gray.
2. The Cubs beat the Pirates
3. Diane stood in front of John.
4. The cannibals ate the tour guide.
5. The paper fell on the rock.
6. The dogs dreamed about chasing cats.
7. Planes can fly people.
8. Spiders eat insects.
9. The cat played with the kittens.
10. A bottle is not a can.

Exercise 3-3

Remember, punctuation marks are symbols that help to give meaning to sentences. Read the sentences in Exercise 3-2 again. Imagine that the sentences end with question marks. Read each question aloud. Notice how the question mark changes the meaning of the sentence.

Sentence form

All sentences have special form. That is, they all have a special shape, or structure. We can identify a sentence because of its form. Here is a rule to help us identify sentences.

All sentences begin with a capital letter and end with an end mark of punctuation. There are only three end marks of punctuation:

> . *(period)*
> ? *(question mark)*
> ! *(exclamation mark)*

We do not need to know how to read English in order to identify a sentence. All sentences follow the same form. They begin with a capital letter and end with an end mark of punctuation. Read the nonsense groups of words. Identify the ones which follow the form of sentences.

Exercise 3-4

Number your work paper 1-10. If the group of nonsense words follows the form of a sentence write *Sentence Form*. If the group of words does not follow the form, write *Not Sentence Form*.

Example: Yrw dfg thdjr dkgxxpe?

Answer: Sentence Form

1. Bpor alvnhjrks jsldjf qgjnboe?
2. Nqptaj a dkf w fj;;m.zmnv
3. Qvmpthadkgfjla fjaldk kd fla;
4. A dfjsl vbys gaqlcp jfls vx!
5. zxd posd ghels ww lkj ben?
6. Tdcr fksa bktdf yjspr hf wl
7. Bhx lokkfr slr dstye.
8. S slskdj alfje sthgfls enffba q tpshg t sjkll
9. Gjk!
10. vpor?

Sentences and fragments

All sentences must follow the proper form, but form is not enough.

Remember, sentences are like words. Words have meaning. All sentences must have meaning, too. In the preceding exercise, we identified groups of nonsense words that followed the form of sentences. However, these groups of nonsense words did not have any meaning for us. They are not truly sentences.

Read the following pair of word groups. One is a sentence; the other is not a sentence.

Sentence: *John went to the store.*
Not a sentence: Went to the store.

Notice that both groups begin with a capital letter and end with a period. Only one word group, though, communicates a complete idea:

John went to the store.

This group tells us that someone did something. We know what happened.

The second group, however, only tells us what happened. The words

Went to the store.

do not communicate a complete thought. They do not tell us who went to the store.

A group of words which does not communicate a complete thought is called a *sentence fragment.*

Be careful! A group of words may begin with a capital letter and end with an end mark of punctuation. That is, a group of words may begin with a capital letter and end with either a period (.), a question mark (?), or an exclamation mark (!).

A group of words may look like a sentence, but if the word group does not communicate a complete thought, it is a sentence fragment.

Exercise 3-5

Number your work paper 1-10. Read the following groups of words. All follow the form of sentences. Some, however, are sentence fragments. If the group of words is a sentence write *Sentence.* If the group of words is a sentence fragment write *Fragment.*

   1. Walking very slowly towards the street corner.

2. The President of the United States.
3. Like my friends who enjoy swimming on a hot day.
4. Chasing mice is what cats do.
5. In winter, when we skate on the frozen ponds near our home.
6. What did you say?
7. One of the greatest achievements in human history.
8. The tired athletes stared at the empty field.
9. Together with John, his best friend.
10. It isn't what you say, it's how you say it.

We can often identify sentence fragments when they are standing alone. In the previous exercise, we were able to read each group of words individually and decide whether or not they communicated a complete thought. A group of words which communicates a complete thought, and which begins with a capital letter and ends with a mark of punctuation, is a sentence.

When we write reports or stories, our sentences flow together. In such cases, it is easy to accidentally include sentence fragments. The only way to avoid fragments is to make a conscious effort to focus on reading one sentence at a time. If the sentence communicates a complete idea, it is a sentence; otherwise, it is a fragment. Be careful!

Exercise 3-6

Number your work paper 1-10. Read the following exercises. If they contain fragments write the letter *F* on your paper. If there are no fragments, only sentences, write the letter *S*.

1. The United States has had many Presidents. Including George Washington, Abraham Lincoln, and Teddy Roosevelt.
2. When Washington was President. There were only thirteen States in the Union.
3. Washington helped create a new government. The country would be led by an elected President, not a king.
4. Washington's face can be found on American money. Like the quarter and the dollar bill.
5. Among his many achievements as a young man. Washington was a surveyor.
6. Abraham Lincoln was elected President in 1860. By a majority vote.

25

7. Lincoln led the Union during the Civil War. He kept the United States from becoming two separate countries.
8. Teddy Roosevelt believed in the power of the United States. His motto was, "Talk softly, but carry a big stick."
9. Roosevelt created Yellowstone National Park. Because he believed in conservation.
10. During the Spanish-American War. Roosevelt was a military hero.

Exercise 3-7

Number your work paper 1-10. Each of the groups of words below is a sentence fragment. You will notice three dots (…) either before or after the group of words. On you work paper, add your own words where you see the (…) to make a complete sentence. Follow the example.

Example: …after working in the hot sun.
Answer: We like to drink lemonade after working in the hot sun.

1. …although she didn't want to.
2. Because the TV was so expensive, …
3. If you're going to be late, …
4. …including baseball and football.
5. …as if she were going to faint.
6. Unless you have enough money,…
7. Since Uncle Earl came to live with us, …
8. … while watching TV.
9. When you finish your homework, …
10. … after you take out the trash.

Exercise 3-8

Number your work paper 1-10. Each of the exercises is composed of two word groups. Read each exercise looking for fragments. If the fragment is the first of the two word groups, write *1*. If it is the second, write *2*. If there are no fragments, write *NF*.

1. We couldn't go to the park. Because of the rain.
2. While Tim watched TV. His sister set the table.
3. After the ball game. We all went to a movie.
4. Mary decided to leave early. Because she felt sick.
5. Unless you're sure that you are right. You should remain quiet.
6. James received an "A" in English. He enjoys coming to class.

7. Like everyone else. Joanne enjoys music.
8. Frank has three pets. Including a dog, a cat, and a goldfish.
9. Although he wanted to. Jim was too nervous to ask Kate to the movies.
10. If dimes were dollars. Betty would have five dollars.

When writing paragraphs and reports it is sometimes easy to become careless and include sentence fragments. This usually occurs as a result of trying to write too quickly. Take your time when you write, then check your writing one sentence at a time to be sure that it is free of fragments.

We have spent a lot of time learning about communication. We have learned about verbal, nonverbal, and ambiguous communication. Imagine a world in which you could neither see nor hear. How would you learn to speak? How would you learn to write? How would you communicate your thoughts and feelings?

Helen Keller (1880-1968), was deaf and blind. She overcame her great physical challenges and became an inspiration to millions.

Exercise 3-9

Number your work paper 1-10. Read the article about Helen Keller. There are ten fragments in the article. Write the fragments. (Hint: the number in parentheses in front of each paragraph tells how many fragments are in that particular paragraph.)

Helen Keller

(1)   Helen Keller was born a normal, healthy baby in 1880. At the age of one and a half, though, she suffered a serious illness. As a result of this illness, Helen was left deaf and blind. She was cut off from the world. Although she was just a tiny child.

(2)   Helen's father met with Alexander Graham Bell, the inventor of the telephone. When Helen was five years old. Bell suggested that Mr. Keller contact the Perkins Institution for the Blind. In Boston, Massachusetts.

(2)   A teacher from the Institute, Annie Sullivan, arrived at Helen's house. Helen was six years old. Sullivan communicated with Helen through the sense of touch. Sullivan used a special alphabet. While

pressing her fingers into Helen's hand. She would spell out words. Slowly Helen learned. Three years after Annie Sullivan's arrival, Helen could understand her special sign language. And even read in Braille, a special alphabet for the blind.

(2)   Helen could not learn to speak in the same way other children learn to speak. Because she could not hear. Most children imitate the sounds they hear. When they are learning to speak. Helen hired a special teacher for the deaf to teach her to speak. She learned quickly. By the time she was sixteen, Helen was making plans to attend college. In time, she graduated form Radcliffe College, a famous school.

(2)   Helen Keller devoted her life to helping the blind, and the deaf and blind. She traveled and gave speeches. She became an author and wrote several books. Including <u>The Story of My Life</u>. During World War II. She worked with soldiers who had been blinded.

(1)   Helen Keller became a great communicator. The touch of Annie Sullivan's fingers in Helen's tiny hand opened a new world to the little girl. A world of shared thoughts and dreams. The world is a better place because of Helen Keller.

Exercise 3-10

Number your work paper 1-5. Each of the exercises is composed of two word groups. One of the groups is a sentence; the other word group is a fragment. Write the group that is a sentence on your paper.

1. The story of my life. I was born in Los Angeles, California.
2. Jean collects coins. Including coins from foreign countries.
3. Marty tried to staple his papers. The whole stack of them.
4. Although she hadn't tried. Mary was sure that she could make the jump.
5. I know a lot of people. Like my best friend George.

<u>Another use of the word "There"</u>

We know that the words *their* and *there* are not the same. *Their* shows ownership. *There* begins certain sentences.

There can also be a word of location. Look at the word *there*.

Inside the word *there* you will see the word *here*. This will help you remember that one way to use the word *there* is as a word of location. If you can use the word *here* in a sentence, you can probably use the word *there*. Look.

*I see a dog **here**.*

*I see a dog **there**.*

Exercise 3-11

Number your work paper 1-10. Write the correct word.

1. You will find the volley balls over (their, there).
2. (Their, There) is where we keep the footballs.
3. (Their, There) house is (their, there), on Seventh Street.
4. (Their, There) are many people (their, there).
5. (Their, There) nephew is a student (their, there).
6. (Their, There) uncle lives in (their, there) house.
7. (Their, There) used to be a shopping center (their, there).
8. (Their, There) is a leak in the bucket.
9. (Their, There) car ran over (their, there) lawn.
10. (Their, There) seems to be a candy store (their, there).

Exercise 3-12

Number your work paper 1-10. Write the correct words.

1. (Their, There) cat chased (their, there) dog.
2. (Its, It's) supposed to rain (their, there) tonight.
3. (Their, There) was snow on the ground. (Their, There) driveway was icy.
4. (Their, There), in the field, they found (their, there) cat.
5. (Its, It's) fur was matted and dirty.
6. (Their, There) football helmets are (their, there) pride and joy.
7. (Its, It's) engine screaming, the jet roared into the sky.
8. (Its, It's) hot (their, there) in the summer.
9. (Their, There) are a lot of things to do (their, there).
10. (Their, There) seems to be smoke over (their, there).

Summary

✓ All sentences have a special shape. They begin with capital letters, and they end with end marks of punctuation.

✓ There are three end marks:
     . (period)
     ? (question mark)
     ! (exclamation mark)

✓ Fragments are pieces of sentences.
✓ *There* is a word of location.

Chapter 4

Semicolons

We have learned much, so far. We have learned that there are two types of communication: verbal and nonverbal. We have also learned that words and sentences work in very much the same way. In order for words to make sense, letters must be in the proper order. In order for sentences to make sense, words must be in the proper order. We have learned that sentences must express a complete thought and that fragments are pieces of sentences.

In this chapter we will learn about a new mark of punctuation. It is called the semicolon. A *semicolon* looks like this:

;

One use of a semicolon is to join two closely related sentences. By the end of the chapter, we will be experts in the use of this simple mark of punctuation.

Before continuing, let's take a moment to remember a very important point: words and sentences function in ways which are very much alike. We know that the letters in a word must be arranged in proper order for the word to make sense, and we know that words in a sentence must be arranged correctly in order for the sentence to make sense. Let's look at another way in which words and sentences are alike.

Both words and sentences can form compounds. One meaning of the word *compound* is *put together*. A compound is formed when two or more objects are put together. For this lesson, we will need to examine compound words and compound sentences.

Compound words
Compound words are words that are formed by joining *two or more words together.*

Exercise 4-1
Number your work paper 1-5. Divide the compound words into two separate words.
1. Football
2. Newspaper
3. Sandstorm
4. Butterfly
5. Goldfish

Exercise 4-2
Number your work paper 1-5. Add the two words together to make a compound word.
1. Out + side
2. Over + look
3. Never + the + less
4. Like + wise
5. Book + keeper

Compound sentences
Words can be formed into compound words. Likewise, sentences can be formed into compound sentences. One way to join two sentences into a compound sentence is to use a semicolon.

Let's take a look at a compound sentence. A *compound sentence* is a single sentence formed by putting two complete sentences together. Look at the examples.

Example Sentence #1: John ate the whole cake.
Example Sentence #2: He must have been hungry.

We will combine these two sentences into a compound sentence using a semicolon.

John ate the whole cake; he must have been hungry.

Pay attention to how the semicolon is used. In a way, it is like a period. It signals your reader that a sentence is ending. Unlike a period, it urges your reader to continue reading. The complete meaning of a compound sentence can only be understood if both halves of the compound sentence are read. Look at the two ways these sentences could have been written.

> *John ate the whole cake. He must have been hungry.*
> *John ate the whole cake; he must have been hungry.*

Capitalization

The word that comes after the semicolon does not have to be capitalized.

Also, it is important to know that semicolons are usually used to join two sentences which are closely related. Read the examples.

> *Correct: Phil collects stamps; he has several stamp books.*
> *Incorrect: Phil collects stamps; football is a sport he likes.*

Exercise 4-3

Number your work paper 1-10. Remember that semicolons should be used to join two closely related sentences. Read the following sentences. If the semicolon is used correctly write the letter *C* on your paper. If it is used incorrectly, write the letter *I*.

1. It was windy today; the light bulb in my lamp burned out.
2. The car's engine died; it had run out of gas.
3. Tom's pen ran out of ink; he couldn't finish his homework.
4. Marla sleeps ten hours every night; she must need the rest.
5. Computer technicians work on computers; trains are fascinating.
6. Maria was proud of herself for reading the entire book; it was over three hundred pages long.
7. Mark joined the Navy; Tim, his brother, joined the Army.
8. The train jumped the tracks; a weak rail line was responsible.
9. Patty spent all afternoon baking the cake; it was delicious.
10. The computer screen suddenly went blank; these systems are very complicated.

Look at number 7 in the preceding exercise. Put your finger on the semicolon. Look at the word that comes after the semicolon. The word is *Tim*. Notice that it is capitalized.

Normally, words that come after a semicolon should not be capitalized. Be careful, though. The names of people, countries, cities, and states are always capitalized. The names of the months and days of the week are capitalized, too.

Exercise 4-4

Number your work paper 1-5. If the sentence is written correctly write a *C*. If it is incorrect write *I*.

1. Tom won the track meet; His friend Jim came in second.
2. Everyone thought the money was lost; Jane thought so, too.
3. Texas can be very hot in the summer; Dallas is particularly bad.
4. The price of the bike bothered Tim; It cost nearly one month's pay.
5. January is the first month of the year; December is the last.

In this course, we will never use a semicolon with a joining word like *or*, *and*, or *but*. Look at the examples.

Correct: *Liz twisted her ankle; it swelled like a balloon.*
Incorrect: *Liz twisted her ankle;* **and** *it swelled like a balloon.*

Take care when using semicolons. Do not use them with *or*, *and*, or *but*.

Exercise 4-5

Number your work paper 1-5. If the sentence is written correctly write a *C*. If it is written incorrectly write an *I*.

1. Peppermint tastes good; but I prefer spearmint.
2. Did you say you were going to the doctor; or did you say you were going downtown?
3. The computer discs were lined up in a row; they were neat and tidy.
4. The baby was playing with the scissors; but she didn't hurt herself.
5. Cathy was late for work; her clock was slow.

Actually, you can spot some semicolon mistakes even if you can't read very much English. Simply look at the word that comes after the semicolon. If the word is *or*, *and*, or *but*, the semicolon is used incorrectly.

Exercise 4-6
Number your work paper 1-5. If the sentence appears to use a semicolon correctly write *C*. If it appears that the semicolon is used incorrectly write *I*.

1. Tkps gks tglkuvme gjlkd; or kjd tjss llkfjdks thej.
2. Pqwoei thsl tjlsk tjlkjd; rjfkld llkjsa' thebvn.
3. Q zpedrl vwsprfl tbnyhd; and tklk lkjflskdj thesl.
4. Mvingthar klkj fe q thv; cxmeh thllj tjechgj.
5. Tlqpcv q fjt h lkjd theksl; clk thrkls tjdksl tsllfj.

Exercise 4-7
Number your work paper 1-10. Turn the sentence pairs into compound sentences using semicolons. Pay attention to capitalization.
Example: Try to improve yourself. Do it every day.
Answer: Try to improve yourself; do it every day.

1. Doug is a lawyer. He handles bankruptcy cases.
2. Rain was falling. It pattered on the roof.
3. My friend's name is Maria. She is a student.
4. John Steinbeck is a famous author. He wrote <u>The Pearl</u>.
5. Felix yawned. He was tired.
6. They made their travel plans. Hawaii was going to be great!
7. That old book is boring. It's much too long.
8. Some people love the Super Bowl. Others prefer the World Series.
9. The crowd roared. Dave won the race.
10. Smoke filled the air. A fire was burning in the mountains.

We have learned one basic use of a semicolon: it can join two complete sentences into one compound sentence. Remember, two complete sentences are required to make a compound sentence.
Correct: John and Bob played basketball; then they went to dinner.
Incorrect: John and Bob played basketball; then went to dinner.

Why is the second example incorrect?

Notice that in the first example, two complete sentences can be underlined. The second example does not contain two complete sentences.

John and Bob played basketball; then they went to dinner.

John and Bob played basketball; then went to dinner.

Fragments

Now you will understand why we have been so worried about the difference between complete sentences and sentence fragments.

If we try to underline two complete sentences in the second example, we can't.

The part that says *then went to dinner* is a fragment. Read it to yourself, and see how it sounds. This fragment does not have a complete subject. It does not express a complete thought.

Fragments might appear at the beginning of an incorrect compound sentence, too. Look.

Incorrect: After playing basketball; John and Bob went to dinner.

The words *After playing basketball* make a fragment. Remember, a compound sentence is a single sentence formed by joining two complete sentences.

Exercise 4-8

Number your work paper 1-10. If the sentence is a correctly written compound sentence write *C*. If it is incorrectly written write *I*.

1. The girls went to the movie; after eating dinner.
2. All the students closed their books; the lesson was over.
3. Watching his favorite movie; Mike decided to make some popcorn.
4. The teacher asked a question; he searched for someone to call on.
5. Juan flossed his teeth; then he brushed them.
6. Josh and Bryan play basketball; they are both star players.
7. Joan likes ice cream; her favorite flavor is chocolate.
8. The car roared down the street; its exhaust pipe was broken.
9. A helicopter hovered over the fire; it poured water on the flames.
10. Everything you need is in this box; including paper and glue.

Exercise 4-9

Number your work paper 1-5. Write five compound sentences using semicolons.

Summary
- ✓ Semicolons look like this ;
- ✓ Semicolons join two complete sentences.
- ✓ Compound sentences are formed from two complete sentences.
- ✓ Semicolons are not used with the words *and, but, or*.

Chapter 5

Paragraphs of Fact

We communicate to express our thoughts and ideas. Usually, our communication requires words. We rarely speak or write one word at a time. We speak in groups of words. These groups of words are called sentences.

Paragraphs are groups of sentences. All the sentences in a paragraph deal with the same subject. For example, in a paragraph about airplanes, all the sentences would deal with airplanes.

We have learned that sentences must follow a special form. They must begin with a capital letter, and they must end with a mark of punctuation. Paragraphs must follow a special form, too.

Paragraph form
Paragraphs must be indented. We can see paragraphs. Paragraphs are indented. Look at a sheet of notebook paper. Be sure the holes are on your left.

Notice the pink line that runs from the top to the bottom of the left hand side of the paper. This is called the margin. The margin is considered the border of the page. In a neatly written paper, our writing lines up on the margin line.

Indenting paragraphs
When writing, we must signal our audience when we begin a new paragraph. This is because a new paragraph is a new group of sentences.

38

The new group of sentences will discuss a new topic. If we do not indent, our readers might become confused. Remember, we write for our audience. The most important member of our audience is our teacher.

We signal our audience that a new paragraph is beginning by indenting the paragraph. We indent by moving the first line of a paragraph towards the center of the page, a short distance in from the margin.

The word *indent* is made of two words *in + dent*. We *dent in* the paragraph to signal our audience that we are beginning a new paragraph. A distance about two-fingers wide is enough. Our audience can see the beginning of a new paragraph.

The paragraphs on this page are indented. In fact, you will find indented paragraphs in newspapers, encyclopedias, and nearly everything else you read. By convention, we signal our readers that we are beginning a new paragraph by indenting it.

Before continuing, let's look at some of the conventions this text uses for indenting paragraphs.

Perhaps you have noticed that not all the paragraphs in this text are indented. The reason is simple. In this text, the publishers wanted certain pieces of information to look a certain way on the page.

Therefore, paragraphs that begin directly beneath section headings are not indented.

Furthermore, exercise instructions are not indented.

Please remember that these conventions are conventions of Read Press (*pronounced Red Press*), the company that publishes this book. Different publishing companies use different conventions.

The important point as far as this text goes, is that students must make a habit of indenting paragraphs. We always write for an audience, and at this point in our writing careers, our teachers are the most important members of the audience. Let's keep them happy.

After mastering the basics, we can begin to bend the rules to suit our own particular tastes.

Now, let's continue.

Exercise 5-1

Number your work paper 1-4. Read the article. Then, answer the questions.

Bats

Bats are mammals. They have furry bodies and smooth wings. They do not lay eggs. They give birth to live young. Like all mammals, bats are warm blooded, but a bat's temperature can change greatly depending on whether or not the bat is active.

There are many kinds of bats. Hundreds of species of bats are found all over the world. Two of the world's better known bats are the brown bat and the flying fox. Brown bats live in the United States, but flying foxes are found in Africa and Asia. All together, there are more than 900 species of bats in the world.

1. The article contains how many paragraphs?
2. How can you tell?
3. Write the first sentence of paragraph 1.
4. Write the first sentence of paragraph 2.

Topic sentences

Look at your answers to questions number 3 & 4. These sentences are the main idea sentences of the article. The main idea sentence of a paragraph is often called the topic sentence.

The *topic sentence* of a paragraph tells the main idea of the paragraph. We use a topic sentence when we are writing a paragraph of facts.

A topic sentence may appear anywhere in a paragraph; however, in this course, we will keep things simple and always make the first sentence of a paragraph the topic sentence.

Details

Let's take another look at the paragraphs about bats. Read the first sentence in paragraph 1. It tells us that bats are mammals. Now read the rest of the sentences in the first paragraph. These sentences give details about bats. They are called detail sentences. *Detail sentences* help us to better understand the main idea sentence. In this case, the detail sentences help us understand the main idea. They tell us that bats have the characteristics of mammals.

Exercise 5-2

Read the paragraphs about bats again. Answer the questions.

1. Look at the first sentence of paragraph 2. This sentence has a special name. What is it called?
2. What are the remaining sentences called?
3. Write two details from paragraph 2 that help clarify the topic sentence.

We know that words are made of letters, and we know that sentences are composed of words. Likewise, paragraphs are built from sentences. Just as with words and sentences, everything must be in its proper place in order for a paragraph to make sense.

Exercise 5-3

Number your work paper 1-6. Examine the following nonsense paragraphs, then answer the questions.

Ikssk fjls lskdj askdj fjk dkfjsls. Skdslskfs dslddlk. Sldjskdjsl fjsjsdk. Llsdjs oiwpfjf . Dlslkdjs. Tjsoeo fsldkfj! Alf thxp fnsldmskfn slikfj. Oe pefj dkfskfm.

Ghdkle akad ldk sdlf fkdalsd sjfdf fnm. Skdf sjdf l Lsdkfldkf fj f seif klj dk djl lf sk kfjll f skf kj! Lkkfldkfl f. Skd fjsldl fdlfkjd, fjdkslkr.

Cdx kdls lsfjs. Fjsldkrh f jmfg ldfkg ladkjae ds? lskdjiejdfj Sjfhdsdjh I fhdj dskjfk sdk ehf s euf k wi k idf d dfsdk skjf sk Sk ddls d fsd fhfj f.

1. How many paragraphs in the article?
2. How many topic sentences?
3. Write the first letter of the first word of the first topic sentence.
4. Write the first group of letters in the second topic sentence.
5. How many groups of letters are in the third topic sentence?
6. How many detail sentences are there in the first paragraph?

We know that sentences must follow a special form. They must begin with a capital letter and end with an end mark of punctuation. Likewise, we know that paragraphs must follow a special form, too. They are indented from the margin line. The indentation tells us that a new paragraph is beginning.

Compositions

When we sit down to write a story or an essay, we are like musicians who sit down at a piano to compose a song. From nothing, we will compose something.

A *composition* is a piece of writing. Notice that the word *compose*, meaning create, is the root of the word *composition*. That is because a composition is something we create.

Usually, a composition consists of several paragraphs. However, in high school, there will be many times when you will be required to write a one paragraph answer to a question. Social studies, literature, and science classes often require such answers.

Let's look at a model of a one-paragraph composition of fact.

Question
What is a paragraph?

Answer

A paragraph is a group of sentences all talking about the same thing. A paragraph begins with a topic sentence. The topic sentence is the main idea sentence of the paragraph. Detail sentences follow the topic sentence. They help explain the topic. All the sentences in a paragraph should deal with the same topic.

Notice how the question is answered in the first sentence. The answer to the question is your topic sentence. The remaining sentences, the detail sentences, simply help to make your answer more clear. Sometimes we add a concluding sentence.

The concluding sentence helps to sum up your answer. It also restates the topic sentence. For example, if we were to write a concluding sentence to the above paragraph, we might write something like this: *In conclusion, paragraphs are groups of sentences all discussing the same topic.*

Writing a paragraph of information

Follow four simple steps to ensure that you compose an excellent paragraph of facts:

1) *Indent the topic sentence. It must be a complete sentence.*
2) *Add several details. The details should help clarify the topic.*

3) *Be sure the details discuss the topic sentence.*
4) *Add a concluding sentence to sum up your paragraph.*

Exercise 5-4

Number your work paper 1-3. Three of the following sentences would make good topic sentences. The remaining sentences would not make good main idea sentences. Write the letters of the three good topic sentences.

- A. You do not seem to understand.
- B. A well-written composition must contain a topic sentence.
- C. First, break an egg into a bowl.
- D. Owls, eagles, and even sparrows are examples of this.
- E. The preceding was a paid announcement.
- F. Trains were important in the development of the United States.
- G. Some of these can be found on the bottom of the sea.
- H. Begin by moistening the area.
- I. A hammer is a kind of tool.
- J. For example, notebooks, rulers, papers, and pencils.

Look again at Exercise 5-4. One group of words is a fragment. Which one is it?

Exercise 5-5

Number 1 on your work paper. The following sentences could be combined to form a short paragraph. Write down the only sentence that could be a topic sentence.

- A. Then the gills sweep oxygen from the water.
- B. Fish breathe using gills.
- C. First, water enters the gills.

Exercise 5-6

Read the list of sentences below. They can be rearranged to make a paragraph. Write the paragraph on your work paper. Be sure to indent the topic sentence.

- A. Millions of people the world over have benefited from his inventive mind.
- B. He is known as the king of inventors because of the many useful devices he invented.
- C. He also invented the motion picture camera.

D. Thomas Edison was one of the world's greatest inventors.

E. For example, he invented the phonograph and the electric light bulb.

Organizing information

We can easily write paragraphs if the information we want to present is organized correctly. Read the following topic sentence and the detail sentences. Examine the paragraph to see how everything is combined.

Topic Sentence:

Fingerprints can be categorized into three main groups.

Details:

A. *The groups are divided according to patterns formed by fingerprint ridges.*

B. *The loop pattern is the most common pattern.*

C. *Another pattern is call the whorl.*

D. *A third pattern is known as the arch.*

We can write a paragraph from this information. Some of the words change, but the topic sentence is still the first sentence. It is indented. The detail sentences help explain the topic. The concluding sentence sums things up.

Fingerprints can be categorized into three main groups. The groups are divided according to patterns formed by fingerprint ridges. The most common of the three fingerprint patterns is the loop pattern. Another pattern is called the whorl. The third pattern is known as the arch. In conclusion, fingerprints can be divided into three main categories.

Exercise 5-7

Read the following topic sentence and details. Compose one paragraph that brings all the information together.

Topic Sentence:

Fingerprints serve many purposes.

Details:

A. *They help police identify crime suspects.*

B. *They are used to check the backgrounds of people applying for jobs in the military.*
C. *They aid in the identification of disaster victims.*

Exercise 5-8

Write the following topic sentence on your work paper. Underneath the topic sentence, number 1-5. Write five details about the topic. Then join it all together by writing a paragraph. Congratulations! You know how to write a paragraph of information.

Topic Sentence:
Dogs make great pets.

Exercise 5-9

Let's review the use of the words *there* and *their*.

Their shows ownership.

There might mean a location (here and there)

There might be used simply to start a sentence.

Number your work paper 1- 5. Write the correct words.

1. (There, Their) books are in (there, their) bags.
2. When is (there, their) plane going to arrive?
3. Did you see the accident over (there, their)?
4. (There, Their) are many species of animals.
5. (There, Their) is where we left (there, their) bikes.

Exercise 5-10

Let's review homophones. Number your work paper 1-5. Read each sentence. Correct each misspelled word.

1. John went two the store.
2. I called my ant on the phone.
3. That evergreen tree looks like a seeder.
4. Give this message to kernel Smith.
5. She has a fir coat.

Exercise 5-11

They're means *they are*.

There is often used to start sentences.

Number your work paper 1-5. Write the correct word.

1. _____ going on vacation.
2. _____ is a dog in our yard.
3. _____ are pencils in the cup.
4. _____ in the classroom.
5. _____ helping the teacher.

Summary

✓ Paragraphs must be indented.
✓ The topic sentence tells the main idea of the paragraph, and the topic sentence is always the first sentence in the paragraph.
✓ Detail sentences give information about the topic.
✓ A composition is a piece of writing.
✓ Composing paragraphs is easy when we take the time to organize our thoughts before we begin writing.
✓ *They're* means *they are*.
✓ *There* often starts sentences.

Chapter 6

TIGER Writing

In order to write well, we must be organized. Writing is not the same as speaking. However, in many ways, writing is like thinking on paper. If our thoughts are well organized, our audience will understand what we are thinking. We must organize our thoughts, *before* we begin writing. When our thoughts are well organized, we will write well-organized compositions.

We will use a simple method for organizing our thoughts. This method is called TIGER.

Prewriting

TIGER is simply a tool to help us collect our thoughts before we begin writing. TIGER is a prewriting strategy. We use TIGER before we begin writing our paragraphs or compositions. Prewriting will focus our thoughts, allowing us to write better compositions.

Remember, clear thinking leads to clear writing.

Before continuing, it is important to keep in mind that any writing assignment will require at least two sheets of paper. One sheet of paper will be used like scratch paper. It will be used for prewriting. In other words, it will help us focus our thoughts. The other sheet will be used for the actual writing which will be graded. Let's begin.

Each letter in the word TIGER stands for a step in the writing process.

T = Topic sentence
I = Ideas
G = Group
E = Enumerate
R = wRite

The TIGER process

Notice that this is a five step process. Even though it involves five steps, the entire prewriting method can be done on a single sheet of paper.

The first step in the process involves writing a clear topic sentence. Our topic sentence is a promise to our audience that we will discuss only one topic in our paragraph. The topic sentence is our main idea sentence.

Next, under the topic sentence, we will list ideas. Our ideas are our details. We will only list ideas that are closely related to our topic. After that, we will group our ideas into logical groups.

Then, we will enumerate our ideas. *Enumerate* means number. You can see part of the word *number* in *enumerate*. Enumerating our ideas means that we will put them into numerical order.

For example, we will put the number *1* in front of the sentence which will come first in our paragraph. This sentence will always be the topic sentence. Then, we will write a number *2* in front of the next sentence. This will be one of our details. We will number all the details.

Finally, we will write our paragraphs.

We have learned that every paragraph must have a topic sentence. We have also learned that the topic sentence must be followed by detail sentences. The details explain the topic. The details help your audience understand the topic. A concluding sentence sums everything up.

Let's practice using TIGER to write a one paragraph summary. A *summary* is a short piece of writing that captures the most important points of something we have seen or read. For example, a teacher might want you to write a summary of a lesson you have just watched, or she may require that you write a summary about something you have read. Earlier we read about Helen Keller. Today, we will summarize that article with a one paragraph summary. The article is reprinted below. This time, it contains no mistakes.

Helen Keller

Helen Keller was born a normal, healthy baby in 1880. At the age of one and a half, though, she suffered a serious illness. As a result of this illness, Helen was left deaf and blind. She was cut off from the world although she was just a tiny child.

When Helen was five years old, her father met with Alexander

Graham Bell, the inventor of the telephone. Bell suggested that Mr. Keller contact the Perkins Institution for the Blind in Boston, Massachusetts.

A teacher from the Institute, Annie Sullivan, arrived at Helen's house. Helen was six years old. Sullivan communicated with Helen through the sense of touch. Sullivan used a special alphabet. While pressing her fingers into Helen's hand, she would spell out words.

Slowly Helen learned. Three years after Annie Sullivan's arrival, Helen could understand her special sign language. She could even read in Braille, a special alphabet for the blind.

Because Helen could not hear, she could not learn to speak in the same way other children learn to speak. Most children imitate the sounds they hear when they are learning to speak. Helen hired a special teacher for the deaf to teach her to speak. She learned quickly.

By the time she was sixteen, Helen was making plans to attend college. In time, she graduated form Radcliffe College, a famous school.

Helen Keller devoted her life to helping the blind, and the deaf and blind. She traveled and gave speeches. She became an author and wrote several books including The Story of My Life. During World War II, she worked with soldiers who had been blinded.

Helen Keller became a great communicator. The touch of Annie Sullivan's fingers in Helen's tiny hand opened a new world to the little girl: a world of shared thoughts and dreams. The world is a better place because of Helen Keller.

Let's begin. We will use the TIGER method to prewrite our paragraph. Look at the next page. A student named Kristen has completed her own TIGER prewrite.

Don't let all the lines and numbers confuse you. In fact, study the lines and numbers carefully. You will notice that the lines act like threads. The lines help to tie related ideas into logical groups.

Here's what Kristen did. She read the article. Then, she decided on a topic sentence. After that, she wrote down ideas about her topic. She didn't worry about writing her ideas in the correct order; she just wanted to get her thoughts onto paper. Later, she joined her ideas with lines, and numbered them in the order she wanted to write about them.

TIGER

TOPIC - [1]Helen Keller was a great communicator.

IDEAS-

7 → She wrote books and gave speeches.

She was born in 1880.

2 → When she was born she was healthy.

3 → She became deaf and blind after an illness when she was two.

Helen's teacher was Annie Sullivan.

5 → Annie taught Helen a special sign language.

Helen's life was spent helping the blind.

6 → Helen learned to speak and attended Radcliffe college.

4 → Helen's father hired a special teacher for his daughter

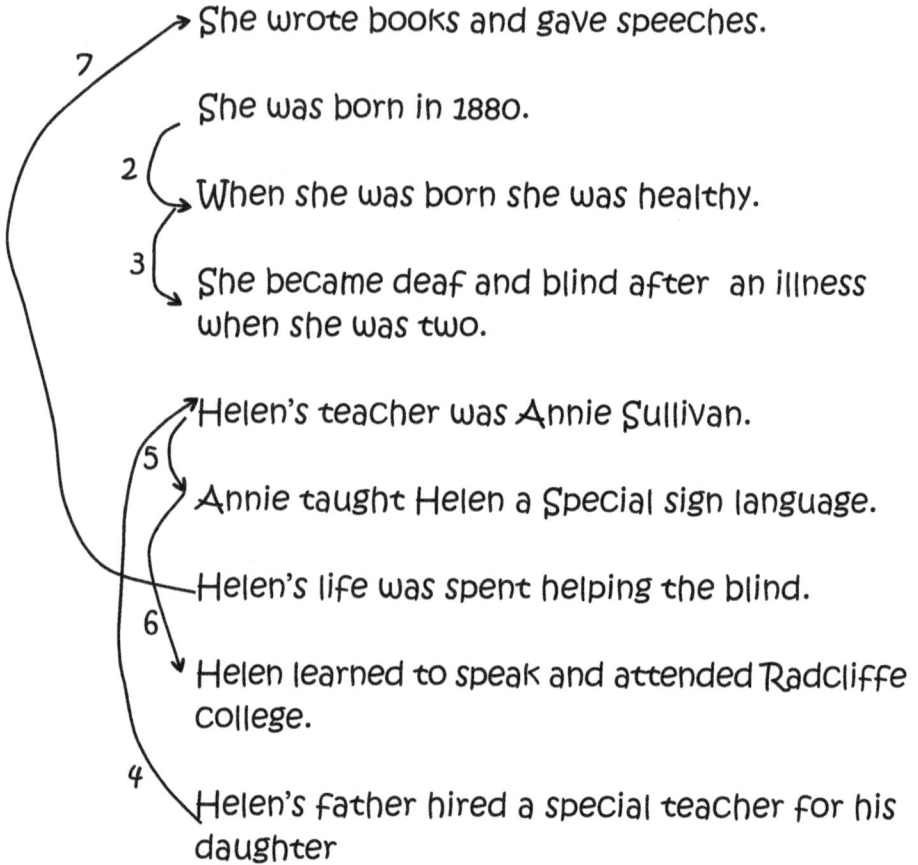

When Kristen was done prewriting, she was ready to write her summary. Notice how closely it matches her prewriting. Kristen begins with a clear topic sentence. There are no fragments, and she included not one, but two a semicolons to show her teacher that she understands how semicolons are used. She did a great job.

Helen Keller

Helen Keller was a great communicator. She was born in 1880. She was a normal, healthy baby until she turned two. An illness caused her to become deaf and blind. Helen's father hired a special teacher to help his daughter; the teacher's name was Annie Sullivan. Annie taught Helen a special sign language. Helen learned how to speak and attended Radcliffe College. Helen wrote books and gave speeches; she devoted her life to helping the blind.

Notice one more point about Kristen's writing. Compare sentences 6 and 7 on Kristen's prewriting list to the final two sentences of her summary. She has reversed their order. This is perfectly natural. As Kristen was writing, she realized that her summary would sound better if she made this simple change. Kristen was thinking clearly as she wrote; the result was a clear summary.

Checklists

When writing a summary, the first step in using the TIGER process is to write a topic sentence. The topic sentence should be the most important information communicated by the article.

We will be writing a paragraph about Helen Keller. We know that a paragraph must be indented. We also know that a paragraph needs a topic sentence and supporting details. Furthermore, we have learned that sentence fragments are unacceptable, and that our sentences must be unambiguous. We have also practiced using semicolons to make compound sentences. Let's look at a checklist that will help us understand what is expected in the paragraph.

_____ *indented paragraph*
_____ *topic sentence (states the most important fact about Helen Keller)*
_____ *detail sentences that support the topic*
_____ *clear writing that is unambiguous*
_____ *no fragments*
_____ *compound sentence using a semicolon*
_____ *concluding sentence*

Above all, our writing must make sense. The checklist will help us focus on showing what we know about good writing. If our writing makes sense, and if we are able to check off each of the requirements, we can be pretty certain that we have done a good job.

It's time to begin prewriting. As we work through this lesson, let's refer to Kristen's prewriting (TIGER) model so we understand what is expected.

Exercise 6-1
T - Topic
First, write the word *Topic* on the margin of the top line of your prewriting paper. Next to this, write your topic sentence. This should be the most important fact about Helen Keller. It must be a complete sentence.

Exercise 6-2
I - Ideas
Now it is time to list ideas, details that help explain the topic sentence. Skip a line under the word *Topic*. Write the word *Ideas*. Look into the article and gather at least seven ideas about Helen Keller. Do not number them; in fact, don't even worry about the order. Simply list the ideas on your paper. For now, write your ideas as complete sentences.

Exercise 6-3
G - Group
Look at your ideas. Maybe it seems to you that certain ideas should go together. Connect these ideas into logical groups by drawing connecting lines.

Exercise 6-4
E - Enumerate
Enumerate means *to number*. Look at your prewriting paper; you will notice that some ideas should be written into a paragraph before other ideas. For example, you will probably want to write about Helen Keller's early years before you write about her accomplishments.
Your topic sentence will always be the first sentence in your paragraph, so put a *1* in front of it. Now decide which sentence should come second and put a *2* in front of it. Do the same for the remaining

sentences until all sentences are in their proper order. If you grouped your ideas clearly, this step will be quite easy. If you're not sure how your paper should look, turn back to the example.

You may also use the sample below to help get started.

Topic: Helen Keller is remembered as a great human being.

Ideas: Helen was born a normal, healthy baby. She became deaf and blind because of a childhood illness.

Annie Sullivan was Helen's teacher.

Helen went to Radcliffe.

She wrote several books including The Story of My Life.

Helen learned to read, write, and speak.

She died in 1969.

Exercise 6-5

R - wRite

Now comes the most important step of the writing process, actually writing. On a clean sheet of paper, write your paragraph of facts, your summary, about Helen Keller.

The TIGER process helps you organize your thoughts. You will think more clearly about your topic. When you think clearly, you will write clearly.

Remember, work hard and work smart.

Exercise 6-6

Read the following article about Alexander Graham Bell. Write a summary paragraph about it. Use two sheets of paper. One sheet is for the TIGER pre-write, and the other is for the actual summary paragraph.

Use the checklist to ensure that you write the best paragraph you can.

Checklist
_____ *indented paragraph*
_____ *topic sentence (states the most important fact about Bell)*
_____ *detail sentences that support the topic*
_____ *clear writing that is unambiguous*
_____ *no fragments*
_____ *compound sentence using a semicolon*
_____ *concluding sentence*

Alexander Graham Bell

Alexander Graham Bell, the inventor of the telephone, was also a skilled musician and scientist.

Early Years

Bell was born in Scotland in 1847. He and his two brothers were home schooled until the age of thirteen. Bell's father was interested in helping the deaf; his mother was a painter and musician. Bell's early education at home influenced the rest of his life.

Because he was fascinated by sound, Bell read all that he could on the subject. He became very knowledgeable on the subject.

Accomplishments

Bell began experimenting with electricity. He was particularly interested in working with telegraphs, which were a new invention of the time.

Bell's experiments required money. Fortunately, Bell, was a teacher of the deaf. During the time he was experimenting with electricity, he had two students whose families were willing to help pay for his studies.

Thomas Watson, a skilled scientist, began working with Bell. The two of them continued to conduct experiments with telegraphs and sound.

On March 10, 1876, Bell spoke into a telephone that was connected to a second phone in another room. Bell had spilled some acid, and he wanted his assistant to help him clean it up. The first words ever spoken into the phone are as famous as Bell, himself. "Mr. Watson, come here, I want you."

With those words the telephone was born.

Later Years

Bell spent the rest of his life working on experiments with sound. He also worked on early airplanes.

He died on August 2, 1922. In honor of all his accomplishments, the telephones in North America were silent in his honor.

Summary

✓ TIGER is a five step writing process.
✓ Each of the letters in TIGER stands for a step in the writing process:

$$T = \underline{T}opic\ sentence$$
$$I\ = \underline{I}deas$$
$$G = \underline{G}roup$$
$$E\ = \underline{E}numerate$$
$$R = w\underline{R}ite$$

✓ We can use this checklist to help us become better writers:

_____ *indented paragraph*
_____ *topic sentence (states the most important fact about the subject of our writing)*
_____ *detail sentences that support the topic*
_____ *clear writing that is unambiguous*
_____ *no fragments*
_____ *compound sentence using a semicolon*
_____ *concluding sentence*

Chapter 7

Appositives

We have been learning to write paragraphs of information. Now it's time to look at simple way to add extra life to our writing. We will learn to use appositives (pronounce *up-POSitives*). Appositives are interesting, easy-to-use groups of words that can make our writing sound more polished.

Before looking at appositives, though, let's review a few points.

We have learned how to use the semicolon. The semicolon is used to join two sentences. Two sentences joined together are called a compound sentence. The two sentences should be closely related in meaning. When using semicolons we show an advanced knowledge of writing.

One excellent reason for using semicolons is to show our audience that we know how to use them; it is always important to show our teachers what we know.

Additionally, we have learned that as writers we have two specific tools we use to make our meanings clear. Our tools are words and punctuation.

Mechanics

Mechanics is the way words and punctuation work together.

We have all seen mechanics at work. They have large toolboxes. Inside the toolboxes, they keep the tools they need to do their job.

As writers, our toolboxes are our thoughts, and inside our toolboxes we keep all our tools: the words and punctuation necessary to make our thoughts clear to others. For writers, the word *mechanics* has a special meaning. Mechanics is the way words and punctuation work together.

Mechanical Mistakes

Sometimes, as writers, we work like mechanics. Just as a mechanic inspects an engine looking for problems, we must inspect our writing. Problems often occur in writing. Our writing mistakes even have a special name. Some writing mistakes are called *mechanical mistakes*. Here are some examples of mechanical mistakes.

Did you see the game last night   (no endpoint of punctuation)
Did you see the gam lasst night? (misspelled words)
did you see the game last night? (no capital letter)
At the game last night. (fragment)
I watched the game; at home. (incorrect semicolon)

Mechanical mistakes are often caused by carelessness. We may be in a hurry to finish a project. We may not pay attention to details. Remember, as writers, we are responsible for making our meaning clear to our audience.

Of course, some mechanical mistakes are caused because writers do not know the proper rules of writing. For example, the proper use of the semicolon was explained in a previous chapter. Semicolons are used to join two sentences with closely related meanings. Now you know how to use semicolons. You can impress your audience and your teachers by using semicolons correctly.

Exercise 7-1

Number your work paper 1-10. The following sentences may contain mechanical mistakes. List the mistakes on your work paper. If there are no mistakes write *No Mistakes*. Follow the examples.
Example: John watched the basketball game; at the gym.
Answer: Incorrect semicolon
Example: John watched the basketball game; he was at the gym.
Answer: No Mistakes

1. All the students walking back and forth in the hallways.
2. The bell rings; classes begin

3. anyone who tries hard will succeed.
4. The teacher talked about the complete subject.
5. Pencils and paper are required; in this class.
6. The teacher pointed to an equation.
7. Was the answer right or wrong.
8. Carl accidentally stapled his finger.
9. Although everyone agreed that the answer was correct.
10. Everyone stared working on the test.

Exercise 7-2

Number your work paper 1-10. Read the following sentences carefully. If you spot a mechanical mistake write the words *Mechanical Mistake* on your work paper. Do not abbreviate. If there are no mistakes, write *No Mistakes*.

Example: tom likes mechanical things.
Answer: *Mechanical Mistake*
Example: Tom likes mechanical things.
Answer: *No Mistakes*

1. We all decided to go to the park
2. What did Nancy tell Shelly about the party?
3. Karen ate dinner; and after that she watched TV.
4. James has a new computer; he uses it to write reports.
5. Tom flies kites on windy days.
6. Beginning with the third paragraph.
7. Baseball; hockey; and football are his favorite sports.
8. David reads one book a week.
9. Did you know that the Japanese use a writing system called Kanji.
10. Every sentence must contain a complete subject; and a complete predicate.

Mechanical mistakes often occur because writers are in a hurry and are not paying close attention to what they are doing. We must take care to avoid mechanical mistakes. We must get our writing right the first time.

Sometimes we make mistakes because we do not know the proper rules. If we do not know the proper rules, we will make mechanical mistakes. Mechanical mistakes can lead to ambiguous sentences. Our writing may become very confusing.

An ambiguous sentence

Read this sentence. It is ambiguous. It has at least two meanings. Can you figure out what the two meanings are?

John a doctor came to visit my house.

This sentence is ambiguous because of a mechanical mistake. The mistake is easy to fix. If we do not know the rule, however, it will be impossible to make the proper correction. Let's look at the sentence again, and examine the possible meanings.

John a doctor came to my house.

(Possible meaning #1) John (who is a doctor) came to my house. In other words:

Dr. John came to my house.

(Possible meaning #2) (You're writing a letter to your friend whose name is John). In other words:

Dear John,
A doctor came to my house. I was very sick.

This sentence:

John a doctor came to my house.

is ambiguous because of a simple mechanical mistake. The mistake involves the use of commas. *Commas* are marks of punctuation often found inside sentences. They look like this (,). Commas act like road signs. They tell us to slow down for a moment as we read.

Let's look at how commas can change the meaning of the sentence we have been examining:

John a doctor came to my house.

If you want to say that Dr. John visited your house you must write the sentence this way: (when you read the sentence, slow at each comma.)

John, a doctor, came to my house.

If you are writing to a friend named John, and you want to tell him that a doctor came to your house, you must write the sentence this way:
John, a doctor came to my house.

How many commas do you see in the first example? How many in the second example?

By subtracting one comma, the meaning of the entire sentence is changed.

Mechanical mistakes are often made because writers do not know how to use commas correctly.

In this chapter we will begin to study the proper use of commas. We will examine one very common use of commas called the appositive (remember to pronounce it *up-POSitive*). An *appositive* is a word or group of words that is placed directly after another word or group of words that mean the same thing. Does it sound confusing?

It isn't. In fact, appositives are often used in textbooks to help define or explain new words.

Look at the following examples. The appositives are underlined.
Hawaii, the fiftieth state, is located in the Pacific Ocean.
Latin, an ancient language, is a fascinating subject.
Thomas Edison, the famous inventor, invented the light bulb.
Helen Keller, the well-known writer and speaker, was deaf and blind.

Examine the above appositives carefully. They all use different words, but they are all arranged in the same way.

First of all, the appositive part of each sentence always talks about the words that come directly in front of it. Look at the sentence about Thomas Edison. The appositive, *the famous inventor*, talks about Thomas Edison.

Look at the sentence about Helen Keller. What does the appositive talk about?

What is Latin? The appositive that defines Latin comes directly after the word *Latin*.

Let's look at the rules for using appositives.

The first rule of appositives is this: an appositive must always talk about the words that come directly in front of it. Look. The appositive tells about Maria.

Maria, an honor student, graduated at the top of her class.

The second rule of appositives is this: an appositive must always be set off from the sentence with commas. When we say the appositive must be *set off* we mean that it must be separated. We separate the appositive from the sentence with commas. In the preceding example, the words *,an honor student,* are set off with commas.

Exercise 7-3

Number your work paper 1-10. Read each of the following sentences. Each contains an appositive. Write the appositive on your work paper. Be sure to include all commas.

Example: Dr. Thomas, a brain surgeon, works at East Hospital.
Answer: , a brain surgeon,

1. Mary, my best friend, lives in Oakdale.
2. Photosynthesis, the process by which green plants create their own food using sunlight, is very complicated.
3. Synonyms, words that mean nearly the same thing, are often used so that common words are not repeated.
4. Kanji, a form of Japanese writing, uses symbol pictures.
5. My dad, a security guard at the airport, works six days a week.
6. Vampire bats, the most feared kind of bats, do not actually suck blood.
7. Alexander Graham Bell, the inventor of the telephone, was a teacher of the deaf.
8. DVD's, digital video discs, hold huge amounts of information.
9. The B-2, a stealth bomber, is difficult to spot on radar.
10. The Rosetta Stone, an enormous stone discovered in Egypt, holds the key to understanding ancient languages.

Appositives may sound strange to you at first. It may seem that an appositive should begin with a word like *was* or *is*. Look what happens if you add one of these words.

     Correct: Mary, my best friend, lives in Oakdale.
     Incorrect: Mary, is my best friend, lives in Oakdale.

Adding the word *is* makes the entire sentence sound awkward.

Appositives never begin with words like *is* or *was*.

Appositives sound strange because they interrupt a sentence. When we say that appositives interrupt a sentence, we mean that they shift our attention from the main body of the sentence. They interrupt the main thought of the sentence, but they add extra information to help the audience better understand the sentence.

We can see how appositives interrupt a sentence by doing a simple exercise. Read this sentence. The sentence contains an appositive.

Mr. Holmes, my science teacher, always wears a tie.

What is the appositive?

The appositive is ,my science teacher,

Notice that the appositive is surrounded by commas. Imagine for a moment that the commas are hooks. Imagine that the hooks can be used to lift the appositive out of the sentence. Here is what is left.

, my science teacher,
Mr. Holmes   always wears a tie.

Now, throw away the appositive, and put the main sentence back together. This is what you will get:

Mr. Holmes always wears a tie.

This is the *main sentence*, sometimes called the *root sentence*. It is a complete sentence. The part that we threw away was the appositive. The appositive interrupted the main sentence in order to give us a little more information about Mr. Holmes.

Now look at the part we threw away.

,my science teacher,

This is not a complete sentence. It is a fragment. Appositives are never complete sentences.

This is a writing course, and we don't want to get confused by technical definitions; therefore, in this course, almost any group of words that interrupt a main sentence, and talk about a word right in front of the group, will be called an appositive.

Exercise 7-4

Number your work paper 1-10. Read the sentences. Each sentence contains an appositive. The appositive interrupts the main sentence. Throw out the appositive. Be sure to throw out the commas, too. Write the main sentence on your paper.

Example: Tim, my brother, sells insurance.
Answer: Tim sells insurance.

1. Mr. Jones, my next door neighbor, drives a Viper.
2. Ernest Hemingway, one of the greatest American writers, was an outdoorsman.
3. Ice, water in solid form, forms at thirty-two degrees.
4. Hydrogen, the first element listed on the periodic table, is very light.
5. George Washington, the first President, commanded forces during the Revolutionary War.
6. The telephone, invented by Alexander Graham Bell, changed the world.
7. Mechanics, the way words and punctuation work together, will be graded in this class.
8. Appositives, sentence interrupters, are easy to use.
9. Physics, the study of the natural world, is a fascinating science.
10. Tim, a doctor, writes well.

We can start appositives with words like *who* or *which*, but before doing so, let's check to make sure the words are really necessary. Generally, appositives sound much better when we DON'T use *who* or *which*.

> *Example:*   *Kimberly likes spaghetti. (my sister)*
> *Possible answer: Kimberly, who is my sister, likes spaghetti.*
> *Better Answer: Kimberly, my sister, likes spaghetti.*

Exercise 7-5

Number your work paper 1-10. Read each of the following main sentences. Each main sentence is followed by an appositive in parentheses. Insert the appositive into the correct place in the sentence. Write the sentence. Be sure to include commas.

1. Ron drives a four wheel drive. (my cousin)
2. That man likes ice cream. (Mr. Jones)
3. The knife dropped to the floor and stuck. (a cleaver)
4. Tsunamis are common after earthquakes. (tidal waves)
5. Ernest Hemingway wrote "A Day's Wait." (the famous author)
6. Lasers perform many important functions. (concentrated beams of light)
7. Louis Braille gave millions of blind people the ability to read. (the inventor of the Braille system)
8. Braille allows the blind to read using their sense of touch. (a system which uses raised dots to represent printed letters)
9. Two famous inventors helped make the world a better place for millions of people. (Alexander Graham Bell and Louis Braille)
10. One famous writer and speaker devoted her life to helping others. (Helen Keller)

Combining sentences with appositives

It is important to begin using new knowledge as quickly as possible.

One of the great advantages of using appositives is that they help to combine information from what might be two sentences into one single sentence. Let's look at an example.

Two sentences

Ken is a reporter for the school newspaper. He is a freshman.

One sentence using an appositive

Ken, a freshman, is a reporter for the school newspaper.

You could also write about Ken this way:

Ken, a reporter for the school newspaper, is a freshman.

Both of the sentences with appositives give the same information about Ken. They both combine two sentences into one. Appositives are extremely useful when it comes to constructing excellent sounding sentences.

We now know two ways to combine sentences:

1. Compound sentences (created with a semicolon ;)
2. Single sentences (created from two sentences using appositives)

Exercise 7-6

Number your work paper 1-10. Combine the following sentence pairs into one sentence using appositives. Be sure to include commas. Underline the appositive.

Example: The car raced around the track. The car was a Ford.
Answer: The car, a Ford, raced around the track.

1. Joan works after school. Joan is a senior.
2. Appositives can be tricky. Appositives are sentence interrupters.
3. John Steinbeck wrote <u>The Pearl</u>. He was a famous American author.
4. <u>Cannery Row</u> was made into a movie. <u>Cannery Row</u> is another of John Steinbeck's books.
5. The history of the people of Japan goes back thousands of years. The people of Japan are called the Japanese.
6. Kanji can be difficult to learn. Kanji is one form of Japanese writing.
7. The aorta carries an enormous amount of blood. The aorta is the main artery leading from the heart.
8. The femur is one of the heaviest bones in the body. The femur is sometimes called the thigh bone.
9. Paintings by Fredrick Remington are worth thousands of dollars. Remington was a cowboy artist.
10. Emeralds are green. Emeralds are valuable gemstones.

So far we have been looking at appositives that appear in the middle of a sentence.

Appositives may appear at the end of a sentence, too. Look at the examples. The appositives are underlined.

Example: That man is my brother John, <u>a lawyer</u>.
Example: We bought a new watchdog, <u>a German shepherd</u>.

Exercise 7-7

Number your work paper 1-10. Each of the following sentences has an

65

appositive at the end. Write the appositive on your work paper.

1. Helen Keller wrote <u>The Story of My Life</u>, her autobiography.
2. Everyone has heard of Thomas Edison, the king of inventors.
3. Mary's computer monitor has an LCD, liquid crystal display.
4. We traveled the Mississippi, the longest river in the United States.
5. We have been reading <u>The Pearl</u>, a great story by John Steinbeck.
6. Jim washed the truck, a Ford.
7. The sick man called his doctor, Dr. Samuels.
8. Paul Tibbits piloted the Enola Gay, the plane that dropped the atomic bomb on Hiroshima.
9. The cage held two kinds of reptiles, lizards and snakes.
10. We have been studying communication, the exchange of thoughts or information.

Exercise 7-8

Number your work paper 1-10. Combine the following sentence pairs into one sentence by adding an appositive to the end. Follow the example.

Example: Give the screwdriver to that man. He is my father.
Answer: Give the screwdriver to that man, my father.

1. Jack never misses a chance to play basketball. It is his favorite sport.
2. Carol gave her new dog a name. The name she chose was Shep.
3. The library subscribes to <u>Time</u>. <u>Time</u> is a weekly news magazine.
4. Andrew bought a new painting. It was a watercolor.
5. Special equipment can be used to examine the aorta. The aorta is the largest blood vessel leading from the heart.
6. Paul Tibbits piloted the Enola Gay. The Enola Gay was a B-29 bomber.
7. Margaret loved to wear her favorite piece of jewelry. It was a string of pearls.

8. The students appreciate Mr. Thompson. He is their science teacher.
9. The house had a terrible design flaw. The flaw was a wooden chimney.
10. That truck has a V-12. A V-12 is a type of engine.

Exercise 7-9

Number your work paper 1-10. Each of the sentences below has one or more appositives. Copy the sentences. Insert commas where necessary to set off the appositives.

1. Jerry a dentist graduated from college in two years.
2. My dad spends every Saturday morning doing what he loves most mowing the lawn.
3. Jane the school's top student wrote a report about photosynthesis the process which plants use to convert sunlight into food.
4. Nelly enjoyed her favorite morning drink hot chocolate.
5. The Enola Gay a B-29 bomber was piloted by a famous American Paul Tibbits.
6. Kanji a form of Japanese writing uses pictures to represent words.
7. Sewers people who sew for a living make bows ribbons for girls to wear in their hair.
8. We have learned how to use the semicolon a mark of punctuation.
9. A compound sentence two sentences joined to form one may be made using a semicolon.
10. Our English teacher a graduate of Harvard says that John Steinbeck the author of <u>The Pearl</u> was one of America's greatest writers.

It is important to remember that we are learning to improve our writing. We have learned about compound sentences, and we have learned about appositives. We can easily write compound sentences that contain appositives. Look at the example.

Example sentence #1: Paul, an artist, traveled to France.
Example sentence #2: He toured Paris, the capital.

Compound Sentence:
Paul, an artist, traveled to France; he toured Paris, the capital.

The semicolon makes the compound sentence! We must always put what we are learning into practice as soon as possible. In this way, we will better remember our lessons.

Exercise 7-10

Number your work paper 1-5. Each sentence pair contains at least one appositive. Combine the sentences using a semicolon, and set off all appositives with commas. Follow the example.

Example: Jim my brother plays football. He is a guard a lineman.
Answer: Jim, my brother, plays football; he is a guard, a lineman.

1. Mrs. Ames our science teacher collects butterflies. She has been adding to her collection since she was five years old.
2. Thomas Edison the king of inventors invented the electric light bulb. He also invented another common tool the motion picture camera.
3. One common metal steel is used in the production of automobiles. Another metal titanium is used for building aircraft.
4. Hurricanes swirling storms that begin over warm water always travel toward the earth's poles. They are called typhoons in Japan.
5. Tim my younger brother plays quarterback on the junior varsity football team. Next year his sophomore year he expects to start on the varsity squad.

Using "however" and "in fact"

In this course we will learn many rules. Here is an important one:
*Don't begin sentences with **And** or **But**.*

We can write much better sentences using the words *In fact* and *However*. One way we use the words *in fact* is to replace the word *and*.

Incorrect: John went home. And he did his homework.
Correct: John went home. In fact, he did his homework.

Sometimes we add *In fact* to the beginning of a sentence to help strengthen a point.

> *John eats breakfast. He always eats eggs.*
> *John eats breakfast. In fact, he always eats eggs.*

The word *however* means the same as *but*. Look.

> *John went home. But he didn't watch TV.*
> *John went home. However, he didn't watch TV.*

Exercise 7-11

Number your work paper 1-5. Copy the sentence pairs. Add either *In fact* or *However* to the beginning of the second sentence. Be sure to use a comma. Follow the examples.

Example: Mary was late for school. But she caught up quickly.
Answer: Mary was late for school. However, she caught up quickly.

1. John didn't like the heat. But he hated the cold.
2. John didn't like the heat. He really hated it.
3. Mary wanted to get an "A." But she got a "B."
4. Mary hoped for an "A." She got an "A+."
5. Tim was hungry.   He was very hungry. But he didn't have enough money to buy lunch.

Exercise 7-12

Number your work paper 1-5. Write either *However* or *In fact*. Be sure to use a comma. Follow the example.

Example: Tim plays soccer. _____ he plays every day.
Answer :   In fact,

1. Jane and Mary love school. _____ they never want to leave.
2. That boy is a great hitter. _____ he can't catch.
3. Mr. Jones teaches English. _____ he prefers to teach math.
4. My grandmother visited last week. _____ she stayed a full seven days.
5. John liked the movie. _____ he was so tired, he fell asleep while watching it.

Review

Let's take a quick review quiz to measure our progress.
Answer the questions on your work paper.

1. The _____ is a mark of punctuation used to join two complete sentences into one sentence.
2. Two sentences combined into one are called a _____ sentence.
3. _____ are words or groups of words that help explain other groups of words.

Write the appositive on your work paper. Be sure to include all commas.

4. Dr. Jones, my neighbor, works at the hospital.
5. The Purple Heart, an award for bravery, is given to soldiers wounded in combat.
6. The theory of relativity was discovered by Albert Einstein, the famous physicist.

Combine the sentences using appositives.

7. The TV finally stopped working. The TV was an old one.
8. Mr. Smith's classroom is usually loud. It is the last one in the corridor.

Summary

✓ Mechanics is the way words and punctuation work together.
✓ Appositives are groups of words that describe other words in a sentence.
✓ Appositives always come directly after the word or words they are describing.
✓ Appositives are always set off with commas.

Chapter 8

Paragraphs of Opinion

We know that when writing a paragraph of facts, we must include a topic sentence. The topic sentence tells our audience what we will be writing about. In fact, the topic sentence is a promise to our audience. From the very beginning, we tell our audience what we intend to write about. We keep our promise by including only details that match our topic sentence.

Paragraphs of fact work well when we are writing reports or summaries. Our teachers can check our understanding of what we have read or watched by asking us to write a paragraph of facts. When writing paragraphs of facts we always begin with a topic sentence. The topic sentence is a fact. It is the most important fact in the paragraph.

Sometimes we are asked to write paragraphs that express opinions. Like a paragraph of fact, a paragraph of opinion must contain a main idea sentence. The main idea sentence will come at the beginning of the paragraph. It will state an opinion. We call this sentence the thesis statement.

Thesis statements

A *thesis statement* is a sentence that expresses an opinion. It is the *main opinion* of a paragraph or even a longer piece of writing. Oftentimes, your teachers will require that you write opinions. Knowing how to write a thesis statement is very important. A well-written thesis statement immediately informs your audience of your opinion.

Exercise 8-1

Number your work paper 1-2. Next to the 1 write the words *Topic Sentence*. Next to the 2 write the words *Thesis Statement*. Write a definition for each of these two key terms.

1. Topic sentence
2. Thesis statement

Although thesis statements may appear anywhere in a paragraph, in this course we will always write the thesis statement first. We want our audience to know our opinions right away.

Fact and opinion

Before writing about facts or opinions, it is important to be able to explain the difference between a fact and an opinion.

Generally speaking, a fact is any piece of information that is known to be true. Here are some examples of facts: dogs are animals, Montana is a state in the United States, cookies can be dunked in milk.

An opinion, on the other hand, is a point of view. An opinion is usually based on a person's feelings about a particular topic. Here are some examples of opinions: dogs make the best pets, Montana is the most beautiful state in the United States, and the only way to truly in enjoy cookies is to dunk them in milk.

Notice that it is usually very simple to turn a fact into an opinion. As writers, we simply need to step back from the fact and ask ourselves how we feel about it. We can then write our opinion.

Exercise 8-2

Number your work paper 1-10. Write an *F* if the statement gives a fact. Write an *O* if it gives an opinion.

1. Amelia Earhart was a pilot who lived in the early twentieth century.
2. She was the greatest aviator who ever lived.
3. Amelia learned to fly in 1921.
4. She was also a fantastic writer.
5. She wrote a book, <u>20Hrs. 40 Min,</u> describing the flight in which she became the first woman to cross the Atlantic Ocean.
6. Amelia probably married George Putnam, a book publisher,

in order to sell more books.

7. Amelia once said that flying was perhaps one of the most important advances in science.
8. In 1937, Amelia attempted to fly around the world with Fredrick Noonan, a navigator.
9. The disappearance of her plane on July 2, led to the greatest mystery of all time.
10. To this day, no one can say for certain what happened to Amelia, Noonan, and their plane.

Facts into opinions

As writers, we can become skilled at turning facts into opinions.

Exercise 8-3

Number your work paper 1-10. Rewrite the facts as opinions. Try to write sentences that clearly state your opinion. Use the examples.

Fact: *Amelia Earhart was a pilot.*
Opinion: Amelia Earhart was the greatest pilot the world has ever seen.

Fact: *Some people eat ham and eggs for breakfast.*
Opinion: Only people who don't care about their health eat ham and
            eggs for breakfast.

Fact: *Electricity has changed the world.*
Opinion: In my opinion, electricity is the greatest discovery in the
            history of the world.
Opinion : In my opinion, electricity, which is usually produced by
            burning fossil fuels, has helped destroy the earth.

1. Bicycles are a form of transportation.
2. Jet aircraft can fly faster than the speed of sound.
3. Most people watch TV.
4. Skiing is a winter sport.
5. Red and blue are colors.
6. One type of dessert is apple pie.
7. We follow conventions when we write.
8. Ambiguous writing is confusing.
9. Homophones are words that sound the same.
10. People talk, read, write, and think.

<u>Opinion into fact</u>

We can also change opinions into facts. Look.

> *(Opinion) All students should be required to wear uniforms.*
> *(Fact)   Some students are required to wear uniforms.*

Exercise 8-4

Number your work paper 1-10. Change the opinions into facts.
Example:

Opinion: Mashed potatoes are delicious.
Fact: Mashed potatoes are often served with dinner.

Opinion: Ford makes the best trucks.
Fact: Ford makes trucks.
1. Everyone likes panda bears.
2. Painting with watercolors is extremely difficult.
3. Homophones can be funny.
4. It's easy to remember that stop signs are red.
5. Everyone knows that the sun is a star.
6. Amelia Earhart, one of the earliest female fliers, was the greatest pilot ever.
7. Helen Keller wrote wonderful books.
8. Chocolate chip cookies are the best.
9. Newspapers are the best way to get the news.
10. In my opinion, football is better than baseball.

Each of the sentences in the preceding exercise states an opinion. Each of these sentences could be the thesis statement for a paragraph. Look at the paragraph of opinion that Kristen wrote using the sentence *Everyone likes panda bears* as a thesis statement.

Everyone likes panda bears. People flock to zoos to see these cute animals. When new panda cubs are born they are often shown on the news. People like pandas because they look so friendly. There are even international organizations dedicated to saving the panda from extinction. Pandas always make people smile.

Kristen wrote a paragraph of opinion. She started her paragraph with a thesis statement that gave an opinion. As a student, you may agree with Kristen when she says that *Everyone likes panda bears.* You must bear in mind, however, that this is an opinion, not a fact. As difficult as it may be to believe, there might be someone, somewhere, who *hates* pandas. Agreeing with an opinion does not make the opinion a fact.

Let's look again at Kristen's paragraph. She didn't write only opinions. She mixed her opinions with facts.

Exercise 8-5
Number your work paper 1-2. Write two facts that Kristen included in her paragraph.

Combining opinion with fact
When writing a paragraph of opinion, it is not enough to simply state opinions. You must base your opinions on facts.

Imagine a courtroom scene. It is the end of the trial and the prosecutor is addressing the jury. Read the two speeches the prosecutor might give. One speech is all opinion. The other is opinion combined with fact. Which do you feel makes the best case?

Opinion speech:
"Ladies and gentlemen of the jury, the accused is guilty. He is so guilty that I can't believe how guilty he is. He's the guiltiest guilty man I have ever seen. You must send him to prison because he is as guilty as guilty can be."

Opinion and fact speech:
"Ladies and gentlemen of the jury, the accused is guilty. Video cameras show him committing the crime. Ten eyewitnesses saw him commit the crime. He denies the crime in court, but admitted it to all his friends. You must send him to prison. He is guilty."

When you state an opinion, you want others to see things your way. The best way to do this, is to use facts to help strengthen your opinion.

Let's use an analogy. An *analogy* is a comparison. Analogies can help make ideas clear and meaningful.

Let's make this analogy: a paragraph of opinion is like a sandwich. The opinion is the bread, and the facts are slices of meat. We can make a huge sandwich if we want to, just as long as we don't make it completely out of bread or completely out of meat. We should try to make layers. We'll call this type of layered writing *sandwich writing*.

Look again at Kristen's paragraph about pandas. She begins with an opinion, her thesis statement. Next, she adds two facts, one about people visiting zoos, and the other about pandas being shown on the news. Then she adds another opinion, this one about pandas looking friendly, and she adds another fact, as well - international organizations are helping the panda. Finally, she concludes by stating her opinion one last time.

Kristen has made an opinion sandwich. She has layered her opinions (bread) with facts (meat). If we were to make a sandwich of Kristen's paragraph we would have layers of bread and meat. We would have an opinion sandwich.

Let's practice making some opinion sandwiches.

The TIGER method will come in handy. Of course, before we begin, we have to make a simple change. Remember, when we were first introduced to TIGER, the *T* stood for *Topic*.

Today, since we are writing a paragraph of opinion, we must change the meaning of the *T*. What do you suppose its new meaning will be?

Today, the *T* will stand for *Thesis*. Remember, a paragraph of opinion begins with a thesis statement.

The rest of the letters in TIGER remain unchanged. Look.

$$T = \underline{T}hesis$$
$$I = \underline{I}deas$$
$$G = \underline{G}roup$$
$$E = \underline{E}numerate$$
$$R = w\underline{R}ite$$

The subject of today's paragraph of opinion will be lunches at the school cafeteria. You can write about anything having to do with the lunches at your cafeteria (or even your lunches at home if you'd like!). As a model, we will be using Brad's paper.

The important thing to remember when we are writing a paragraph of opinion is that we want to convince people that our opinion is a solid one. Let's imagine that we will be presenting this piece of writing to an audience that is a group of people on a jury.

Our job is to convince the jury that our opinion is correct. In order to do this, we must support our opinions with facts. We will use TIGER to help us prewrite. Our goal is a sandwich paragraph, one that combines fact and opinion. Of course, our thesis statement, the first sentence in the paragraph, will be used to state our opinion.

Here is a checklist to ensure that we turn in a completed paper that shows what we know. It is much like the checklists for the Helen Keller and Alexander Graham Bell papers. Of course, we must always put new knowledge into practice. This time, the checklist requires that an appositive be used.

_____ *indented paragraph*
_____ *thesis statement (states our opinion)*
_____ *fact and opinion sentences that support the thesis*
_____ *clear writing that is unambiguous*
_____ *no fragments*
_____ *compound sentence using a semicolon*
_____ *appositive*
_____ *concluding sentence*

We will now write a paragraph of opinion. TIGER prewriting is important to organize our thoughts. Look at how Brad got started. Compare the first step in his prewrite to his final paragraph. Do you see how he grouped and numbered his ideas?

Thesis: The cafeteria should stop selling meatloaf.

Ideas: We have it every Wednesday.
        Nobody buys it.
        We should have Pizza, instead.
        The meatloaf is too salty
        Pizza is more nutritious (the tomato sauce)
        Everyone loves pizza.
        Pizza is healthy.

No More Meatloaf!

In my opinion, the cafeteria should stop selling meatloaf. It looks awful and tastes even worse. We have it every Wednesday and hardly anyone buys it. Most people complain that it is too salty. I think we should replace meatloaf with pizza. Everyone loves pizza, don't they? The tomato sauce is full of vitamins. Talk about healthy! Let's have pizza!

Brad has made a few mistakes in his paragraph, but they will be easy to correct. His paragraph is good enough to serve as a model for our own paragraphs. Let's get to work on our papers.

Exercise 8-6
T – Thesis

Write the word *Thesis* at the top of your paper. Now, write an opinion about lunch at the school cafeteria or somewhere else.

Exercise 8-7
I-Ideas

List your fact meat and opinion bread sentences. Write at least seven sentences.

Add a final opinion. This opinion should closely match the thesis statement, but it should not be an exact copy.

Exercise 8-8
G-Group

Draw lines to make logical groups. Try to pair opinions with facts that support them.

Exercise 8-9
E-Enumerate

Enumerate the order in which you want your sentences to appear. Remember, the thesis statement is always 1.

Exercise 8-10
R-wRite

Write your paragraph of opinion.

The important point to remember when writing a paragraph of opinion is this: opinions alone don't count. Opinions must be supported by facts.

Let's take another look at Brad's paragraph. It offers a mix of facts and opinions, and also follows the conventions, the rules, of proper writing. Brad's paragraph offers a variety of sentences that will keep his audience interested. He gets started with the words "In my opinion," to let us know that he is writing an opinion piece. Overall, Brad has written a fine paragraph. Let's read it.

No More Meatloaf!

In my opinion, the cafeteria should stop selling meatloaf. It looks awful and tastes even worse. We have it every Wednesday and hardly anyone buys it. Most people complain that it is too salty. I think we should replace meatloaf with pizza. Everyone loves pizza, don't they? The tomato sauce is full of vitamins. Talk about healthy! Let's have pizza!

This is a pretty good paragraph, but it could be improved. The first sentence expresses an opinion, and Brad uses facts to strengthen the opinion.

Take a look at the underlined portion. Brad has written a sentence that looks like a question. In fact, he is expressing an opinion. He is saying, "Everyone loves pizza."

Rhetorical questions

We call the question Brad asks a rhetorical question. *Rhetorical questions* are questions we ask, but without expecting an answer. Actually, when we ask a rhetorical question, we are often stating an opinion. We'll look at rhetorical questions more closely in a little while.

Brad has done a good job following the conventions of written English, but he could improve his paragraph. The major problem is this: Brad's thesis statement calls for the cafeteria to stop selling meatloaf, but it is clear that what he really wants is pizza. Therefore, he should change his thesis statement a little.

In my opinion, the cafeteria should serve pizza on Wednesday instead of meatloaf.

Additionally, Brad should show what he knows. For example, he should show that he knows about semicolons and appositives. Inserting these into the paragraph will take a little rewriting, but that is no trouble. The reward of a well written paper is worth the extra time. When people read good writing, they understand that the writer is a clear thinker. They form a good impression of the writer.

Let's take a look at the changes Brad made.

No More Meatloaf!

In my opinion, the cafeteria should serve pizza on Wednesday instead of meatloaf. The meatloaf looks awful; it tastes even worse. We have it every Wednesday, but hardly anyone buys it. Most people, including teachers, complain that it is too salty. I think we should replace meatloaf with pizza Everyone loves pizza, don't they? The tomato sauce is full of vitamins. Talk about healthy! Let's have pizza!

Check Brad's writing against the checklist. He has done everything that is required.

_____ *indented paragraph*
_____ *thesis statement (states our opinion)*
_____ *fact and opinion sentences that support the thesis*
_____ *clear writing that is unambiguous*
_____ *no fragments*
_____ *compound sentence using a semicolon*
_____ *appositive*
_____ *concluding sentence*

Furthermore, notice the underlined portions. Changing the original word *It* into the two words *The meatloaf* makes Brad's meaning clear. The sentence is not ambiguous. Brad has also added a semicolon and an appositive. The result is an excellent paragraph.

As previously discussed, rhetorical questions are questions which are asked, but for which no answers are expected. We almost always ask rhetorical questions in order to express an opinion.

Rhetorical question: Who doesn't like donuts?
Opinion: Everybody likes donuts.

Exercise 8-11
Number your work paper 1-5. Change the rhetorical questions into declarative sentences.
1. Who hasn't heard of Benjamin Franklin?
2. Why don't they sell something we could actually use?
3. What has happened to good manners?
4. How long should we have to stand here and wait?
5. Is there anything better than peanut butter and jelly?

Exercise 8-12
Number your work paper 1-5. Change the opinions into rhetorical questions.
1. I think they're making us wait too long.
2. Everyone has heard about Amelia Earhart.
3. Everyone has a TV.
4. We would all like to see less crime.
5. We all like to get presents.

Exercise 8-13
Return to your paragraph of opinion about the school cafeteria. Find a place where you could insert a rhetorical question. Skip two lines below the paragraph. Write the rhetorical question, then draw an arrow from the rhetorical question into the paragraph, indicating where you think it would best fit.

Before closing this chapter, let's take another look at our paragraphs of opinion about the school cafeteria. We'll know that we've done a good job if can answer "yes" to these simple questions:

Did I begin with a thesis statement?
Did I make a sandwich of fact and opinion?
Did I follow the conventions of written English?
Did I include a rhetorical question?
Did I conclude with an opinion sentence that matches my thesis?

Exercise 8-14

Be sure that you can answer "yes" to all the above questions. Rewrite your paragraph on a clean sheet of paper. Include the rhetorical question you just wrote.

Exercise 8-15

Number your work paper 1-5. Write the correct word.
1. (Its, It's) time to start reading.
2. (There, Their) car won't start.
3. Tim was angry. (In fact, However,) he didn't show it.
4. (There, Their) are more than ten people in line.
5. John did his homework. (In fact, However,) he even did the extra credit.

Summary

✓ A paragraph of opinion begins with a thesis statement.
✓ A thesis statement is an opinion.
✓ Opinions must be supported by facts.
✓ Sandwich writing involves layering facts and opinions.
✓ Rhetorical questions are questions that state an opinion. No answer is expected to a rhetorical question.

Chapter 9

Varied Sentences

Vary means *change*. If we live in a place where the weather is constantly changing, we might say, "The weather varies."

The word *various* is a form of the word *vary*. *Various* means "kinds of." Look.

> There are *various* flowers in the garden.
> John has a collection of coins from *various* countries.

Sometimes the word *various* is used alongside the words *kinds of*. Look.

> There are *various kinds of* flowers in the garden.

Another form of *vary* is *varied*. We can guess that *varied* has something to do with *kinds of* and *change*. Look.

> The weather *varied* from day to day.
> John had a stamp collection. The stamps *varied* by country.

As writers, we must use different kinds of sentences. We must vary our sentence types. Sometimes we need a particular kind of sentence to help us make a point. For example, we might choose to use a rhetorical question to express an opinion.

Other times, we might use an exclamation to show our audience that we have strong feelings about a subject.

Sometimes we will use long sentences, and other times we might use very short sentences.

We vary our sentences as we write. We use various kinds of sentences to help us make our thoughts clear. Varied sentences also help to keep our audience interested in our writing.

Four types of sentences

Generally speaking, we can say that there are four types of sentences:

Declarative sentences give information.
Interrogative sentences ask a question.
Exclamatory sentences show strong emotion.
Imperative sentences give a command or make a request.

Let's look at how the sentences are used.

Declarative

Bats are found on every continent except the Antarctic.
Helen Keller became a great communicator.

Interrogative

Who was Helen Keller?
When did Amelia Earhart learn to fly?

Exclamatory

How nice the weather is!
What a wonderful person Helen Keller was!

Imperative

Read that report by tomorrow morning.
Please give me a call before you leave.

Pay particular attention to exclamatory sentences. Almost any group of words can be made into an exclamatory sentence just by tacking an exclamation point to the end. Look.

Jim was late.
Jim was late!
Mary likes tomato soup.
Mary likes tomato soup!

In the above sentences the exclamation point was added to show that the writer considered the sentences to be particularly exciting. In these cases, we say the exclamation point is optional. An *option* is a choice. Therefore, we can say that the writer made a choice to end his sentences with an exclamation point, even though he could have ended them with a period.

There are some sentences, though, in which the exclamation point is required. It is not optional. These sentences follow the pattern of the examples below. Look.

<u>What</u> a wonderful day it is!
<u>How</u> delicious this is!

Notice the underlined words. These words normally begin interrogative sentences. In fact when you first read a sentence like this one:

<u>What</u> an expensive looking vase!

You might think you are about to read a question. Exclamatory sentences often start with the question words *What* and *How*. In these cases the exclamation point is required. Look.

It's a nice day today.   *<u>What</u> beautiful weather we're having!*
That was a good dinner.   *<u>How</u> delicious that dinner was!*

Exercise 9-1
Number your work paper 1-10. List the sentence type: declarative, interrogative, exclamatory, or imperative.

1. Alexander Graham Bell invented the telephone.
2. Have you ever heard of him?
3. What a change he made on society!
4. Bell was fascinated by sound.
5. You should read his biography.

6. His experiments in sound led to the invention of the phone.
7. What was the name of Bell's assistant?
8. Please research this on the web.
9. Helen Keller, who was deaf, turned to Bell for help.
10. How lucky it was that Bell knew Annie Sullivan!

Exercise 9-2

Number your work paper 1-10. Read the sentences. Decide which end mark of punctuation should be used. Write the mark on your paper.

1. Amelia Earhart was a famous aviator
2. What an exciting life she led
3. When did Alexander Graham Bell invent the telephone
4. Thomas Edison is known for his many inventions
5. Did you know that he invented the movie camera
6. He is respected as the King of Inventors
7. How hard he must have worked
8. Thomas Edison said that invention is one per cent inspiration and ninety-nine per cent perspiration
9. Do you understand what he meant
10. All inventors work hard

Exercise 9-3

Number your work paper 1-10. Follow the instructions for each item.

1. The classroom is cold. (write this as an exclamatory sentence)
2. How tall you are! (write this as a declarative sentence)
3. How tall you are! (write this as an interrogative sentence)
4. We will leave soon. (write this as an interrogative)
5. Dinner was delicious. (write as an exclamatory sentence)
6. I think we saw Bill at the movies. (write as an interrogative sentence)
7. Will you wash your hands? (write as an imperative sentence)
8. You will open your book. (write as an interrogative)
9. This is an interesting composition. (write as an exclamatory sentence)
10. Will you please remember to buy bread? (write an imperative sentence)

Look at number 8 and number 10 in the preceding exercise.

Will you open your book?
Will you please remember to buy bread?

These two interrogative sentences act something like rhetorical questions, don't they. They seem to be asking questions, but they are really giving commands. The commands are softened by phrasing them as questions. We'll call these types of sentences interrogatives, but let's keep in mind their real purpose. Their real purpose is to give a command.

Why are you interrupting me? (interrogative)
Stop interrupting me. (imperative)

Exercise 9-4

Number your work paper 1-5. Eeach interrogative sentence could be making a command. Write the command.
1. Do you think that you will be on time?
2. Will you be prepared to take a test tomorrow?
3. Would you please take a seat?
4. Could you tell me who said that?
5. Why are you chewing gum in the classroom?

Writing about an opinion

It's time to put what we've learned to work.

We will write a paragraph about a place that we would like to visit. Since we'll be writing opinions, we'll be sure to start with a thesis statement. Use this thesis statement as a model for one of your own:
In my opinion, the Grand Canyon is the most beautiful place on earth.

Let's put everything we have learned into this paragraph. Use the checklist to help you.

_____ ;
_____ *rhetorical question*
_____ *sandwich construction*

Remember to use varied sentences, too.

_____ *declarative*
_____ *interrogative*
_____ *imperative*
_____ *exclamatory*

Kristen used the TIGER method to prewrite her paragraph. It

only took a couple of minutes, and she was able to focus her thinking on the assignment. Read her paragraph. You may want to use it as a model for your own. Notice that she has met all the conditions of the checklist.

A Place I Would Like to Visit

In my opinion, the Grand Canyon is the most beautiful place on earth. I wish I could visit there someday. The Canyon's history is fascinating. It was formed by erosion through millions of years. In pictures that I have seen, there are beautiful layers of colorful rock. Could anything be more wonderful? I think that everyone should visit the Grand Canyon; it's one of the great wonders of the world. How I wish I could go!

Notice that Kristen used a variety of sentences in her paragraph. She wrote for her audience, and that is why her writing sounds so good!

Exercise 9-5
Now it's your turn! Write a paragraph about a place you would like to visit. Be sure to prewrite to organize your thoughts. TIGER is an excellent way to organize thoughts. Also, be sure that you can put a check mark in front of each requirement in the check list.

Exercise 9-6
Sometimes the word *too* has the meaning *also*. When *too* is used to mean *also* it must be set off with commas. Look.
> *He also bought beans.*
> *He bought beans, **too**.*

Sometimes *too* means *very*. When *too* means *very*, do not use commas. Look.
> *It was very cold. We couldn't play baseball.*
> *It was **too** cold to play baseball.*

Number your work paper 1-10. If the sentence is correct write *C*. If it is incorrect write *I*.

1. It was too hot to go outside.
2. I, too, love pizza.
3. John said that he was, too, tired to watch TV.
4. Mary wondered if Tim liked her, too.
5. Too many cooks spoil the broth.
6. Did you go to the movies too?
7. Kimberly said that she, too, wanted to go to the movies.
8. That game ended in a two-to-two tie too.
9. We wondered if they were reading, too.
10. I was interested in science, too.

Summary

✓ *Vary* means *change*.
✓ There are four types of sentences:
> **Declarative sentences** *give information.*
> **Interrogative sentences** *ask a question.*
> **Exclamatory sentences** *show strong emotion.*
> **Imperative sentences** *give a command or make a request.*

✓ Exclamatory sentences often begin with *How* or *What*.
✓ The word *too* has two meanings:
> too = also (requires commas)
> too = very (no commas required)

Chapter 10

Narratives

A *narrative* is a story. It may be made up, or it may tell about something that actually happened. The important thing to remember is that narratives tell stories.

Chronological order

One way to tell a story is in chronological order. When we tell a story in *chronological order*, we tell the events of the story in the *time order* in which they happened. The word chronological has the root *chrono* meaning *time*. When we tell a story in chronological order, we are telling the events of the story in the order that the events occurred.

A narrative has a beginning, a middle, and an end. A narrative may be as short as one paragraph or as long as a book. In this chapter, we will focus on writing one paragraph narratives that clearly explain a situation in chronological order.

Let's begin by looking at some words and expressions that help us undertand the order in which things happen. We will call these words *time transitions*. Some examples of time transitions are words like *then*, *next*, and *finally*.

We are all familiar with using time transitions to tell stories in chronological order. We use these words and expressions all the time. For this lesson, we will attach these time transitions to the beginning of sentences. We will attach them using commas.

Time Transitions

Remember, as writers we have two tools to help us make our meaning clear. We have words, and we have punctuation. When writing time transitions we will use both. Time transitions are words that are attached to sentences with commas. The commas tell our audience to slow slightly in their reading. The comma helps to make the meaning of the sentence clear. Be careful when attaching time transitions. Generally speaking, only the first word of a sentence gets capitalized.

Later, we had dinner.

Notice that *we* is not capitalized.

Exercise 10-1

Number your work paper 1-10. Rewrite each sentence using the time transition in parenthesis. Be sure to use a comma to help set off the transition words.

Example: Open the box. (First)
Answer: First, open the box.
1. We got up early to go to the park. (First of all,)
2. We ate a good breakfast. (Secondly,)
3. We loaded up the car. (Next,)
4. We headed out onto the highway. (After that,)
5. Dad said that he saw the exit sign. (Then,)
6. We got off the freeway. (Finally,)
7. The day was ours to enjoy. (At last,)
8. We played volleyball. (Later,)
9. The dog ran away. (In the middle of the game,)
10. We drove back home. (After we found him,)

Let's take a closer look at three of the time transitions from the preceding exercise:

First of all,   After that,   At last,

What makes these time transitions different from the others in the list? These time transitions use more than one word.

Often, transitions require more than one word. Here are some more transitions from the preceding exercise.

By then,   In the middle of the game,

Some time transitions require more than just one word to make sense. Others require more than one word because if they stand alone they lead to sentence fragments. Look.

Sentence: *We drove to the park.*
Fragment: *When we drove to the park.*
              After we drove to the park.
              While we drove to the park.

Let's look at one of the fragments:
              While we drove to the park.

It is clear that this group of words is a fragment. A complete sentence would have to look like this:

<u>While we drove to the park</u>, we listened to the radio.

Note how the underlined fragment has been attached to a complete sentence with a comma. Also notice that the comma is placed exactly where it seems we must take a short break in order for our reading to make sense. Remember, a comma is like a road sign telling our audience to slow down.

Exercise 10-2
Number your work paper 1-5. Rewrite the sentences inserting commas where necessary.

1. When I was walking to school this morning a strange thing happened.
2. First of all a man wearing a mask and carrying a burlap sack ran down the street.
3. After that a barking police dog passed me.
4. Next a policeman ran by blowing his whistle.
5. Just then I realized a movie crew was trying to make a movie.

Exercise 10-3

Number your work paper 1-10. At the beginning of each sentence, you will see time transition words. On your work paper, write the word that needs the comma. Follow the example.

Example: While he was exercising Phil listened to music.
Answer: exercising,

1. After winning the game the team celebrated.
2. When answering questions do you sometimes get confused?
3. First remove the foil packaging.
4. After you have removed the cover label the box.
5. Next be sure to put the serial number in a safe place.
6. While studying math it is a good idea to be in a quiet room.
7. When we got home from school we went to swimming practice.
8. After the dance Mary went to a movie.
9. Later we all went to the baseball game.
10. After that we walked home.

Exercise 10-4

Number your work paper 1-10. The sentences in this exercise are in the correct chronological order to form a short narrative. Rewrite each sentence using the time transition words that help your audience understand the chronological order of the story.

1. We went to Lake Smith. (last week)
2. We picked out a camping spot. (when we got there)
3. We unloaded the car. (after that)
4. Our dog, Rex, ran away. (while we were busy)
5. We searched for him. (for three hours)
6. We found him. (finally)
7. We were ready to set up camp. (after getting back to the camp site)
8. Dad set up the tent. (first)
9. We all moved our sleeping bags inside. (then)
10. We were set up and ready to camp. (at last)

   Transition words help us understand the chronological order of a narrative. Narratives are stories. They may be true, or made up.

Exercise 10-5

Number your work paper 1-10. Write sentences that go together to form a short narrative. Execise 10-4 can be your guide. Use the transition words to begin your sentences. Be sure to include commas.

1. last summer
2. at first
3. while
4. then
5. when
6. next
7. after
8. later
9. finally
10. at last

Kristen wrote a narrative about her science fair project. Read it and notice how she used time transitions to show chronological order. She also used a variety of sentence types.

Last year, I decided to do a science fair project on solar energy. First, I went to the library to read about solar power in an encyclopedia. Who would have thought there was so much to read? After that, I realized I had to narrow my topic; in fact, I decided to concentrate on using solar energy to boil water. What a great idea! I made a solar reflector from a reflector inside an old flashlight. Next, I took my new reflector outside and pointed it at a small glass of water. At first, nothing seemed to happen, but then, the water began to boil. I had created a successful project.

Exercise 10-6

Number your work paper 1-10. Answer the questions.

   1-6. List all the time transitions Kristen used in her paragraph.
   7. Kristen uses a rhetorical question. Write it on your paper.
   8. Kristen uses an exclamatory sentence. Write it on you paper.
   9-10. Kristen uses two compound sentences. Write both on you paper.

      Kristen has written a fine paragraph. Notice that she does not use transition words to begin every sentence. She uses the sandwich method of writing. She lists events (facts) and her feelings (opinions) about them. This is a good strategy to follow when writing narratives.

      Sandwich writing is a very useful method of getting our readers to understand exactly what happened and how we feel about it.

Exercise 10-7

Write a narrative paragraph. Remember a narrative may either be real or made up. Tell your story in chronological order. Let's start our paragraphs with a fact, like Kristen did. Prewrite using the TIGER method. Use the checklist to ensure that you have written a good paragraph.

        _____ *indented paragraph*
        _____ *topic sentence (fact) to get started*
        _____ *fact and opinion sentences that support the thesis*
        _____ *clear writing that is unambiguous*
        _____ *no fragments*
        _____ *compound sentence using a semicolon*
        _____ *appositive*
        _____ *concluding sentence*

Chapter 11

Interrupters

Read this sentence:

My cousin John is I think living in fact in New York.

The sentence is difficult to read. Several ideas seem to be jumbled together. At first, you might think this is a run-on sentence. A *run-on sentence* is two or more sentences joined incorrectly. The example is not a run-on. This sentence is an example of a sentence with interrupters.

We have already learned about one special type of interrupter. It is called an appositive. Remember, appositives are words or groups of words that help to explain other groups of words.

Commas

We use commas to set off appositives. When we say that we set off appositives with commas, we mean that we separate the appositive from the rest of the sentence using commas.

Commas tell us to slow down for a moment as we read. When reading a sentence with an appositive, the commas help us to better understand the meaning of the sentence. Commas are used to set off appositives.

Look at the two examples. The first is incorrect. Commas have not been used to set off the appositive. The sentence is difficult to read. It must be read at least twice in order to be understood.

Incorrect: People all insurance agents gathered at the convention.
Correct: People, all insurance agents, gathered at the convention.

Notice how commas help to set off the appositive in the correct version. They tell us to slow down when we see them. The sentence is much easier to understand.

Appositive review
Let's quickly review appositives. When we are expert at appositives, we will be able to recognize and use other types of interrupters.

Exercise 11-1
Number your work paper 1-5. Each sentence contains an appositive. Write the appositive. Include the commas.
1. The clouds, thunderheads, ruined the picnic.
2. We, all of us, wanted to leave.
3. That dog, a German shepherd, loves to play.
4. The scissors, stainless steel, were sharp as razors.
5. Alaska, the largest state, is located partly in the Arctic.

Remember, when dealing with an appositive, the commas act like hooks. We can use the hooks to lift the appositive part out of the sentence. A complete sentence will remain. We call this the main, or root, sentence. Look at the example.

With appositive: The girl, **a student,** studies every day.
Remove the appositive: **, a student,**
The main sentence is: The girl studies every day.

Exercise 11-2
Number your work paper 1-5. Each of the following sentences contains an appositive. Remove the appositive. On your work paper, write the main sentence.
1. John, my older brother, lives in Las Vegas.
2. Cathy, a paralegal, works every day.

3. That woman, a teacher, loves to read.
4. Dreadnaughts, battleships, were fierce weapons in World War II.
5. Jumbo jets, large aircraft capable of carrying large amounts of cargo, are getting larger and larger.

Now, let's try something new. Test your ability to spot appositives when no commas are present. The key to finding the appositive is locating the spot where you must pause in your reading in order for the sentence to make sense.

Example: Tim our neighbor likes to eat dinner at our house.

Listen for the pauses.

Example: Tim (pause) our neighbor (pause) likes to eat dinner at our house.

To correct the sentence, simply insert commas where you naturally pause during reading.

Example: Tim, our neighbor, likes to eat dinner at our house.

Exercise 11-3

Number your work paper 1-10. Each of the sentences has an appositive, but there are no commas to help set off the appositive. Rewrite each of the sentences, adding commas where necessary.

1. Jane likes truffles chocolates with soft centers.
2. The photograph a black and white one was fuzzy.
3. That woman the one in the red dress dances well.
4. Helen Keller the famous writer was deaf and blind.
5. The way words and punctuation work together is known by a simple word mechanics.
6. Semicolons marks of punctuation used to join two sentences into one compound sentence make sentences interesting.
7. Sewers pipes that carry waste water are buried deep in the ground.
8. Sewers people who operate sewing machines work hard.
9. The pen old and dry could barely write.
10. Thomas Edison the king of inventors was born over 100 years ago.

We can often tell where an appositive begins and ends by the sound of the sentence. Sentences with appositives sound like they need commas. The commas tell the reader to slow down slightly.

Interrupters

Appositives are a kind of interrupter. They are called interrupters because they interrupt a sentence. Commas set off appositives. We can use the commas to lift the appositive out of the sentence. The main sentence remains. This is an important point.

The following sentences all contain interrupters. The interrupters are not appositives. Appositives are groups of words that describe other groups of words. Interrupters do not necessarily describe other words in the sentence. Read the examples. The interrupters are underlined.

As a matter of fact, your answer is correct.
Your answer, as a matter of fact, is correct.
Your answer is correct, as a matter of fact.

What do you notice about interrupters?

In the first place, interrupters require commas. Interrupters are set off by commas.

Also, interrupters can occur almost anywhere inside a sentence. An interrupter might occur at the beginning of a sentence, or it might occur somewhere in the middle. Interrupters can appear at the end of sentences, too. Let's look at some more interrupters.

By the way, did you remember to send that letter?
Well, I forgot all about it.
Mary, you really should try harder to remember things.
I, you know, just forgot.
You'll do better next time, I'm sure.

Interrupters interrupt the flow of the main sentence. Remember, appositives also interrupt the flow of the main sentence. An appositive is set off by commas. The commas tell the reader to slow down slightly. Slowing down helps the reader more clearly understand the meaning of the sentence.

An appositive may be removed from a sentence by using the commas as hooks. The main sentence remains.

Interrupters work exactly the same way! This is why learning to use interrupters is so easy.

Let's practice with interrupters.

Exercise 11-4

Number your work paper 1-10. Each sentence contains an interrupter. Write the interrupter on your paper. Be sure to include all commas.
Example: Bill, of course, will be the team captain.
Answer: , of course,

1. To tell the truth, I have never really thought about it.
2. Sue wanted to go on the trip, however.
3. Prime numbers, for example, are studied in algebra.
4. By the way, your homework will be due on Monday.
5. Jim's brother, I believe, plays football.
6. All words are symbols, I believe.
7. It was raining. Nevertheless, we went to the picnic.
8. On the contrary, I disagree completely with your opinion.
9. That book, on the other hand, looks brand new.
10. Many people, in my opinion, don't listen carefully.

Here is an important point. Interrupters can be removed from a sentence. Remember, commas can act like hooks. They can pull the interrupter completely from the sentence.

Read the sentences in Exercise 11-4 aloud. Leave the interrupters out. You will find that the sentences make perfect sense, even without the interrupters.

Exercise 11-5

Number your work paper 1-10. Each of the following sentences contains at least one interrupter. Use the commas as hooks to remove the interrupters. Rewrite the main sentence on your paper.

1. Frank, I believe, gets straight A's in math.
2. In fact, Helen Keller was born a healthy baby.
3. Football is the greatest sport, in my opinion.
4. A bad dinner is better than no dinner, I suppose.
5. We must, on the other hand, consider opposing views.
6. John, by the way, will be arriving late.
7. We weren't happy, however.
8. However, it rained.

9. Helen Keller, deaf from an early age, learned to speak, nevertheless.
10. Philosophers, for example, study knowledge.

In order to communicate clearly, let's name interrupters according to their position in a sentence. An *interrupter first*, for example, would be an interrupter that appears at the beginning of a sentence. Look at the examples of interrupter first sentences.

> *To tell the truth, I can't answer that question.*
> *Of course, I want what's best for you.*
> *However, you should check your answers first.*

An *interrupter middle* is an interrupter that occurs somewhere inside the sentence. Look at the examples.

> *I can't, to tell the truth, answer that question.*
> *I want, of course, what's best for you.*
> *You should, however, check your answers first.*

An *interrupter last* is an interrupter that appears at the end of a sentence.

> *I can't answer that question, to tell the truth.*
> *I want what's best for you, of course.*
> *You should check your answers first, however.*

How many commas do interrupter first sentences require?
How many commas do interrupter middle sentences require?
How man commas do interrupter last sentences require?
Remember, commas are hooks. We can drag an interrupter first out of a sentence by pulling the hook to the left. We can drag an interrupter last out of a sentence by pulling the hook to the right.
An interrupter middle requires two hooks, commas, to pull it free of the sentence.

An interrupter can be added almost any place in a sentence. The three sentences below illustrate this point.

> *Of course, Jose is an excellent student.*
> *Jose, of course, is an excellent student.*
> *Jose is an excellent student, of course.*

In the above examples, the main sentence is always the same. The main sentence is "Jose is an excellent student". The interrupters help add power to the main sentence.

Exercise 11-6
Number your work paper 1-10. Each of the sentences contains an interrupter. Use the letters below to identify the type of interrupter.

F - Interrupter first
M - Interrupter middle
L - Interrupter last

Example: Our English teacher, by the way, reads a book a week.
Answer: M

1. However, the first choice is still the best.
2. My older brother, in fact, lives in Germany.
3. The movie begins at 8:00, I believe.
4. You are, I suppose, ready to begin.
5. Jane, on the other hand, enjoys listening to music.
6. In my opinion, the movie needed a different ending.
7. On the contrary, you should always follow the rules.
8. The television was expensive. Nevertheless, I bought it.
9. I'd like another dessert, I believe.
10. Mary, by the way, told me to tell you hello.

In the following exercises you will be adding interrupters to sentences. Notice how the new sentences sound better than the originals.

Exercise 11-7
Number your work paper 1-5. Rewrite the sentences with an interrupter first.
Example: John will be late. (by the way)
Answer: By the way, John will be late.

1. She is an excellent cook. (to tell the truth)
2. A red light signals stop. (for example)
3. I don't want to. (however)
4. Baseball is better than football. (in my opinion)
5. Tadpoles become frogs. (in fact)

Now, let's rewrite the sentences from the preceding exercise. This time, we'll write the sentences with an interrupter middle. Be careful when adding an interrupter to the middle of a sentence. An interrupter in the wrong place sounds awkward. On the other hand, there are usually at least two places where an interrupter middle can be placed. Look at the examples.

Incorrect: *The, in fact, doctor was a specialist.*
Correct: *The doctor, in fact, was a specialist.*
Correct: *The doctor was, in fact, a specialist.*

Exercise 11-8
Number your work paper 1-5. Rewrite the sentences from Exercise 11-7. This time, change each interrupter to an interrupter middle.

Exercise 11-9
Number your work paper 1-5
Rewrite, again, the sentences from Exercise 11-7. This time, change each interrupter to an interrupter last.

Summary
   ✓ Interrupters are individual words or groups of words that interrupt the main thought of a sentence.
   ✓ Interrupters are set off with commas.
   ✓ Appositives are one type of interrupter.

Chapter 12

Examining Sentences

We have learned that a paragraph is a group of related sentences. It is a collection of sentences about a single topic. We have also learned that a paragraph has a special shape. It must be indented from the edge of the page. In the previous chapter, we wrote one paragraph narratives.

Word order

Paragraphs are made of sentences. It is important to remember that the meaning of a sentence is determined by the order of the words in the sentence. Changing the word order can change the meaning of the sentence.

Sharks eat swimmers.
Swimmers eat sharks.

Of course, this is a simple example. Other examples, though, may not be so easy to recognize. Read the following example sentence and see if you can find the mistake.

John found the dog who was a doctor.

Misplaced modifiers

The above sentence contains a misplaced modifier.

Modifiers are words that add extra information to a sentence. The term *misplaced modifier* is a special term writers use to help identify a specific kind of problem in sentences. *Misplaced modifiers* are words that are out of place.

Let's look at the original sentence one more time.
John found the dog who was a doctor.

What the writer wanted to say was this:
John, who was a doctor, found the dog.

Try this one:
The fireman rescued the cat wearing a heavy coat.

What do you think the writer was trying to say?

Mistakes in writing happen when we are in a hurry. We are not thinking clearly. We are not writing for our audience. We must always keep our audience in mind. Clear thinking leads to clear writing. Read this sentence. Be prepared to explain what it means.
The book was read by the entire class, a big one.

This sentence seems to be saying that a large-sized class, a class of maybe forty students or more, read a book.

Unfortunately, this is not what the writer wanted to say. The writer wanted to say that the book was big. In fact, it was over four hundred pages long. The writer made a simple mistake. The appositive words *a big one* are in the wrong place. The appositive should come after the word *book*, not after the word *class*.

Here is a simple way to fix the sentence:
The big book was read by the entire class.

When writing, we must take care to say exactly what we mean. We only get one chance to make our meaning clear to our audience. Remember, the order of the words in a sentence gives the sentence its meaning. If some words are out of order, the sentence may be confusing or ambiguous.

Mechanics
Actually, sentences may contain many problems. In order to correct the

problems in sentences, we must learn how sentences work.

Think of the engine in your car. It is a complicated piece of machinery. It is made of hundreds of parts, all working together. If a single part breaks, the engine may stop working. A trained mechanic understands how the parts of an engine work together. He can repair engine trouble. He has been trained to spot problems.

In this course we will learn how the parts of a sentence work together. We will learn how to repair broken sentences. We will be trained to write proper sentences. We will learn proper mechanics. Remember, in this course, mechanics is the way words and punctuation work together.

Before we begin taking apart sentences, let's have fun with a few more misplaced modifiers.

Exercise 12-1

Number your work paper 1-10. The following sentences have misplaced modifiers. Rewrite each sentence so that it makes better sense.

1. The car is parked in the driveway which is a Viper.
2. The TV is in the corner with the thirty-seven inch screen.
3. John drinks his coffee in a blue mug black.
4. A window is on the side of the house which is broken.
5. The clock is on the desk that runs fast.
6. The milk is in the refrigerator which is spoiled.
7. Mary bought a turtle who is a soccer player.
8. The painting was admired by a man on the wall.
9. Janice always carries a notebook who is a good student.
10. A man was working on a truck with long hair.

Exercise 12-2

Number your work paper 1-3. See if you can come up with misplaced modifier sentences of your own. Write them on your paper. Then, rewrite the sentences so that they make better sense. Feel free to use the sentences in Exercise 12-1 as a guide.

Example (misplaced modifier): People watched the blimp on the
curb.
Answer (corrected): *People on the curb watched the blimp.*

We have learned that word order in a sentence can change the meaning of the sentence. We have also learned that words are symbols, and that words have meaning. It is now time to begin looking at how everything works together to create sensible sentences.

Complete subject and predicate

Just as a mechanic begins his studies by learning the basic workings of an engine, we will begin with the basic parts of a sentence. All sentences have two basic parts. The basic parts of a sentence are the *complete subject* and the *complete predicate*.

All sentences must have two parts. One part names what the sentence is about. The other part tells what is happening in the sentence. Look.

Bill | eats cheese.
Naming part   Telling part

The wind | is hot.
Naming part   Telling part

The *complete subjec*t is the *naming part* of the sentence. It names who or what the sentence is mainly about.

The *complete predicate* is the *telling part* of the sentence. It tells what the subject does, or gives more information about the subject.

Look at this sentence. What is the complete subject?

The sky was dark.

The complete subject is *The sky*. Remember, the complete subject names who or what the sentence is mainly about.

The complete predicate is *was dark*. Why? Because the words *was dark* tell about the sky.

Exercise 12-3

Number your work paper 1-5. Skip lines between numbers. Rewrite the following sentences onto your work paper. Underline the complete subject once. Underline the complete predicate twice. Follow the example.
Example: The tall man plays basketball.

    1. John reads the newspaper every day.

    2. He turns to the sports section.

3. Football is his favorite sport.
4. Baseball and hockey interest him, too.
5. That young man played high school football.

You should notice that every word in the preceding exercise was underlined. All the words in the complete subject were underlined once, and all the words in the complete predicate were underlined twice.

Point to any word in any sentence. It must be either part of the subject or part of the predicate.

Every sentence must contain a subject and a predicate. In fact, every sentence is a combination of a complete subject and a complete predicate. We can make a simple mathematical equation from this fact.

Complete Subject + Complete Predicate = Complete Sentence

Any word in any sentence is either a part of the subject or a part of the predicate.

Exercise 12-4
Number your work paper 1-10. List the complete subjects. Remember, the complete subject tells who or what the sentence is mainly about. Follow the example.
Example: The women play tennis.
Answer: The women

1. The pictures in hieroglyphics represent words.
2. Ancient Egyptians used hieroglyphics to represent thoughts and ideas.
3. Hieroglyphics can be found in ancient Egyptian tombs.
4. People called scribes wrote the hieroglyphics.
5. The meaning of Egyptian hieroglyphics remained a mystery for centuries.
6. A French soldier discovered an interesting stone in Egypt in 1799.
7. The stone was a large, flat tablet.
8. It was engraved with three languages, including hieroglyphics and Greek.
9. This famous stone came to be called the Rosetta Stone.
10. The Rosetta Stone helped investigators unlock the mysteries of Egyptian hieroglyphics.

We have learned that any word in any sentence is either a part of the complete subject, or a part of the complete predicate. In the preceding exercise we identified the complete subject of each sentence. What does this tell us about the rest of the words in each of those sentences? It tells us that the rest of the words belong to the complete predicate.

Exercise 12-5

Number your work paper 1-10. Look at the sentences in Exercise 12-4. Write the first word of the complete predicate for each of the sentences. The first one is done for you.

1. Represent

Fragments

We now know that a complete sentence must contain a complete subject and a complete predicate. What do you suppose a sentence would be called if it only contained a complete subject?

It would be called a sentence fragment!

What do you suppose a sentence would be called if it only contained a complete predicate?

It would be called a sentence fragment, too!

Now for a quick review.

Exercise 12-6

Number your work paper 1-10. If the group of words is a sentence write an *S*. If it is a fragment, write an *F*.

1. Running wildly down the street.
2. The engine roared.
3. Mary reads.
4. The three men who were wearing suits.
5. For example, the Monarch butterfly.
6. You should be careful.
7. John assembled the model very carefully.
8. After gluing the wings together.
9. Joanne decided to bake brownies.
10. She bought the brownie mix.

Exercise 12-7

Number your work paper 1-6. For each complete sentence in Exercise 12-6, list the complete subject. You should have six answers. Follow the example.

Example: 1. The engine

Remembering that we must always write complete sentences will greatly improve our writing. Beware of fragments!

Exercise 12-8

Write a paragraph of facts about your family. Be sure to include only facts. Opinions are not allowed. You will need two sheets of paper: one for prewriting with TIGER and the other for your final draft. One possible topic sentence might look like this:

There are eight people in my family including me.

Summary

- ✓ Misplaced modifiers are words out of place.
- ✓ Misplaced modifiers can lead to ambiguous sentences.
- ✓ All sentences are made of two parts: the complete subject and the complete predicate.
- ✓ The complete subject is the naming part of a sentence.
- ✓ The complete predicate is the telling part of a sentence.
- ✓ A sentence fragment is a piece of a sentence.

Chapter 13

Subjects and Simple Subjects

The subject of any piece of writing is what the writing is about. For example, the subject of a science report on clouds, is clouds. The subject of a report about George Washington, is George Washington. The subjects always tells who or what the composition is about.

Simple subjects

We have learned that sentences have subjects, too. The subject of a sentence names who or what the sentence is mainly about. Earlier, we identified the complete subject of sentences. In this chapter we will learn to find the single most important word in the complete subject, the simple subject. The *simple subject* is the most important word in the complete subject.

Finding the simple subject is important. Many writers make mistakes because they do not know the subjects of the sentences they are writing. Look at the two example sentences. Only one of them is correct. Do you know which one is the correct one? Can you explain why?

The earrings or the bracelet <u>are</u> gold.
The earrings or the bracelet <u>is</u> gold.

We are working towards being able to answer questions like these. When we misuse the English language, we show that we are not knowledgeable about English. With hard work, we can improve our knowledge of English. By the way, in the preceding example, the second sentence is the correct one.

The earrings or the bracelet is gold.

Let's begin to learn why. In this chapter, we will learn to identify the simple subject of a sentence. Knowing what words make up the simple subject will help us correct some of our problems in writing.

First, let's review the four different types of sentences. These sentence types are tools for us to use. The more we write, the more we will come to appreciate these tools. By using a variety of sentences in our writing, we will keep our audience interested.

Four types of sentences

The word *declare* means *say*. When we declare something we say it out loud. We give information.

A declarative sentence gives information. Notice that the word *declarative* comes from the word *declare*. Declarative sentences always end with a period (.). The following are declarative sentences.

Dad arrived home late today.
Insects have six legs.
Ernest Hemingway is a famous author.

Almost every sentence you write will be a declarative sentence. In fact, this sentence is a declarative sentence.

The word *interrogate* means *question*. When we interrogate someone, we question them.

An interrogative sentence asks a question. The word *interrogative* comes from the word *interrogate*. Interrogative sentences always end with a question mark (?). Look at the following interrogative sentences.

What will the weather be like today?
Who asked that question?
How did you manage to build that?

We are used to calling interrogative sentences by another name. We usually call them questions. In this text we will use both terms.

When we *exclaim* something, we show strong emotion.

An *exclamatory sentence* shows *strong emotion*. Exclamatory sentences end with an exclamation mark (!). This mark is also called an exclamation point. Look at the exclamatory sentences.

> *Look out!*
> *What a beautiful day!*
> *How well you write!*

One meaning of *imperative* concerns giving orders. *Imperative sentences* give *orders or commands*. Generally, imperative sentences end with a period (.). There are times, though, when a writer wants to show a strong command. In these cases, an imperative sentence might end with an exclamation mark (!). Look at the imperative sentences.

> *Please pass your papers forward.*
> *Sit down right now!*
> *Hand me that screwdriver.*

Exercise 13-1

Number your work paper 1-10. Read each of the following sentences. You will notice that each is missing the correct endpoint of punctuation. In the space next to the number on your work paper, write the correct endpoint.

Example: Do you have your keys
Answer: ?

1. Will you please get ready to read
2. Some compositions require several paragraphs
3. Words are important to writers
4. What a nice paragraph
5. Your teacher will not allow ambiguous sentences
6. Misplaced modifiers cause confusion
7. Do you remember what a homophone is
8. Please compose a paragraph
9. The teacher asked the class if they could compose a paragraph
10. The class declared that they could

Finding simple subjects
We want to find the simple subject of a sentence in order to correct certain writing mistakes. We will find the simple subject inside the complete subject. Remember, the equation for a sentence looks like this:

Complete Subject + Complete Predicate = Complete Sentence

In other words, every complete sentence has a complete subject (the naming part) and a complete predicate (the telling part).

Converting interrogatives into declaratives
Normally, the complete subject comes at the beginning of a sentence. What about questions, though? What is the complete subject of this question:

Did every student turn in a homework paper?

To find the complete subject, we must rearrange a few words. We will try to make the question sound like a declarative sentence. Look at how we make the change.

Question: *Did every student turn in a homework paper?*
Declarative: *Every student did turn in a homework paper.*

True, the sentence sounds strange, but by rearranging the words we find the complete subject. The complete subject tells us who or what the sentence is mainly about.

We can easily see that the complete subject is

Every student

The simple subject is one of these two words. Common sense tells us that the word *student* is more important to the subject than the word *every*. Therefore, the simple subject of the sentence is *student*. A little common sense will go a long way when it comes to learning the conventions of English.

Let's look at another question and try to decide what the simple subject is.

Do you remember what a homophone is?

First, we will find the complete subject by rearranging the words a little to make a declarative sentence.

You do remember what a homophone is.

We can now see that there is only one word in the subject. The word is *You*. Therefore, the complete subject and the simple subject are the same: they are both the word:

You

Let's practice finding the complete subject of questions.

Exercise 13-2

Number your work paper 1-10. Make declarative sentences from the interrogative sentences. Underline the complete subject of each sentence. Look at the example.

Example: Who is he?
Answer: He is who.

1. Where are you going?
2. Did Mary see Phil?
3. What is the teacher saying about English?
4. When did the newspaper arrive?
5. Is the fan on the table?
6. Were John and Mary at school?
7. How do birds find worms?
8. Are bats mammals or birds?
9. How hot is boiling water?
10. When were Mary and Jane at the mall?

Converting imperatives into declaratives

We can also find the complete and simple subjects of imperative sentences. Imperative sentences, sentences of command, give orders. Sometimes the subject is given to us, but other times it is not. Look.

(Subject "John" is given):   John, please pick up your papers.
(No subject given):   Please pick up your papers.

When no subject is given in an imperative sentence we can often imagine that the word *You* is the subject. Look.

John, please pick up your papers.
***You**, please pick up your papers.*

What is the subject of this imperative sentence?
Call home.

The subject is *You.* We could rewrite sentence this way:
You, call home.

Exercise 13-3

Number your work paper 1-10. Some of the word groups below are fragments. Others are sentences. If the word group is a fragment, write the word *Fragment*. If the word group is a sentence, tell whether it is *Declarative*, *Interrogative*, *Exclamatory*, or *Imperative*. Do not abbreviate your answers. Writing full answers only takes a second or two longer than writing abbreviations, and it will help you remember these very important words.

1. Who told the teacher that?
2. After everyone was seated.
3. When did you find out?
4. Study these words!
5. The foot bone is connected to the ankle bone.
6. Do you believe everything you hear?
7. I think so.
8. For example, bloodhounds make good pets.
9. Watch for red lights.
10. Is everyone listening?

Exercise 13-4

Number your work paper 1-5. Look at the form of these nonsense sentences. If they look like interrogative sentences, write the word *Interrogative*. If they look like declarative sentences, write the word *Declarative*. If they look like exclamatory sentences, write *Exclamatory*. Remember, a sentence must begin with a capital letter, and end with a mark of punctuation. If the nonsense group looks like a fragment, write *Fragment*.

1. Qghy dcr thalsdk tpoi ghedkt?
2. cvglsj slf nomaa ghe.
3. Bllkjd sl gjsl hj teksl.
4. Ccngh ty sdproef tjlelpp thws;l?
5. Cnsls glslsdj gjdk sl fjfjls qpzpx!

We are learning about various kinds of sentences. This will help us improve our writing. In order to improve, we must practice every day. The next exercise is a short writing exercise. Before beginning, let's talk for a moment about checklists. In this class, the word checklist refers to specific pieces of information the teacher is looking for in a piece of writing.

By using a variety of sentences, appositives, semicolons, and other writing tricks, we can make our writing clear and interesting. We want to make using these simple tricks a matter of habit. Therefore, we use checklists. Checklists remind us of the skills we have learned, and they help us develop good habits of writing.

Our writing must always make sense. If a question has been assigned, our writing must answer the question. Our teachers will be looking for specific features in our writing. Look at the checklist.

_____ *indented paragraph*
_____ *topic sentence (or thesis statement if writing an opinion)*
_____ *detail sentences that support the topic*
_____ *clear writing that is unambiguous*
_____ *a variety of sentence types (including interrogatives)*
_____ *no fragments*
_____ *appositives and interrupters*
_____ *compound sentence using a semicolon*
_____ *concluding sentence*

If our writing makes sense, and if we are able to check off each of the requirements on the checklist, we can be pretty certain that we have done a good job.

Exercise 13-5
Read the thesis statement and the detail sentences. Put them together and write a paragraph on your work paper. Use the model as your guide. Be sure to start each sentence with a capital letter. Include a rhetorical question in your paragraph.

Thesis statement: *The home chore I most dislike is mowing the lawn.*
Ideas: *it takes up half of Saturday morning*
                          during the summer the heat makes the job almost
                          unbearable

117

I get covered with grass clippings
Does anyone else have to spend Saturday mornings
mowing the lawn?

Here is a model of a well-written paragraph. Notice that it meets all the requirements of the checklist.

Model

The home chore I most dislike is mowing the lawn. Could there be anything worse? Doing it right, the way my dad wants it, takes up half of Saturday morning. In summer, the heat is so bad, I practically melt. Talk about hot! I get covered with sweat; grass clippings stick to my body. Does anyone else live this kind of a life? I hate mowing the lawn.

Using the same facts, write your own paragraph. Be sure that it meets the requirements of the checklist.

Exercise 13-6
Let's take a closer look at sentence subjects. We have learned that the complete subject of a sentence tells who or what the sentence is about. Number your work paper 1-5. List the complete subject of each sentence.
1. The jetliner hit heavy winds over Kansas.
2. All members of the team voted on the new captain.
3. Where did John's dad park the car?
4. That old computer went on the blink.
5. Why did the cat chase the dog?

We have listed the complete subject of the sentences. We will now look at the simple subjects of these sentences. The simple subject is the most important word in the complete subject. It tells who or what the complete subject is talking about.

Exercise 13-7
On your work paper, you have listed the complete subjects for each of

the sentences in Exercise 13-6. Read the complete subjects carefully. Ask yourself this question, "Who or what is this complete subject mainly talking about?" The single word that answers this question is the simple subject.

Go back to the list of complete subjects for Exercise 13-6 and circle the word you think is the simple subject. Use common sense as your guide.

Exercise 13-8

Number your work paper 1-10. Read each sentence. Ask yourself who or what the sentence is mainly speaking about. The answer to your question will be the simple subject. List the simple subject for each sentence. Each answer will be only one word.

Example: The very old men in the shed played cards.

Answer: men

1. The first chapter was the most interesting.
2. A school of fish swam near the reef.
3. Do students at that school wear uniforms?
4. Many museums are famous for their art collections.
5. The little boy will pick up that box.
6. Three cars on the train were empty.
7. The vacant, old motel looked dangerous and spooky.
8. How much does a box of feathers weigh?
9. Notebook paper has blue lines and pink margins.
10. We should be careful with scissors.

Let's do one more exercise with subjects and predicates.

Exercise 13-9

Number your work paper 1-10. Copy the sentences. Draw a vertical line between the complete subject and the complete predicate. Underline the simple subject.

Example: The ancient vase broke on the floor.

Answer: The ancient vase | broke on the floor.

1. We never expected to find you here.
2. The object of the game is to win.
3. Many people have visited Washington D.C.
4. The pencil lead broke.

5. Ron cut his hand while doing yard work.
6. That newspaper is one of the country's largest.
7. Dogs are social animals.
8. A very large truck passed us on the highway.
9. The smoke made us cough.
10. Basketball players are often very tall.

Exercise 13-10

Let's do a quick review to measure our progress.

Number your work paper 1-3. Answer the questions.

The (1)_____ tells who or what the sentence is about.

A (2)_____ sentence gives information.

An interrogative sentence always ends with a (3) _____.

Number your work paper 4-6. Each of the following sentences is missing the correct end point of punctuation. In the space next to the number on your work paper, write the correct end point.

4. Tim declared that he was a millionaire
5. We all wondered if it would rain
6. Did you see the game last night

At the beginning of this chapter we tried to answer which of these two sentences was written correctly:

1) The earrings or the bracelet are gold.

2) The earrings or the bracelet is gold.

Although we are not yet able to give a clear reason why the answer is 2, we have made much progress. We will continue to make progress in the next chapter.

Before continuing, let's practice writing a paragraph of opinion. Remember, a paragraph of opinion begins with a thesis statement.

Exercise 13-11

In Chapter 6, we read about Amelia Earhart and Alexander Graham Bell. We wrote summaries, paragraphs of fact, about each of the articles we read.

This time we will write an opinion about Alexander Graham Bell. We will base our opinion on what the article (p. 54) tells us about him. Before beginning, be sure to have two papers in front of you. Title your prewriting paper TIGER. Always do a little prewriting.

On the second sheet, copy the checklist. You will write your paragraph beneath the checklist.

When you have finished writing, place a check mark in front of each of the requirements that you have satisfied.

If you find that you have not satisfied all the requirements, do your best to add what is necessary. We can almost always meet the requirements of the assignment.

Checklist

_____ *indented paragraph*
_____ *thesis statement (states our opinion)*
_____ *fact and opinion sentences that support the thesis*
_____ *clear writing that is unambiguous*
_____ *a variety of sentence types*
_____ *no fragments*
_____ *compound sentence using a semicolon*
_____ *appositive and interrupters*
_____ *interrupters*
_____ *rhetorical question*
_____ *concluding sentence*

Using the model below will help you meet the requirements of the assignment. You may borrow ideas from the paragraph, but do not copy exact words. Work hard, and work smart. Remember, common sense is your best friend.

Alexander Graham Bell

In my opinion, Alexander Graham Bell is one of the greatest men who ever lived. From an early age, Bell was fascinated by sound. His parents schooled him at home. Was it this individual attention that led him to such greatness? Bell, like his father, became a teacher for the deaf; he also read all that he could about electricity. He was fascinated by electricity. Bell began experimenting with telegraphs and sound. His hard work paid off. In 1876, Bell successfully tested the first telephone. How much better the world is because of Alexander Graham Bell!

Summary

- ✓ The complete subject of a sentence is the naming part of the sentence.
- ✓ The most important word in the complete subject is called the simple subject.
- ✓ The simple subject of some imperative sentences is not written. In these cases, we assume that the simple subject is the word *You*.
- ✓ Good writing is the result of good writing habits.
- ✓ Checklists help us develop good writing habits.

Chapter 14

Subject and Predicate Review

Communication review

Communication is the exchange of thoughts or information. We have written several paragraphs to communicate specific information. We began with paragraphs of fact; then we moved on to paragraphs of opinion. Next we wrote a narrative paragraph. In the previous chapter, we wrote an opinion about Alexander Graham Bell.

We have studied semicolons, appositives, and interrupters. We understand that as writers we have two important tools to help us communicate clearly: words and punctuation. Furthermore, we have also studied the building blocks of sentences: the subject and the predicate.

Complete subject

The complete subject tells who or what the sentence is mainly about. The simple subject is the most important word in the complete subject. The simple subject is usually only one word. It tells who or what the complete subject is about.

Exercise 14-1

Number your work paper 1-5. Write the complete subject of each sentence and underline the simple subject.

    1. The old man declared that he was fit as a fiddle.

2. John read.
3. The well-dressed gentleman insisted that the women precede him through the door.
4. Pete told his dad to grab the thingamajig off his desk.
5. A class of students learned that synonyms are words that mean nearly the same thing.

Complete predicate

Earlier we learned that the telling part of a sentence is called the complete predicate. The complete predicate tells what the subject does, or gives more information about the subject. We also learned a simple equation.

Complete subject + Complete predicate = Complete sentence

We will now build complete sentences by adding complete subjects to complete predicates.

Exercise 14-2

Number 1-5. Rewrite each of the word equations as a complete sentence.
Example: A flock of birds + flies through the sky.
Answer: A flock of birds flies through the sky.
1. Cats and dogs + play together.
2. The girls + jumped rope.
3. The light bulb + burned out.
4. A little boy + is running up the street.
5. Tom + became team captain.

Now let's do it in reverse.

Exercise 14-3

Number your work paper 1-5. Divide each sentence into a word equation.
Example: That girl broke the vase.
Answer: That girl + broke the vase.
1. Tim and his brother share the same books.
2. A sharp pair of scissors cuts through thick paper.
3. The silver vase reflected light.

4. Bill listens to loud music.
5. The pad of paper was written on.

Let's be sure that we can identify the complete subject and the complete predicate.

Exercise 14-4

Number your work paper 1-10. Each of the sentences below has an underlined part. The underlined part is either the complete subject or the complete predicate. If the underlined part is the complete subject, write *CS* on your paper. If the underlined part is the complete predicate write *CP*.

1. <u>A dozen eggs</u> fell and broke on the floor.
2. <u>Was</u> Shirley <u>frying fish</u>?
3. <u>Those puppies</u> run and play all the time.
4. <u>We</u> thought we had the correct answer.
5. The lamp <u>was sold at a garage sale.</u>
6. The junior soccer team <u>won an important game.</u>
7. <u>Very old radios</u> require time to warm up.
8. <u>Everyone</u> knows that the alphabet has twenty-six letters.
9. Everyone in row six <u>stand up.</u>
10. Jane <u>eats.</u>

A complete sentence requires a complete subject and a complete predicate. It must also express a complete thought. A piece of a sentence is called a fragment.

Exercise 14-5

Number your work paper 1-5. Some of the word groups below are fragments. Others are complete sentences. If the word group is a fragment write *Fragment*. If it is a sentence write *Sentence*.

1. After Jimmy entered the classroom.
2. Because he worked hard, Tom passed the class.
3. An interrogative sentence asks a question.
4. If sketching is your hobby.
5. Since we were hungry, we ate.

Exercise 14-6

Number your work paper 1-10. Copy the sentences. Draw a short,

vertical line to separate the complete subject from the complete predicate.
Example: The big dog barks loudly.
Answer: The big dog | barks loudly.

1. Helen Keller was born in 1880.
2. Young Helen suffered a serious illness.
3. The little girl became deaf and blind.
4. Helen's father met with Alexander Graham Bell.
5. The science of sound fascinated Mr. Bell.
6. Alexander Graham Bell invented the telephone.
7. He suggested that Mr. Keller contact the Perkins Institute.
8. The Kellers were visited by Annie Sullivan.
9. Annie Sullivan had great patience.
10. She taught Helen a special sign language.

We know that a sentence must have both a complete subject and a complete predicate. We have also learned that a sentence must express a complete thought. Additionally, we have also learned that the most important word in the complete subject is the simple subject. Let's do one more exercise that combines everything we know.

Exercise 14-7
Number your work paper 1-10. Copy the sentences. Each of the sentences contains a complete subject and a complete predicate. Underline the complete subject once. Underline the complete predicate twice. Circle the simple subject.
Example: These three pages are ripped.
Answer: These three pages are ripped.

1. Words are symbols.
2. We use words to communicate our thoughts.
3. Nonverbal communication may signal our feelings.
4. Nearly everyone can communicate in some way.
5. Deaf football players face a special problem.
6. They can't hear the quarterback's calls.
7. One school found a solution to this problem.
8. A big bass drum is used.

9. The coach pounds the drum.
10. Deaf players feel the vibrations of the pounding drum.

Summary

✓ In this chapter, we reviewed complete and simple subjects. We have also practiced finding complete predicates.

✓ We are on our way to understanding why there is only one way to write this sentence:

> *The earrings or the bracelet is gold.*

✓   Knowing how sentences work will help us improve our writing.

Chapter 15

Expletives

Expletives are strange words. They have no real meaning, but they serve an important purpose. Expetives help round out sentences.

One common expletive that often begins sentences is the word *there*. Be careful. Sentences that begin with the word *there* often lead to a simple mechanical mistake.

Look at this sentence, for example. It begins with *there*, and it contains a mechanical mistake.

There is a lot of people here.

The word *is* is incorrect in this sentence. The sentence should look like this:

There are a lot of people here.

Mechanical mistakes often occur when writers are not aware of certain writing conventions. In this chapter we will begin to examine some rules of writing that we may not be aware of.

To begin, we must return to the basic equation that describes all sentences:

Complete Subject + Complete Predicate = Complete Sentence

We have studied the complete subject and the complete predicate, but before we go any further, it would be a good idea to review.

The naming part of a sentence is the complete subject. The most important word in the complete subject is the simple subject.

The telling part of a sentence is the complete predicate.

Exercise 15-1

Number your work paper 1-10. Write each sentence. Underline the complete subject once. Circle the simple subject. Underline the complete predicate twice.

1. A group of boys from that school started their own football team.
2. The box of books fell from the shelf.
3. The girls missed the bus.
4. Nebraska is one of the fifty States.
5. That baseball bat was used by Babe Ruth.
6. Paul bought a phone with two lines.
7. Happiness can be shared.
8. Mary divided her stamp collection into two halves.
9. The room at the end of the hall was locked.
10. Freedom of thought is the greatest freedom.

The simple subjects in each of the sentences in the preceding exercise have something in common. They are all words which name people, places, things, or ideas

Exercise 15-2

Number your work paper 1-10. Below you will find a list of the simple subjects from the preceding exercise. Copy the list. Next to each word, write whether the word names one of the following:

person
place
thing
idea

The first one is done for you.

1. group - thing
2. box
3. girl

4. Nebraska
5. bat
6. Paul
7. happiness
8. Mary
9. room
10. freedom

Nouns

Nouns are words which name *people, places, things or ideas*. Everything in the world that you can see, hear, touch, smell or taste is a noun. In sentences, nouns are found in both the subject and the predicate.

Exercise 15-3

Number your work paper 1-10. Read each sentence. List all the nouns from each sentence. Separate the words in your list with commas.
Example: The big, red balloon rose through the clouds and into the blue sky.
Answer: balloon, clouds, sky

1. The repairman took three months to fix the computer.
2. Sharp scissors can be dangerous weapons.
3. Hank bought new running shoes.
4. The new speakers delivered deep bass.
5. The shelf was made of wood and weighed seventy-five pounds.
6. The jet made white trails in the sky.
7. Anger can be a destructive emotion.
8. The smell of onions was thick in the kitchen.
9. Some people say that patience is a virtue.
10. Writing is a skill that anyone can develop.

Read this sentence:
   Twenty people waited in line to buy tickets.

The word *people* is the simple subject of this sentence. The simple subject of a sentence must always be a noun.
   From now on, we will refer to the simple subject as the *subject*.

This will help make our discussions about sentences easier to understand. Think back to the original problem sentence that started this chapter:

There is a lot of people here.

We are trying to understand why that sentence is incorrect. To help us understand, we must be able to locate the subject of a sentence. We should be able to describe the subject as a person, place, thing, or idea. Let's work one more exercise.

Exercise 15-4

Number your work paper 1-10. List the subject of each sentence. Tell whether the subject is a person, place, thing, or idea.

1. Apples turn red.
2. The black widow spider eats her mate.
3. Members of the team made the trip.
4. The color TV was hooked to a satellite dish.
5. Running shoes might cost hundreds of dollars.
6. The spinning blades of a propeller cut easily through the water.
7. Push ups are a basic exercise.
8. Dan told Dave about the movie.
9. The dusty attic held long forgotten treasures.
10. Doubt causes delay.

The subject of a sentence is always a noun. The subject of a sentence usually comes near the beginning of the sentence. We usually find the subject in front of the predicate. The following sentence is a typical sentence. It shows the usual position of the subject and the predicate. The subject is underlined. The predicate is circled. Notice that the subject comes before the predicate.

A team of baseball players practiced on the field.

Reversed subjects and predicates

Sometimes, the usual order of subject-predicate is reversed. Sometimes the predicate comes before the subject. This often happens when a sentence begins with an expletive. The most common expletive is *there*.

Read the following examples. The subject in each sentence is underlined. The predicate is circled.

There are apples in the tree.
There is the milk.

The key to fixing many incorrect sentences is understanding that the subject sometimes comes *after* the predicate.

You can easily locate subject of a sentence that begins with *there*. Use common sense. Simply ask yourself one of these two questions:

Who is the sentence mainly about?
What is the sentence mainly about?

Let's give it a try.

Exercise 15-5

Number your work paper 1-10. Each of the following sentences begins with the expletive *there*. Find the subject of each sentence. Write it on your paper.

1. There are a dozen eggs in the carton. (Hint: What is the sentence mainly about?)
2. There are many boys in this class. (Hint: Who is the sentence mainly about?)
3. There are invitations to be ordered.
4. There are new coats on sale.
5. There is static on the radio.
6. There is money on the floor.
7. There seems to be too much noise in here.
8. There were too many clouds to see the moon.
9. There are some people in the library.
10. There are some umbrellas here.

Expletives

Before continuing, let's recall that expletives are words which have no real meaning. They help to introduce, or fill out a sentence.

We have learned that words have meaning. The expletive *there* seems to be an exception to the rule.

Be careful, though! The word *there* might be an expletive with no real meaning. On the other hand, the word *there* might be used to tell the location of someone or something. Read the examples. The subjects are underlined and the predicates are circled.

> *There* (*is*) *a reason for this.* (expletive)
> *There* <u>*I*</u> (*fell*) *(location)*

Notice that in the sentence using the expletive, the subject comes after the predicate. In the sentence where *there* is used as a location, however, the subject precedes the predicate.

The same thing happens with these examples:

> *There* (*are*) *many* <u>*players*</u> *on the team.* (expletive)
> *There, in the woods,* <u>*I*</u> (*lost*) *my wallet.* (location)

Notice the appositive in the second sentence. It helps describe the location where the wallet was lost.

Use care when searching for subjects in sentences that start with *there*.

When a sentence begins with an expletive, the subject will usually be found after the predicate.

When a sentence begins with a word of location, the subject will usually be found before the predicate.

Let's practice understanding the difference between expletives and words of location.

Exercise 15-6

Number your paper 1-10. Read each sentence. If the sentence begins with an expletive, write the word *expletive* on your paper. If the sentence begins with a word of location, write *location* on your paper. Also, write the subject of each sentence. Use commas to separate your answers.

Example: There the people watched the movie
Answer: Location, people
Example: There are too many rules.
Answer: Expletive, rules

1. There we played football.
2. There he stood and waited.
3. There are winds swirling in the desert.
4. There we saw something unusual.
5. There is something strange in that house.
6. There are some coins in the fountain.
7. There, in Mr. Hawley's class, we learn English.
8. There were many ants crawling around the nest.

9. There the keys fell.
10. There wasn't any time left.

We started this chapter by looking at an incorrect sentence:
There is a lot of people in here.
We wanted to correct that sentence. More importantly, we wanted to understand why the sentence was incorrect. We have come a long way towards understanding the problem.

We know, first of all, that it contains a mechanical mistake. Mechanical mistakes are easily corrected.

We also know that the subject of a sentence must be a noun. We learned that nouns are words that name people, places, things, or ideas. We learned that anything in the world that can be seen, heard, touched, smelled, or tasted is a noun.

We have learned that in sentences the subject usually comes before the predicate. Sometimes, however, it comes after the predicate.

We have learned that words called expletives seem to have no meaning at all. They introduce or help to round out sentences. In sentences that begin with expletives, the subject usually comes *after* the predicate.

We are not yet able to explain why the example sentence is incorrect, but we are on the way.

"There sentences"

In this book, we will use a special name for sentences that begin with the expletive *there*. We will call them "There sentences."

Here is the rule for dealing with "There sentences." It comes in two parts.

WRITING "THERE SENTENCES"

Part 1: When writing a sentence about one thing use "There is."
Part 2: When writing a sentence about more than one thing use "There are."

Let's look at some examples.

(One thing):   *There is a boy in the library.*
(More than one): *There are two boys in the library.*
(One thing):   *There is a team of boys ready to play.*
(More than one): *There are teams of boys ready to play.*

Exercise 15-7
Number your work paper 1-10. Read each of the "There sentences."
Decide whether the missing word should be *is* or *are*. Write the word
on your work paper.
Example: There (is, are) five boys on the field.
Answer: ar*e*

    1. There (is, are) a pizza on the counter.
    2. There (is, are) cookies in the cookie jar.
    3. There (is, are) students waiting in the classroom.
    4. There (is, are) people standing in line.
    5. There (is, are) something wrong here.
    6. There (is, are) a movie playing in that theater.
    7. There (is, are) a gas station on the corner.
    8. There (is, are) boxes in the storeroom.
    9. There (is, are) posters all over the walls.
    10. There (is, are) one more thing I should mention.

Exercise 15-8
Number your work paper 1-5. Read the sentence fragments. Decide
whether each fragment requires *There is* or *There are*. Write your
answer on your paper.
Example: _____ *a dog in the yard.*
Answer: There is

    1. _____ one lamp in the room.
    2. _____ many men on that team.
    3. _____ few cars in the parking lot.
    4. _____ an egg in the nest.
    5. _____ some things everyone should know.

Exercise 15-9
Number your work paper 1-5. Write five sentences beginning with *There is*.

Exercise 15-10
Number your work paper 1-5. Write five sentences beginning with *There are*.

<u>Summary</u>
    ✓ We learned about the expletive *there*. We learned how to
    correctly write "There sentences."

✓ We learned that mechanical mistakes can be easily corrected once we know the proper conventions.

✓ We continue to make good progress on our way to becoming excellent writers.

✓ Soon we will learn the convention that leads to correct sentences like this one:

> *The earrings or the bracelet is gold.*

Chapter 16

Descriptive Paragraphs

In this chapter we will write paragraphs of description. In fact, we will write paragraphs of description about our rooms at home. We will need two sheets of paper out and ready. One will be for TIGER prewriting, and the other will be for the finished paragraph.

Spatial description

There are many ways to write a paragraph of description. In today's paragraph, we will use a type of description called spatial description. Spatial description uses words to describe where things are. The word *spatial* comes from the word *space*. Our rooms are our spaces. We will use spatial description to tell where things are.

When using spatial description, we need to begin at a certain place, the reference point. Next, we pick a direction in which we will let our eyes travel. Our eyes will always travel in one direction, and we will describe what we are seeing as our eyes move. Imagine that we are holding a movie camera on our shoulders. The camera turns, but our feet never move. We never leave the reference point.

Read this example of spatial description for a typical classroom. The reference point is the doorway. Notice how the description travels around the room, as if the writer were turning in a circle while writing. Look for appositives, interrupters and a "There sentence."

My English Classroom

My English classroom looks like any other classroom. When you first walk into the room, you will see that you are in the front, right corner. To the left, the entire front wall is a long whiteboard. Moving your eyes clockwise, you will see that the wall adjacent to the white board is crowded with computer tables and computers. On the wall opposite the door, the back wall, there are large windows. They let in lots of light. The teacher's desk is in the back corner directly opposite the doorway. The wall next to the teacher's desk is a giant bulletin board that displays examples of student work. There are thirty desks crammed into the room. It isn't very big, but a lot of learning goes on in there.

Before we begin, it will help to become familiar with a few terms we use when writing spatial description.

First, we can describe the way we are moving our eyes as either clockwise or counter clockwise. When we say something is moving in a *clockwise* direction, we mean that it is moving in the direction of the hands of a clock.

Counter clockwise describes the motion we would see if the hands of a clock suddenly began to turn backwards.

Reference points

When describing a room, we also need to know how we can describe where the walls are. To make our meaning clear, it is best to begin with our reference point. A *reference point* is a point that never moves. In this case, it will be the place where we imagine we are standing while we write our spatial description. For this paragraph we will use the doorways to our rooms as our reference points.

Adjacent

One important word when writing a spatial description is the word adjacent. *Adjacent* means *next to*. For example, if you wanted to say that the bank was next to the supermarket, you could say, "The bank is adjacent to the supermarket." Using the word *adjacent* will help make your writing sound more intelligent.

Opposite

Another word we will use is opposite. When writing spatial description, the word *opposite* usually means *across from.* For example, when writing a description of your room, you will probably notice that there is one wall opposite the doorway. For any wall, there will be an opposite wall.

Likewise, there are actually two walls adjacent to the doorway. Remember, the word adjacent simply means "next to."

We know that we will be writing a spatial description of our rooms, and we have an idea of some of the words and expressions that will help us write a good paragraph.

Before we begin writing, though, it will help us to know what the teacher is looking for in our writing. As we know, a checklist lists specific pieces of information the teacher is looking for. As always, the most important point to keep in mind is this: our writing must make sense.

Let's look at the checklist for our paragraph of description.

_____ *indented paragraph*
_____ *topic sentence (thesis statement if writing an opinion)*
_____ *detail sentences that support the topic or thesis*
_____ *clear writing that is unambiguous*
_____ *a variety of sentence types (including interrogatives, etc.)*
_____ *no fragments*
_____ *spatial transitions (adjacent, opposite, etc.)*
_____ *appositives and interrupters*
_____ *compound sentence using a semicolon*
_____ *concluding sentence*

The checklist looks nearly the same as the one we used for our previous paragraph on page 121. The most important addition to this checklist is that, in this paragraph, we will be held responsible for the use of spatial transition words.

Spatial transitions

Look at the list of transition words you may want to use in your paragraph.

Spatial transition words:

in	*next to*	*near*	*over*
in front of	*between*	*beside*	*above*
inside	*adjacent to*	*alongside*	*under*

Spatial transition words are words that allow the sentences in our spatial descriptions to flow smoothly together.

Read the following writing examples. The first set of sentences does not include transition words. The second set of sentences does. The transition words are underlined. Notice how the second set of sentences seems to flow much more smoothly and creates a better picture than the first.

No transition words:

My room is small. It is cramped. There is a small table. There is a desk. My bed is pushed up against one of the walls. A painting hangs on the wall. I have a dresser. There is a closet, too.

With transition words:

My room is small and cramped. <u>To the left of</u> the doorway, you see a small table in the back corner. <u>Adjacent to it</u> is my desk. <u>Beside</u> the desk is my bed, which is pushed up against the wall. <u>Over</u> the bed hangs a painting; <u>opposite</u> the foot of my my bed is my closet. <u>To the right of</u> my closet is my dresser. My room might be cramped, but I like it.

In the description of your room, you will use transition words to help make the sentences in your paragraph flow smoothly. Furthermore, the transition words you use will help your audience understand where various objects are located in your room.

Spatial transitions do not necessarily need commas. Insert commas only if you feel that a pause would help clarify things for your audience.

We have already covered the TIGER writing process. By now, you know the steps of the process. Let's review them quickly.

T = <u>T</u>opic sentence
I = <u>I</u>deas
G = <u>G</u>roup
E = <u>E</u>numerate
R = w<u>R</u>ite

As always, we will begin our new paragraph with a two sheets of paper and the checklist in front of us. For this assignment, we may write either a thesis statement (if we want to write a paragraph of opinion) or a topic sentence (if we want to write a paragraph of fact).

Next, we will list ideas. After that, we will draw lines to connect our ideas into logical groups. Then we will enumerate the groups the way we want them to appear in the paragraph. Finally, we will write our paragraph.

We will write a spatial description. When writing a spatial description, think of using a movie camera. Use the camera to focus your audience's attention. Move the camera slowly. Describe what the camera sees.

If you were watching a movie of your room, the first thing you would expect to see is a shot of the entire room. This shot sets the scene. We get a general impression of your room. Is it big? Is it small? Is it clean or messy? Is it your own room, or do you share it with other brothers or sisters? The camera is set up in the doorway. This is the reference point.

After the first shot, the camera will begin to turn. It will begin at some point in your room and move slowly around, providing details, and close-ups. The camera will not jump back and forth from one wall to another. This would confuse your audience. Your job as a writer is to use words to create the pictures the camera would see.

You must remember your audience. Your audience does not know what your room looks like until you describe it. If you describe your room accurately, your audience will be able to picture it in their minds. If, however, your camera jerks back and forth and up and down, your audience will become confused. They will not be able to picture what you are describing.

Let's look at Carl's description of his room. It is well written, but it has some problems. Can you spot them? Compare Carl's paragraph to the checklist. How would you score his paragraph?

My Room

My room is small, but it isn't too cramped because I don't have to share it with anyone. There's several posters on the walls. A window that looks out onto the backyard. My bed is in the back corner; it's pressed against the wall to make more room. Next to my bed is my desk with a computer, a Compaq, on it. Would you believe it's five years old? I can still use it, though. To the right of my desk is my dresser, on top of it is a model truck I made when I was in seventh grade. My closet is on the wall opposite my bed. The doors are covered with posters of cars. So is my bedroom door, which is on the wall adjacent to the closet. I guess I like cars. All the posters on the wall make my room look more cramped than it really is.

Here's the checklist one more time. Check for everything. What score would you give Carl?

Checklist

_____ *indented paragraph*
_____ *topic sentence (thesis statement if writing an opinion)*
_____ *detail sentences that support the topic or thesis*
_____ *clear writing that is unambiguous*
_____ *a variety of sentence types (including interrogatives)*
_____ *no fragments*
_____ *spatial transitions*
_____ *appositives and interrupters*
_____ *compound sentence using a semicolon*
_____ *concluding sentence*

Let's look at this sentence from Carl's paragraph:
> *"There's several posters on the walls."*

We have a problem with the word *there's*, but we are on our way to taking care of it. Carl's "There sentence" is talking about more than one thing. He should have written it this way:
> *There are several posters on the walls.*

Also this group of words from the middle of the paragraph is a fragment:
> *A window that looks out onto the backyard.*

Now, it's your turn. Plan your paragraph carefully on your TIGER prewriting paper. Be sure you include everything required by the checklist.

Exercise 16-1

Write a paragraph of spatial description about your room. When you have finished your paragraph compare it to the checklist one more time, just to be sure. Work hard, work smart, be successful.

Summary

- ✓ Spatial description describes a space.
- ✓ When writing spatial description, start with a reference point. Pretend to move a camera across the space. Write what you see.
- ✓ Your imaginary camera may move in either a clockwise or counter clockwise direction.
- ✓ Spatial transition words help to paint a clear picture.

Chapter 17

Quotations

Quotations tell us what people say. There are different types of quotations, and different ways of punctuating quotations. The conventions of writing tell us how to deal with quotations. In this chapter we will become familiar with some of the conventions regarding quotations.

Direct and indirect quotes

To begin with, there are two basic types of quotations. One type of quotation, called *direct quotation*, tells the exact words that a speaker says.

Another type of quotation, called *indirect quotation* gives information about what a person says.

We can easily compare the two types of quotations.

Direct Quotation: Dad said, "It's time to leave."
Indirect Quotation: Dad said that it was time to leave.

Direct Quotation: Mike said, "I'm hungry."
Indirect Quotation: Mike said that he was hungry.

Direct quotations always tell the *exact words* a speaker says. Direct quotations are like voice recordings. The speaker is speaking, and we are recording every word we hear. Direct quotations are always enclosed in quotation marks.

Indirect quotations do not tell a speaker's exact words. *Indirect quotations give information about something a speaker says.* We often use indirect quotations when we are telling friends about a conversation we had with somebody else. We don't tell our friends the exact words the other person used, we simply report what they were talking about. We do not use quotation marks with indirect quotations.

Exercise 17-1

Number your work paper 1-10. If the sentence contains a direct quotation write the word *Direct* on your paper. If the sentence contains an indirect quotation, write the word *Indirect*.

1. "Let's get ready to take a test," said Mr. Michaels.
2. The student stated, "I don't feel well."
3. John said that he was too tired.
4. Mrs. Smith asked if anyone else was going to be late.
5. The old man yelled at the kids to get out of his yard.
6. "May I have your name?" the nurse asked.
7. The patient explained that he had a headache and a sore throat.
8. The doctor said, "That sounds serious."
9. "I hope," he said, "that you'll be better soon."
10. He told the patient to get plenty of rest.

Using "that" in indirect statements

It is helpful to be able to change direct quotations into indirect quotations. For example, a writer may want to summarize what a speaker has said. Indirect quotes allow the writer to do this. Read this direct quotation:

"The price of gas goes up and down," said the oil man.

We can change this into an indirect quotation by following a three step process:

First: Place the speaker at the beginning of the sentence.
Second: Use the word "that."
Third: Summarize what was said.

We will begin with this direct quotation:
"The price of gas goes up and down," said the oil man.
We will end with this indirect quotation:
The oil man said that gas prices go up and down.

Let's look at the steps we follow to go from the direct quotation to the indirect quotation.

First: *Place the speaker at the front of the sentence.*
<u>*The oil man said*</u>

*Second: Add the word **that**.*
The oil man said <u>*that*</u>

Third: Summarize what was said:
The oil man said that <u>*gas prices go up and down.*</u>

Notice that the speaker is named at the beginning of the sentence. The word *that* is used. The speaker's exact words are summed up.

Let's try another. There are many possible answers. They all begin with the same words. They all begin with the person who is speaking and the word *that*.

Direct Quote:
"It looks like it's going to rain," said the weatherman.

Indirect Quote:
<u>*The weatherman said that*</u> *it looked like rain.*
<u>*The weatherman said that*</u> *it would probably rain.*
<u>*The weatherman said that*</u> *we could expect rain.*

Be careful when you are converting direct quotations into indirect quotations. Keep in mind the meaning of what you are writing. One common mistake writers make is that they forget who's doing the talking. Read the example.

Direct Quote:
Phil said, "I'm going to the movies."

In this quote Phil is talking. He is saying that he plans to go to the movies. Now, read how a student might make a mistake when changing this direct quote into an indirect quote.

Indirect Quote:
Incorrect: Phil said that I'm going to the movies.

This indirect quote is wrong. Why? The indirect quote says that the person writing the sentence is going to the movies. Look carefully:

I'm going.

According to the direct quote, Phil is the one going to the movies; however, according to the indirect quote *I* am the one going to the movies.

What the writer wanted to say was that Phil was going! The indirect quote should be written this way:

*Phil said that **he** was going to the movies.*

Using "if" in indirect questions

Sometimes direct quotes are questions. In order to change a direct quote question into an indirect quote, we use the word *if.* The end mark of punctuation changes from a question mark (?) to a period (.). The direct quote is a question, but the indirect quote is a declarative sentence. This is because indirect quotes report what others say. They are almost always declarative sentences.

Direct quote: The teacher asked, "Does everyone have a pencil?"
Indirect quote: The teacher asked if everyone had a pencil.

Be careful, take your time, and think about sentence meaning when writing indirect quotes. Common sense is your best friend.

Exercise 17-2

Number your work paper 1-10. Change the direct quotes into indirect quotes.

1. "It's time for a test," the teacher said.
2. Mary said, "I'm hungry."

3. The teacher asked, "Is anyone absent?"
4. The mechanic said, "The job will cost two hundred dollars."
5. Mary asked me, "Do you like ice cream?"
6. I said, "I have ten dollars."
7. I told Phil, "You'll have to wait a few minutes."
8. Bob shouted, "This water is cold!"
9. "I'd like some French fries," Tim said.
10. "Is Liz home?" dad asked.

Direct quotations are the exact words a speaker uses. They are like tape recordings. Direct quotations always require quotation marks. Sentences with quotation marks might look complicated, but they aren't. Here's why: quotations work almost exactly like interrupters.

Remember the three types of interrupters.
Interrupter first
Interrupter middle
Interrupter last

Three types of direct quotes

Direct quotations work nearly the same way. There are three types of direct quotations.
Speaker first
Speaker middle
Speaker last

In this course, we will focus mainly on speaker first direct quotes. Look at the examples:
Speaker first:
Dan said, "I'm going home."
John shouted, "Let's get out of here."
Donna whispered, "Can you hear me?"

We call these quotes *speaker first* because the person who is doing the talking comes at the beginning of the sentence. The name of the speaker is always set off with a comma.

Notice how a speaker first sentence is much like an interrupter first sentence. The speaker, like the interrupter, is set off from the main sentence with commas.

(Interrupter first) As a matter of fact, it's expensive.
(Speaker first)   John said, "It's expensive."

Remember, when writing direct quotes, the speaker is set off with a comma, just like an interrupter.

Exercise 17-3

Number your work paper 1-5. The sentences are all examples of speaker first quotations. Rewrite the sentences on your work paper. Put commas where they belong.

1   The policeman said "Clear the area."
2   That girl asked "How much is the gold necklace?"
3   Tom said "I'm a mechanic."
4   The golfer shouted "My club is bent."
5   Maria wondered "How will I pay for that?"

The conventions for quotation marks are simple to understand if you think of interrupters. Let's begin by looking at this sentence:
Don't touch that.

We can add an interrupter to change the sentence. Look.
Please, *don't touch that.*

Notice how the interrupter is set off with a comma.
Now let's change the interrupter *Please* to *Mary said*.
Mary said, *don't touch that.*

We're not done making a quote yet, but we're close. First of all, remember that direct quotes, the exact words a speaker uses, always require quotation marks. Let's add them.
*Mary said, **"***don't touch that.**"***

Our final touch involves what we will call the *"The Golden Rule of Direct Quotations."* All direct quotations must begin with a capital letter. Let's make the change.

*Mary said, "**Don't** touch that."*

We're done. Let's look at the final sentence again. The words *Mary said* are treated like an interrupter first. They are set off from the rest of the sentence with a comma.

In this course, the direct quote will always be treated like the root, or main sentence, and the person doing the speaking will be treated as an interrupter.

The Golden Rule of Direct Quotations

Let's pay special attention to The Golden Rule of Direct Quotations. Here it is:

Direct quotes always begin with capital letters.

Read this sentence one last time:

Mary said, "Don't touch that."

The speaker, Mary, is the interrupter. She is set off from the direct quote with a comma. Her direct quote begins with a capital letter.

Exercise 17-4

Number your work paper 1-5. All of the sentences contain speaker first direct quotes. Rewrite the sentences onto your paper. Insert all necessary commas and quotation marks.

1. Our English teacher said My best friend is a doctor.
2. Mr. McGee asked Will anyone donate to this charity?
3. The judge told the convict You are guilty.
4. The newsman reported Stocks took a fall today.
5. Jim said Everyone should be as lucky as me.

Now let's put it all together. This time you will not only be inserting commas and quotation marks, but inserting capital letters, as well.

Exercise 17-5

Number your work paper 1-5. All of the sentences contain speaker first direct quotes. Rewrite the sentences onto your paper. Insert all necessary commas, quotation marks, and capital letters.

1 The repairman said it will cost ten dollars for me to look at it.
2 The attorney said this man is innocent.
3 Everyone looked when Mary screeched no toothpicks?
4 Donald said English and Latin are related.
5 The sewer said the sewers are backed up again.

Exercise 17-6
Number your work paper 1-5. Listed below are five quotations. Using your own words, make them into speaker first quotations.
Example: "I think I'm going to like this."
Answer: Pete said, "I think I'm going to like this."

1. "This is going to be great!"
2. "Did you see that?"
3. "We all feel that way sometimes."
4. "What is the difference between an impression and an idea?"
5. "You're next."

Speaker first direct quotes are the easiest to learn and use. Let's practice finding the difference between direct quotes and indirect quotes. Remember, indirect quotes do not tell a speaker's exact words.

Exercise 17-7
Number your work paper 1-10. The following sentences contain indirect quotes and speaker first direct quotes. If the sentence contains an indirect quote write *Indirect* on your paper. If the sentence contains a direct quote, write *Direct*. Correct the direct quote sentence. Be sure to include all commas, quotation marks and capital letters.
Example: John said that he was sick.
Answer: Indirect
Example: John said I'm sick.
Answer: Direct. John said, "I'm sick."

1. Mary said that she was going to do her homework.
2. Phil asked are you going to the park?
3. The old man said things were different in my day.

4. We listened to what the man said.
5. The radio announcer said that it would be cold today.
6. Jane wondered if she would like the movie.
7. My uncle told me that his knees ached before a rainstorm.
8. The salesman said you look like a man who deserves the best.
9. Tom told his boss I quit.
10. John argued that he shouldn't be punished.

Now, we will convert indirect quotes into speaker first direct quotes. There are several correct answers for each problem.

Exercise 17-8
Number your work paper 1-5. Convert the indirect quotes into speaker first direct quotes. Notice that there may be several possible answers for each problem. You only need to write one.

Example: Tim said that he had no money.
Answer: Tim said, "I don't have any money."
Answer: Tim said, "I'm broke."
Answer: Tim explained, "I'm out of money."

1. The reporter said that there would be a parade on Monday.
2. Jim asked his English teacher if he could borrow a pencil.
3. Andrea wondered if the lasagna was good.
4. Ted said that he'd be early.
5. My dentist told me I needed braces.

When people speak, they often interrupt themselves. We can easily insert interrupters into direct quotations. Read the examples. The interrupters are underlined. Pay attention to the commas.

John said, "Of course, I will probably be late."
The mechanic said, "I think, uh, I think I can fix it."
Mr. Edwards told the class, "This is the most important assignment of the year, in my opinion."

Exercise 17-9
Number your work paper 1-5. Beside each direct quote is an interrupter in parentheses. Rewrite the quote onto your work paper, inserting the interrupter

into the direct quote. Be sure to put the interrupter in the correct position and include all necessary commas and capitalizations.

Example: Tim said, "I can't guarantee it." (of course) (interrupter first)

Answer: Tim said, "Of course, I can't guarantee it."

1. Dan asked, "Does anyone have a nickel?" (I wonder) (interrupter first)
2. The student said, "I don't know." (uh) (interrupter middle)
3. Professor English remarked, "Thomas Edison was a great thinker." (in my opinion) (interrupter last)
4. Sandy said, "The score was tied." (I think) (interrupter last)
5. The plumber answered, "It's going to cost you." (however) (interrupter first)

We often use quotations when we are writing stories. Our stories sound more believable when we are able to show the exact words that a character says.

Before we continue let's do a quick check.
What is the Golden Rule of Direct Quotations?
The Golden Rule of Direct Quotations is this:
Direct quotations always begin with capital letters.

The Silver Rule of Direct Quotations

There is a Silver Rule of Direct Quotations, too. Here it is.
Indent a new paragraph each time the speaker changes.

We indent each time the speaker changes. We indent to signal our audience that a new speaker is about to begin speaking. When you are watching a movie, the camera usually shifts back and forth from face to face as people speak. Indenting new paragraphs to show that a speaker is changing is like swiveling a movie camera back and forth. For writers, this is a requirement.

Dialogue is another word for *conversation*. It is a synonym for conversation. Dialogue and conversation mean nearly the same thing. Look at the examples of dialogue. The first example is incorrect. The writer has not indented a new paragraph each time the speaker changed.

Incorrect

John said, "I'm planning on going to the movies tonight. I haven't decided what I want to see, though." His friend Phil asked, "What time do you want to go? I could be ready to go any time after, uh, let me think, seven thirty." John said, "How about eight o'clock?" Phil thought about it for a moment. He said, "Great. I'll go, too."

Correct

John said, "I'm planning on going to the movies tonight. I haven't decided what I want to see, though."

His friend Phil asked, "What time do you want to go? I could be ready to go any time after, uh, let me think, seven thirty."

John said, "How about eight o'clock?"

Phil thought about it for a moment. He said, "Great. I'll go, too."

Notice the number of indentations in the second version. This is exactly how written dialogue is supposed to look. Remember, indent a new paragraph each time the speaker changes.

Exercise 17-10

The following three dialogues are incorrectly written. The writer did not indent each time the speaker changed. Correctly write the dialogues on your work paper.

1. Mary said, "My brother is rolling in dough." Her friend Sylvia asked, "Is he a banker?" Mary answered, "No, he's a baker."

2. Tom said, "I can't believe my cousin got an 'A' for cutting class." Tim, Tom's friend, said, "Uh, what kind of school gives an 'A' for cutting class?" Tom said, "Barber school."

3. Little Billy told his mother, "Today at school, I was the only one who knew the answer to one of the teacher's questions." His mother asked proudly, "What was the question?" Little Billy said, "Who threw the baseball through the window?"

Exercise 17-11

It's your turn. On your work paper, write three dialogues. Each dialogue should contain at least three speaker first quotations. Remember to indent a new paragraph every time the speaker changes. Do your best to use everything you've learned.   Your teacher will be checking for these things:

Dialogue Checklist
___*Proper indentation*
___*Proper use of quotation marks*
___*Proper use of commas*
___*Proper capitalization*
___*Proper use of periods and question marks*

Summary

- ✓ There are two types of quotations.
- ✓ Indirect quotes report what someone says.
- ✓ Indirect quotes do not require quotation marks.
- ✓ Direct quotes show the exact words a person says. They <u>always</u> require quotation marks.
- ✓ Direct quotes always begin with capital letters.
- ✓ When writing direct quotes, always indent a new paragraph when the speaker changes.

Chapter 18

Subject-Verb Agreement

Remember this sentence from a previous lesson:
There's a lot of people in here.

Contractions

This sentence contains a mechanical mistake. The word *There's* is not used correctly. The word *There's* is a special kind of word. It is called a contraction. A *contraction* is formed when two words are shortened and joined with an apostrophe to create one word.

In fact, the word *There's* is a contraction formed from two words:

There is

(Notice that *There* is an expletive, and also notice that this is the beginning of a "There sentence.")

What if we rewrote the example sentence without the contraction? Now, we have a very clear "There sentence."
There is a lot of people in here.

This sentence contains a mechanical mistake. The mistake involves what is called *subject-verb agreement.*

In this chapter we will learn what we mean by subject-verb agreement.

Just like mechanics can fix problems with cars, we can fix problems with sentences. Before mechanics can fix cars, they must understand how cars work. Good mechanics understand how the different parts of a car work together.

Good mechanics can fix any car, and good writers can fix any sentence.

It would not help us to try and fix sentences one at a time. Think of how many sentences have been spoken and written since the beginning of time. Think how many more will be spoken and written in the future. The number is infinite. The number grows larger as more and more people speak. In fact, today you will speak and write sentences that no one has ever written or spoken before. How can we be sure that our sentences are correct?

Conventions

We use basic rules to make sure we are speaking and writing correctly. These basic rules are called conventions. *Conventions* are the rules that control the way we speak and write. Without these rules, everyone would speak and write as they please. It would be impossible to communicate.

Here are some simple conventions we have learned to help us become better writers:

1. A complete sentence must have a complete subject and a complete predicate.
2. The most important word in the complete subject is the simple subject.
3. The simple subject is always a noun.
4. A noun is a word that names a person, place, thing, or idea.

Verbs

Here is a new rule.

*The complete predicate contains the **verb**.*

Look at these example sentences. The complete predicate is bold. The verb is underlined.

> a) *Tim **<u>runs</u>** around the track.*
> b) *That table **<u>leans</u>** to the left*
> c) *Small dogs **<u>bark</u>** at big dogs.*

One job that *verbs* do is *tell what someone or something does.*
> *In example (a) what does Tim do? He runs.*
> *In example (b) what does the table do? It leans.*
> *In example (c) what do small dogs do? They bark.*

Read the following sentence. What kind of word is the word *jumped*?

> *The cow **jumped** over the moon.*

The word *jumped* is a verb.
Why is it a verb? Because it tells what the cow did.

To help improve our writing, we must be able to locate verbs in a sentence. One way to find the verb in a sentence is to ask ourselves, "What is the subject doing?"

Exercise 18-1
Number your work paper 1-10. Write the words that tell what *He* does.
Example: He jumps.
Answer: jumps

1. He coughs.
2. He sees.
3. He thinks.
4. He runs.
5. He explains.
6. He dances.
7. He answers.
8. He wonders.
9. He argues.
10. He believes.

Exercise 18-2
Number your work paper 1-5. From each set of three words, choose the verb. Write it on your paper.

1. yesterday, runs, into
2. words, symbols, screams
3. television, believes, speakers
4. sees, sunlight, whether
5. for, off, learns

Exercise 18-3
Number your work paper 1-10. Write the words that tell what *they* do.

1. They cough.
2. They see.
3. They play.
4. They answer.
5. They think.
6. They argue.
7. They declare.
8. They spin.
9. They stare.
10. They wonder.

In the preceding exercises we were looking for verbs. Let's remember that a complete sentence requires a complete subject and a complete predicate. The verb is part of the predicate.

Exercise 18-4
Number your work paper 1-10. Read the sentence pairs. Write whether the word that changes is the subject or the verb.
Example: Tim runs. Tim jumps.
Answer: Verb

1. Sharon reads. Sharon writes.
2. Randy runs. Tim runs.
3. Scissors cut. Scissors rust.
4. We watch. They watch.
5. They play. They argue.

6. Fires burn. Fires smoke.
7. Jan thinks. Mary thinks.
8. She wonders. Sandra wonders.
9. Computers calculate. Computers run.
10. Dave and Barbara bow. They bow.

Verbs tell what someone or something does. Below, you will find some simple sentences. How are they the same? How are they different?

He coughs.	*They cough.*
He sees.	*They see.*
He thinks.	*They think.*

The verbs in both columns describe the same actions. However, the verbs in the first column end with the letter *s*. The verbs in the second column do not end with an *s*. There is a simple grammar rule at work here. Can you figure it out?

Oftentimes, we can see a rule at work, but we might have trouble putting it into words. That is, we may understand a rule, but be unable to express it. Let's try an exercise to see if we understand the rule, even though we might have trouble stating exactly what the rule is.

Exercise 18-5
Number your work paper 1-10. Each two word sentence is missing the subject. Write either the word *He* or the word *They* to complete the sentence.

Example: _____ *play.*
Answer: *They*

1. _____ explain.
2. _____ argues.
3. _____ wanders.
4. _____ teach.
5. _____ listen.
6. _____ shovels.
7. _____ polish.
8. _____ leads.
9. _____ imagine.

10. _____ sew.

The rule is simple, but before we state the rule, we must look closely at the subject. Here are two facts about the subject of a sentence:

The subject must be a noun.

A noun is a word for a person, place, thing, or idea.

Exercise 18-6

Number your work paper 1-10. Each group of words below contains only one noun. Write the noun on your work paper.

Example: we, were, be

Answer: we

1. vase, into, happily
2. through, chair, around
3. girls, went, to
4. rain, over, should
5. would, gone, wind
6. could, lead, was
7. hammer, a, greenish
8. without, underneath, bow
9. next, has, thought
10. before, idea, in

A noun is a word for a person, place, thing, or idea. A noun may be singular or plural.

Singular means one. Plural means more than one. In English we often change a singular to a plural by adding the letter *s*. Look.

Singular	*Plural*
boy	*boys*
town	*towns*
pen	*pens*
idea	*ideas*

Exercise 18-7

Number your work paper 1-20. Next to each number, write whether the word is singular or plural. Do not abbreviate your answer.

Example: boats

Answer: plural

1. kite
2. planes
3. feet
4. boy
5. team
6. class
7. classes
8. geese
9. bird
10. group
11. cup
12. bones
13. something
14. glasses
15. jeans
16. belt
17. socks
18. book
19. encyclopedias
20. memory

Agreement

Suppose there are five students in a classroom, and there is one desk. Is the number of students equal to the number of desks?

No. There are more students than there are desks. The numbers involved are 5 and 1. We say:

The numbers do not agree.

Suppose there are three textbooks and one student. Is the number of textbooks equal to the number of students?

No. The numbers do not agree.

Suppose there is one horse and five riders. Do the numbers agree?

No. The numbers do not agree.

In English, words have number. Singular words talk about one thing. Plural words talk about more than one thing.

We know that nouns can be singular or plural. Nouns have number.

Verbs have number, too. Verbs can be singular or plural. Let's look. The verbs are underlined. Can you guess the rule for changing singular verbs into plural verbs?

Singular	*Plural*
A boy <u>runs</u>.	*Two boys <u>run</u>.*
A girl <u>jumps</u>.	*Two girls <u>jump</u>.*
A town <u>grows</u>.	*Two towns <u>grow</u>.*

In English we often change the singular form of a verb into the plural form by subtracting an *s*.

Exercise 18-8
Number your work paper 1-10. Compose new sentences by changing singular subjects to plural subjects. Follow the example.
Example: A boy eats.
Answer: Two boys eat.
1. A cow chews.
2. A kite soars.
3. A girl sings.
4. A bear plays.
5. A group of boys runs.
6. A team of girls plays.
7. A bird lands.
8. A boy leads.
9. A student writes.
10. A cup of milk spills.

Suppose we have one cup of milk and two children. Do the numbers agree?

No, the numbers do not agree.

Why? Because the numbers are 1 and 2. One cup is singular. Two children are plural.

Suppose we have one student and three sandwiches. Do the numbers agree?

No, the numbers do not agree.

The numbers are 1 and 3. One student is singular. Three sandwiches are plural.

In English the number of the subject must always agree with the number of the verb. That is, a singular subject must match, agree, with a singular verb. A plural subject must agree with a plural verb. Look at the examples.

Singular subjects

Agree	*Do Not Agree*
A boy runs.	*A boy run.*
A girl sings.	*A girl sing.*

Look at the sentences in the *Agree* column. The subject of each sentence is singular. The verb is singular, too. We say:

The subject agrees with the verb.

Now look at these examples of sentences with plural subjects.

Plural subjects

Agree	*Do Not Agree*
Two boys play.	*Two boys plays.*
Two girls eat.	*Two girls eats.*

Look at the sentences in the *Agree* column. The subjects are plural. The verbs are plural, too. We say:

The subjects agree with the verbs.

The title of this chapter is "Subject-Verb Agreement". When we talk about subject-verb agreement, this is what we mean: a singular subject must match a singular verb, and a plural subject must match a plural verb. Let's practice subject-verb agreement.

Exercise 18-9

Number your work paper 1-10. Choose the verb that agrees with the

subject. Write the entire sentence on your work paper.
Example: Chuck (wants, want) to go home.
Answer: Chuck wants to go home.
  1. That girl (likes, like) milk.
  2. One puppy (barks, bark) playfully.
  3. Many birds (sings, sing) at sunrise.
  4. Three players (throws, throw) the ball.
  5. We (wonders, wonder) about things.
  6. They (answers, answer) correctly.
  7. The flowers (blooms, bloom).
  8. A fish (swims, swim) upstream.
  9. Several papers (falls, fall) on the floor.
  10. Baseball bats (is, are) made of wood.

Subject-verb agreement is important in both writing and speaking. We must always be sure that subjects and verbs agree in number. We say that a subject agrees with a verb when both the subject and the verb have the same number.

Number

Keep in mind that the word *number* has a special meaning for us. In this course, *number* means either *singular or plural*. The only numbers we actually care about are either one, or more than one.

If a subject is singular and the verb is singular, too, we say that the subject agrees with the verb.

Likewise, if the subject is plural and the verb is also plural, we say that the subject agrees with the verb.

Exercise 18-10

Number your work paper 1-10. If the subject and the verb agree write *Agree* on your work paper. If the subject and verb do not agree, write *Do not agree*.
Example: That boy eats quickly.
Answer: Agree
Example: That girl dance well.
Answer: Do not agree.
  1. One boy play solitaire.

2. We play football.
3. Those kittens climbs everywhere.
4. Airplanes soars through the clouds.
5. Scissors cut paper.
6. The tires roll down the road.
7. Bottles breaks on cement.
8. Matches start fires.
9. A raindrop falls.
10. The clock keep time.

One very common verb is the word *be*. As a matter of fact, this verb appears in many different forms. There are singular forms of this word and there are plural forms. Look at the examples.

Singular	*Plural*
One boy <u>is</u> happy	*Two boys <u>are</u> happy.*
One girl <u>was</u> sad.	*Two girls <u>were</u> sad.*

Exercise 18-11

Number your work paper 1-10. Choose the form of the verb that agrees with the subject. Write the verb on your work paper.
Example: The desk (is, are) crowded with papers.
Answer: is

1. Jan (is, are) excited about the party.
2. The team (was, were) expected to win.
3. Computers (is, are) amazing.
4. Many people (was, were) sick.
5. A single duck (is, are) floating on the pond.
6. Most nails (is, are) made of metal.
7. Several clouds (was, were) drifting across the sky.
8. Two telephone poles (was, were) knocked over.
9. Many chairs (is, are) stacked in the utility room.
10. A feather (is, are) light.

Subject-verb agreement is often a problem when sentences begin with expletives. Remember, the word *there* is an expletive. Often, when it is the first word in a sentence, it seems to have no real meaning. Look.
There are many birds in the sky.

The word *there* is an expletive. It is not the subject of the sentence. The subject of the sentence is *birds*. The subject *birds* is plural. The verb is the word *are*. The verb *are* is plural. It is correct to say, *birds are*. The subject and the verb agree.

It would not be correct to say, *birds is*. The subject and the verb do not agree.

Exercise 18-12

Number your work paper 1-10. The following sentences all begin with expletives. Choose the verb that agrees with the subject.

1. There (is, are) many students in school.
2. There (was, were) a coin stuck in the slot.
3. There (is, are) something in the back of the closet.
4. There (is, are) money on the table.
5. There (was, were) too many choices.
6. There (is, are) many ways to communicate.
7. There (was, were) one thing I forgot.
8. There (was, were) many posters on the wall.
9. There (is, are) correct answers and incorrect answers.
10. There (is, are) several people waiting in line.

We began this chapter by looking at this incorrect example sentence.

There's a lot of people in here.

The sentence is incorrect. Why?

Remember, the word *there's* means *there is*. The word *is* is singular. In this sentence a plural subject (people) is matched with a with singular verb (is). It is incorrect to say "people is." The subject and the verb do not agree.

Exercise 18-13

Number your work paper 1. Rewrite the example sentence correctly on your paper. Be sure that the subject agrees with the verb.

Exercise 18-14

Number your work paper 1-5. Write five sentences about the classroom you are in. Use singular agreement. Begin each sentence with the words *There is* or *There was*.

1. There is …
2. There was …
3. There was …
4. There is …
5. There was …

Exercise 18-15

Number your work paper 1-5. Write five more sentences about your classroom. Use plural agreement. Begin each sentence with the words *There are* or *There were*.

1. There are …
2. There are …
3. There were …
4. There were …
5. There were …

Subject-verb agreement is an important area to focus on. The number of the subject should always agree with the number of the verb.

Singular subjects require singular verbs. Plural subjects require plural verbs.

Review

Answer the questions on your work paper.

1. _____ are the rules that control the way we speak and write.
2. One simple convention is that every sentence must have a complete subject and a complete _____.
3. The complete predicate contains a word that tells what someone or something does. This word is called the _____.
4. A _____ is a word for a person, place, thing, or idea.
5. _____ means "one."
6. _____ means "more than one."
7. A plural subject requires a _____ verb.
8. The number of the subject must _____ with the number of the verb.

On your work paper, write *Noun* if the noun changes. Write *Verb* if the verb changes.

   9. The fire smokes. The fire burns.

  10. Those birds fly. Those planes fly.

  11. The painting was beautiful. The painting is beautiful.

  12. The pen writes smoothly. The pencil writes smoothly.

  13. John, a lawyer, reads thick books. Jim, a doctor, reads thick books.

  14. He sees stars. She sees stars.

  15. Puppies sleep. Puppies play.

Write the subject and the verb from each sentence. Follow the example.
Example: The group of boys runs on the track.
Answer: group runs

  16. Eric buys bread at the bakery.

  17. There are three birds in the tree.

  18. Those two girls, twin sisters, look alike.

  19. There is a boy in the classroom .

  20. Dan carved a point onto a stick.

Choose the verb that agrees with the subject. Write the verb on your work paper.

  21. Four boys (shouts, shout) for victory.

  22. Mary (buys, buy) ice cream for dessert.

  23. The class (learns, learn) quickly.

  24. We (thinks, think) the answer is correct.

  25. One puppy (is, are) barking.

If the subject agrees with the verb, write *A* on your work paper. If the subject and verb do not agree write *NA*.

  26. We communicate every day.

  27. Japanese speakers understands Japanese.

  28. There is three empty seats in the back.

  29. There are cars all over the lot.

  30. My friends, all in this school, calls me every night.

Chapter 19

One Page Narratives

It's time to put everything we've learned together. By the end of this chapter we will be able to write a one-page narrative. Remember, a narrative is a piece of writing that describes an event. It's a story, really. The narrative may be true or not true.

Chronological order

One thing all of our narratives should share is the idea of chronological order. *Chronological order* is time order. Our narratives will start at the beginning, move to the middle, and then to the end. With a little planning we will be able to fit our narratives on one page.

Before we start, let's look at the basics of a well-written story. To begin with, every story must include details about where and when the story takes place. A story also needs to have some kind of problem that must be solved.

Setting

We have a special word to describe the where and a when of a story. It is called the setting. The *setting* tells us *where and when* a story takes place.

A writer needs to create a setting quickly. Remember, we write for an audience Our audience needs to know where and when the story is taking place. Read the following story beginnings. Notice how they immediately create a setting.

Story #1
Bill sat in his bedroom watching TV and wondering what to do with the rest of the day.

Story #2
Bill leaned back in his chair, his cowboy hat tilted over one eye, and watched the new folk climbing from the stagecoach. One of them was a killer.

Story #1 contains a *where* and a *when*. The *where* is Bill's bedroom. What is the *when*? Is it a Sunday? Is it last year? We cannot say for certain. But the fact that Bill is watching a TV tells us that this story is probably taking place during modern times. We can say that the setting of Story #1 is Bill's bedroom in modern times.

Story #2 has a *where* and *when*, too. We cannot tell exactly where the story is taking place, but clue words can help us make a guess. Words like *cowboy hat*, *new folk*, and *stagecoach* allow us to guess that the story is taking place in the old West. We can guess that the *where* of the story is a western town. We can also guess about the *when* of the story. It is taking place in the old west over one hundred years ago.

Exercise 19-1
Number your work paper 1-5. Divide your paper into two columns. Label one column *Where* and the other one *When*
Read the following story beginnings. List the setting, the *where* and *when* of each story.
Example: Theodore set the antigravity controls from his position in the space cruiser's pilot's seat. Somewhere behind him, magnetic coils hummed. A strange smell flooded the oxygen system.
Answer: **Where**   **When**
           A spacecraft   The future

1. John was sitting in his favorite chair in the living room, talking to his friend Bob on the phone. Suddenly, the line

crackled with static.

2. The phaser was dead. The energy packs were drained. Here on the surface of the red planet, there was no way to recharge them. Now, it was Captain Stone's turn to sweat.

3. The auditorium was packed. Everyone was watching Sandy as she crossed the stage. She heard the microphone hum. Suddenly, she felt herself tripping over her own feet.

4. The sails snapped loudly as they filled with wind. Commodore Steven's looked through his telescope. Where were the supply ships?

5. Jenny stepped up to the plate and took a couple of practice swings. This was her first time up on the varsity team, and she was feeling nervous.

In addition to a setting, all stories need to begin with the hint of a problem. Reread the beginnings of Story #1 and Story #2.

Story #1 has a setting. The setting is Bill's bedroom during modern times. The story beginning also hints at a problem. Bill is bored. What will he do?

Story #2 has a setting, too. It is the old West. There is a hint of a problem, as well. Bill is on the look-out for a killer.

Conflict

Every story should have some kind of problem that needs to be solved. Problems in stories have special names. They are called conflicts. A *conflict* is a *problem*. The beginning of the story should at least hint at the story's conflict. This will keep our audience interested in what we have written.

Exercise 19-2

Number your work paper 1-5. Reread the story beginnings from Exercise 19-1. List the conflict that is hinted at in each story beginning. For example, if you were to read a story beginning this way:

Theodore set the antigravity controls from his position in the pilots seat. Somewhere behind him, magnetic coils hummed. A strange smell flooded the oxygen system.

You might say that the conflict, the problem, is the hint of trouble caused by the strange smell.

Now, go back and list the possible problems that are hinted at in the story beginnings of Exercise 19-1.

We will be writing one page narratives. We want to launch our stories quickly. We want our audience to be interested in what we have written. Therefore, we should always try to create interesting settings and conflicts at the very beginning of our stories.

Of course, when we write stories, we must follow the conventions of written English. Now, let's look at the checklist we will use to grade our one page stories.

_____ *topic (setting & conflict) described at beginning*
_____ *clear writing that is unambiguous*
_____ *variety of sentence types (interrogatives, etc.)*
_____ *indented paragraphs*
_____ *quotations (direct & indirect)*
_____ *gimmick*
_____ *no fragments*
_____ *spatial transitions*
_____ *appositives*
_____ *compound sentence using a semicolon*
_____ *title*

By quickly creating settings and conflicts, and by following the conventions of written English, we will write stories that others want to read.

Gimmicks

You may have noticed the need for a *gimmick* in this checklist. *Gimmicks* are *tricks* that writers use to keep their audience entertained. We will discuss gimmicks soon.

We have been writing one paragraph compositions. Now we will be writing stories. Stories do not need a thesis statement. They do not need detail sentences that relate to the thesis. Notice that there is no scoring for thesis or detail sentences on this new checklist.

The new requirements involve quickly creating a setting and a problem. Notice that you will also be required to use quotations, both direct and indirect.

Before going any further, let's read a story that Frank wrote. It contains several mechanical mistakes, but that's OK. We want to notice how he gets his story started, and how he uses a gimmick at the end of the story to entertain us.

We can fix all his problems later. Let's just enjoy his story for now.

A Bad Day

John tried to sneak into his house, but his father was sitting right there in the living room. He was in the La-Z-Boy. The tv was off. John's dad never sat in the La-Z-Boy with the tv off unless there was trouble. His dad said, "I've been waiting for you." John swallowed hard.

His dad said, "It's about this." He waved an envelope in the air.

John thought quickly to himself. The school must have sent a letter home. John had been in another fight. His dad had told him that if there was any more trouble at school, John wouldn't be able to get his driver's license. John thought it would be best to confess. Maybe that way he could keep his father on his good side. And still get his license. John said, "I can explain." His father looked surprised. "Explain what?"

John said, "About the fight at school." His father asked, "What fight?"

John knew he'd just made a big mistake. He said, "Isn't that letter about the fight I had at school."

His father said, "No, it isn't. It's an application from the driver's license bureau. I sent away for it last week. I was going to help you fill it out. But now you tell me about this trouble at school. You'll be waiting a long time for that license."

John slumped down on the sofa. Sometimes you just can't win.

Frank has written a good one page story. Let's see how he got his ideas from his head onto his paper.

We begin by using a slightly changed version of the TIGER writing method. This new version is good for writing stories. No matter what we are writing, stories or reports, we should always take the time to get our thoughts organized. Prewriting allows us to explore our thoughts. Our writing will sound much better as a result of a little planning and prewriting.

Here is the TIGER method for writing a story.

T - *Topic*
I - *Ideas*
G - *Gimmick*
E - *Ending*
R - *wRite*

We can see why this new version of TIGER should be used when writing stories. It is slightly different from the version used for writing other types of compositions.

To begin with, a story does not need a topic sentence or a thesis statement, but we do need a topic. The topic is simply what we will be writing about. We can say that we will introduce our topic with a setting and a conflict.

T stands for Topic. The topic will be the setting and the conflict.

I stands for Ideas. We will still need to list ideas. The ideas will move the story forward and keep our audience entertained.

G stands for Gimmick. Gimmicks are tricks. As writers, we use gimmicks to put a little twist on our stories. When reading a story, our audience wants to be entertained. Think of watching a movie. A movie is not interesting if we can guess everything that is going to happen next. The same is true of our writing. Our audience wants to be surprised. Gimmicks are unexpected twists that we place in our stories in order to help keep our audience entertained.

E stands for Ending. Endings are important to a story. The ending of our story must satisfy our audience. We wouldn't walk out of an entertaining movie without waiting for the end, would we?

R, of course, still stands for wRiting, which is something we should get to right away.

175

We have read Frank's story, "A Bad Day." Let's take a look at how he organized his writing for his story.

First he needed to think up a setting and a problem.

Frank writes the word TOPIC near the top of his prewriting paper. He has decided on a setting and a problem.

TOPIC

Setting – John is at home in modern times. Conflict – He is trying to hide a secret from his father.

IDEAS: Now, Frank has to list some ideas. What secret is John trying to hide from his father? Why is he trying to hide it? Frank writes the word IDEAS in the center of his paper and begins answering these questions.

IDEAS

John got in a fight at school.

He has been in fights before.

He wants to get his driver's license.

His dad won't let him get his license if he hears about the fight.

GIMMICK – John is tricked into confessing about the fight.

John confesses to the fight

John doesn't get his license

Frank has listed several basic points about his story. He has also listed his gimmick. In this story, John is going to be tricked into confessing about a fight. It is up to Frank to decide how he will write the gimmick.

Also, Frank has decided on an ending. When writing a short story, it is helpful to know the ending *before* you begin writing. Knowing the ending of the story before you begin writing is like knowing where you plan to go before getting in the car.

When you know the ending of the story, you have a destination to aim for. Try to keep the ending of your story in mind from the very beginning.

Let's see how Frank turns his topic into a story beginning.

TOPIC

Setting – John is at home in modern times. (Conflict – He is trying to hide a secret from his father.

Story Beginning:

John tried to sneak into his house, but his father was sitting right there in the living room. He was in the La-Z-Boy. The TV was off. John's dad never sat in the La-Z-Boy with the TV off unless there was trouble.

Frank has created a story beginning. We get the impression from words like La-Z-Boy and TV that the story takes place in modern times. We also get a hint of a problem. First of all, John tried to *sneak* into the house. Secondly, John's father is sitting in the La-Z-Boy with the TV off. Frank has created an interesting problem. The audience is wondering what will happen next.

Let's reread the entire story. Mechanical mistakes are underlined. We will check the story against the checklist.

A Bad Day

John tried to sneak into his house, but his father was sitting right there in the living room. He was in the La-Z-Boy. The tv was off. John's dad never sat in the La-Z-Boy with the tv off unless there was trouble. His dad said, "I've been waiting for you. John swallowed hard.

His dad said, "It's about this." He waved an envelope in the air.

John thought quickly to himself. The school must have sent a letter home. John had been in another fight. His dad had told him that if there was any more trouble at school, John wouldn't be able to get his driver's license. John thought it would be best to confess. Maybe that way he could keep his father on his good side. And still get his license. John said, "I can explain." His father looked surprised. "Explain what?"

John said, "About the fight at school." His father asked, "What fight?"

John knew he'd just made a big mistake. He said, "Isn't that letter about the fight I had at school."

His father said, "No, it isn't. It's an application from the driver's license bureau. I sent away for it last week. I was going to help you fill it out. Now, you tell me about this trouble at school. You'll be waiting a long time for that license."

John slumped down on the sofa. Sometimes you just can't win.

Compare Frank's work to the requirements of the checklist. How did he do?

He quickly created a setting and a problem.

Did you find any mechanical mistakes?

There were several. They are underlined. We will examine them in a moment.

He used at least one interrogative.

On the other hand, he also wrote an interrogative sentence without using a question mark.

He did not use a semicolon.

He did not use an appositive.

His subjects and verbs all agreed. Almost all his subjects were singular. His verbs were singular, too.

He did use interrupters.

He used speaker first quotations, but did not indent them properly.

He did not use indirect quotations.

He had a title.

Overall, Frank did not meet the requirements of the checklist. This time, he can easily fix his mistakes. In the future, he will have to be more careful.

Let's look at his story one more time. This time everything is fixed.

TV
By the way, note the spelling of TV. It is always capitalized. It does not require periods.

Also note the semicolon. It is underlined so that it can be clearly seen. We can always create compound sentences using a semicolon.

All the indentations are correct. We can expect to see many indentations when we are writing conversation. Remember The Silver Rule of Direct Quotations. We must begin a new line and indent every time the speaker changes.

A Bad Day

John tried to sneak into his house, but his father was sitting right there in the living room. He was in the La-Z-Boy. The TV was off. John's dad never sat in the La-Z-Boy with the TV off unless there was trouble.

His dad said, "I've been waiting for you."

John swallowed hard.

His dad said, "It's about this." He waved an envelope in the air.

John thought quickly to himself. The school must have sent a letter home. John had been in another fight. His dad had told him that if there was any more trouble at school, John wouldn't be able to get his driver's license. John thought it would be best to confess. Maybe that way he could keep his father on his good side; he could still get his license.

John said, "I can explain."

His father looked surprised. "Explain what?"

John said, "About the fight at school."

His father asked, "What fight?"

John knew he'd just made a big mistake. He said, "Isn't that letter about the fight I had at school?"

His father said, "No, it isn't. It's an application from the driver's license bureau. I sent away for it last week. I was going to help you fill it out. Now, you tell me about this trouble at school. You'll be waiting a long time for that license."

John slumped down on the sofa. Sometimes you just can't win.

Exercise 19-3

Write a one page narrative.

Begin by prewriting your topic and ideas on a TIGER prewriting paper.

Try to include a gimmick.

Feel free to use Frank's story, "A Bad Day," as a model. Remember, you may always borrow ideas, but you are not allowed to copy words.

Use the checklist to help you plan your writing.

Finally, write your finished story on a clean sheet of paper.

Congratulations! You have successfully written a one-page narrative.

Summary

- ✓ Narratives are stories. A narrative may be true or not true. Either way, it is still a story.
- ✓ Narratives are usually told in time order.
- ✓ Chronological order means time order.
- ✓ The setting of a story tells where and when the story takes place.
- ✓ Another word for problem is conflict.
- ✓ Gimmicks are tricks. Writers use gimmicks to keep their audience interested and entertained.
- ✓ Endings are an important part of narratives. Endings must satisfy our audience.

Chapter 20

Conventions and Capitalization

Why do we write?

We write to communicate our thoughts. We write to exchange thoughts and information. Writing is a form of verbal communication. When we write, we use words to express our ideas clearly.

Ambiguous sentences

Words, however, are not enough. Words might be confusing. They might be used in an ambiguous manner. Read this sentence:

jim a barber said he was late

What is the meaning of this sentence?

Do you think that it means that a barber named Jim said that he was late?

Let's read a little background information before we answer the question.

Suppose there is a teacher whose last name is Barber. His first name is Jim, and his middle initial is *A*.

Imagine that yesterday, Mr. Jim A. Barber spoke to a woman teacher named Miss Smith. Imagine that he spoke about a student in his

181

classroom. The student's name was Tom.

Mr. Barber said that Tom did not get to class on time.

Miss Smith didn't hear Mr. Barber clearly. She asked, "Tom was what?"

Now, we have the answer to our original question.

Jim A. Barber said, "He was late."

Amazing! Compare the original sentence to the final sentence.

(Original) jim a barber said he was late
(Final) Jim A. Barber said, "He was late."

Maybe you thought that Jim was a barber. If you did, you thought the sentence contained an appositive, like this:

Jim, a barber, said he was late.

The original sentence was ambiguous. We did not clearly understand the meaning of the words. We did not realize that the word *barber*, for instance, was really the name, *Barber*. The sentence was confusing. We, the audience, could not be sure about its meaning.

As writers we have two sets of tools we can use to make our meaning clear: words and punctuation.

Words must follow conventions (for example the word *dog* describes a furry, four-legged creature). Punctuation must follow conventions, too. The rules, conventions, of punctuation help give meaning to sentences.

In this book, we use the word conventions to describe specific rules which must be followed when writing English.

Conventions

Conventions are the rules of writing. For example, all sentences require a capital letter at the beginning, as well as an endpoint of punctuation at the end. The endpoint might be a period, a question mark, or an exclamation point. A sentence which correctly follows the conventions of writing could be called conventional. A sentence which does not correctly use the conventions of writing might be called unconventional. The example sentences help to make this clear.

Conventional: Jim and Tom, his brother, went to West High School.
Unconventional: jim and tom his brother went to west high school

Here is the important point: Children learn to speak English by imitating what they hear, but students must learn and memorize the conventions of proper writing.

A five-year-old girl might say, "I want candy." We understand what she is saying.

On the other hand, if she has not learned all the rules of writing she might write something that looks like this:

iwandknd

Here is the problem: the five-year-old girl knows the conventions for speech, but she doesn't know conventions of writing. In other words, she knows how to speak, but she doesn't know how to write.

Memorization

We learn conventions by memorizing them. For example, this is a common convention:

car

The spelling of the word *car* is a convention of written English. When writing English, we must spell the word *car* correctly. A *car* is not a *cat*. We memorized the spelling of the word *car* early in our lives. Now, the correct spelling of the word *car* is one of our habits.

By memorizing conventions and practicing them often, they become habits for good writing. We use conventions to help make our meaning clear to our audience. In this book we have already studied many conventions. These conventions help us correctly write what we want to say. Some of the conventions we have studied are listed below.

Indented paragraphs
Semicolons to join sentences
Commas to set off appositives and interrupters
Transition words
Subject/Verb agreement

This chapter is titled "Conventions and Capitalization." We will be reviewing some conventions which we have already learned. We will also be learning new rules. We will learn the conventions for capitalization.

Let's begin by remembering what we have learned so far about commas. We can list the conventions.

    1. Use commas to set off appositives.

    2. Use commas to set off interrupters.

    3. Use commas to set off the speaker from a quote.

    Now, let's do an exercise. With constant practice, using commas correctly will become a habit. Read the instructions carefully.

Exercise 20-1

Number your work paper 1-10. Read the sentences. Pay attention to commas. If the commas are used correctly, write the word *Conventional* on your work paper to show that the sentence is conventional. If the commas are not used correctly, write the word *Unconventional*.

Be ready to explain your answers.

Example: *Jan, my older sister, goes to school in San Diego.*

Answer: *(Conventional)*

Example: *Mike the, youngest likes, to go fishing.*

Answer: *(Unconventional)*

    1. By the way Aunt Sally will be here tomorrow.

    2. Dad asked, if we were planning to leave soon.

    3. The man, it seems, is the president of the bowling league.

    4. Thomas Edison, the king of inventors, studied electricity.

    5. Mark wondered ",What are symbols?"

    6. As a matter of fact, we all wonder about things.

    7. Words are symbols for things and ideas.

    8. Bow a heteronym may be pronounced two ways.

    9. Mr. David Smith said, "It's time to go, I think."

  10. Mrs. Jones, our English teacher said "A declarative sentence always ends with a period."

    How did you do? Were you able to spot all the comma mistakes?

    Of course, we have learned more than the proper use of commas. We have also learned these important conventions:

    1. Indent new paragraphs.

    2. End all sentences with an end mark of punctuation.

    3. Semicolons combine two complete sentences.

    4. Fragments are pieces of sentences.

    5. Direct Quotes tell the exact words a speaker says.

The following sentence is unconventional. Can you explain why?
John wrote a report on Thomas Edison; and he read it to the class.

The sentence is unconventional because the joining word *and* is used with the semicolon.

Try this one.

Sara spent her summer vacation working at a restaurant and taking horseback riding lessons; she also read several books, by the way

The sentence requires an end mark of punctuation. Be careful!

Exercise 20-2

Number your work paper 1-10. If the sentences are conventional write *Conventional*. If the sentences are not conventional write *Unconventional*.
Be ready to explain your answers.

1. Later that year, when the cherry blossoms bloomed.
2. The United Kingdom is made up of two major islands; Great Britain and Ireland.
3. The Nile River runs through Egypt. It supplies much water to that desert region.
4. The capital of Nevada Carson City is located north of Las Vegas.
5. Have you heard about Stonehenge.
6. Stonehenge, an ancient monument built of giant stones, is located in England.
7. As a matter of fact, no one really knows who built Stonehenge; or why they built it.
8. You can find pictures of Stonehenge in any encyclopedia.
9. People who study ancient civilizations are called archaeologists.
10. Archaeologists have studied Stonehenge; digging and exploring the ancient site.

Now let's learn some new conventions. We will learn the conventions of capitalization. We use capital letters for a number of reasons. Everyone knows something about capitalization, but let's take a little test to see how expert we are. Read the following paragraph.

None of the words are capitalized. Read carefully; move your finger over each word. When you spot a word that should be capitalized, count it. Some words are repeated. Count every word. You should find 30 words.

The corrected version is right beneath the incorrect version. Play fair! Cover the corrected version so you won't be tempted to look at it.

Now, give the exercise a try.

Exercise 20-3

john and mary took the bus to east twenty-second street. they were looking for the offices of the arizona republic, a well-known newspaper in phoenix, arizona. john had read an article about the sun, the earth, mercury and venus. a famous french professor, dr. simon, had written the article. john wanted to meet him. john's uncle frank had called the newspaper. the doctor said that he would be glad to meet the boy. the bus, a ford, approached the seventh street bridge. soon, john and mary would meet the professor.

Here is the corrected paragraph. The capitalized words are underlined so you can seem them easily.

<u>John</u> and <u>Mary</u> took the bus to <u>East</u> <u>Twenty</u>-second <u>Street</u>. <u>They</u> were looking for the offices of the <u>Arizona</u> <u>Republic</u>, a well-known newspaper in <u>Phoenix</u>, <u>Arizona</u>. <u>John</u> had read an article about the sun, the earth, <u>Mercury</u> and <u>Venus</u>. <u>A</u> famous <u>French</u> professor, <u>Dr</u>. <u>Simon</u>, had written the article. <u>John</u> wanted to meet him. <u>John's</u> <u>Uncle</u> <u>Frank</u> had called the newspaper. <u>The</u> doctor said that he would be glad to meet the boy. <u>The</u> bus, a <u>Ford</u>, approached the <u>Seventh</u> <u>Street</u> <u>Bridge</u>. <u>Soon</u>, <u>John</u> and <u>Mary</u> would meet the professor.

Capitalization

We already know many of the conventions for capitalizing words. For example, we all know that the first word of a sentence must be capitalized. We also know that the word *I* must be capitalized.

People's names and the names of cities are also capitalized. There is a reason for this. Let's learn it.

In a preceding lesson, a lesson before this one, we learned about nouns. Nouns are words which name people, places, things, or ideas. For example, the word *boy* is a noun. So is the word *Dave*.

Why is *Dave* capitalized, but *boy* is not?

Proper nouns

Dave is a special kind of noun. It is called a proper noun. *Proper nouns* are nouns which name *specific people, places or things*. Read the list of proper nouns. All these nouns are proper nouns because they name specific people, places, or things.

> Uncle Jim
> Aunt Mary
> Lake Superior
> Glendale High School
> Federal Bureau of Investigation
> Easter
> Fourth of July
> Third Street
> New York

Exercise 20-4

Number your work paper 1-5. Each of the following sentences contains proper nouns. Write the proper nouns on your work paper.

1. The class took a field trip to the Metropolitan Museum of Art.
2. We all listened to Judge Murphy.
3. Hundreds of children enjoyed this year's Elm City Book Days.
4. The movie was showing at the Cinema Six Theater.
5. Jim and Bob played football on Friday.

Proper nouns are capitalized because they name specific people, places, or things.

Common nouns

There is another type of noun. This noun is called a *common noun*. Common nouns do not name specific people, places, or things. Common nouns are usually *not capitalized* unless they begin sentences.

An example of a common noun is the word *boy*. The word *boy* could mean any boy. It does not talk about a specific boy. That is why we say that the word *boy* is a common noun.

On the other hand, the word *Dave* <u>does</u> name a specific boy. *Dave* is a proper noun, but *boy* is not.

Look at the chart. It helps to show the difference between proper nouns and common nouns.

Proper Nouns	Common Nouns
Glendale High School	high school
Dr. Jones	doctor
Tuesday	day
January	month
Sears	store
Germany	country
Pittsburgh	city
Mount Shasta	mountain

Exercise 20-5

Make two columns on your work paper. At the top of the left-hand column write the words <u>Proper Nouns</u>. At the top of the right-hand column write the words <u>Common Nouns</u>. Your chart should look like the chart above.

Number your work paper 1-10. skip two spaces between the numbers. Read the sentences. List the proper nouns under the heading <u>Proper Nouns</u>. List the common nouns under the heading <u>Common Nouns</u>.

1. John went to the museum.
2. We enjoyed the parade on the Fourth of July.
3. After Tuesday, no applications will be accepted.
4. The car, an old Chevy, still ran.
5. The boy got lost at Wal-Mart.
6. Have you ever wondered about the Loch Ness Monster?
7. The Sixty-seventh Street Bridge will be closed Wednesday, as well as next week.
8. The band at Catskill High marched onto the field.
9. Students cheered Senator Smith.
10. Automobiles are used for transportation.

Proper nouns name specific people, places, and things. For example, the names of cities and states are proper nouns. They must be capitalized. So must the names of continents, countries, oceans, streets, and highways. Generally speaking, any specific name should be considered a proper noun and should be capitalized.

Exercise 20-6

Number your work paper 1-10. The following sentences all contain proper nouns. The proper nouns are not capitalized. Use capital letters, and write the proper nouns on your work paper.

1. The students at central high school wear uniforms.
2. Everyone listened as judge carpenter sentenced the convict.
3. Travelers enjoy the scenery in the rocky mountains.
4. The snake river winds through montana.
5. Our dog, shep, loves to catch tennis balls.
6. That package was sent to an address on river street.
7. The solomon islands are located in the pacific ocean.
8. Have you ever visited the grand canyon?
9. The nile is an important river in egypt.
10. His family bought a new mazda.

Although the names of specific galaxies, planets, and other places and things in outer space are usually capitalized, we never capitalize the words *sun, earth,* or *moon.*

Here is another interesting convention. When we travel, we talk about going in different directions. For example, we might say that we will drive north to get to the high school. We do <u>not</u> capitalize direction words like *north, south, east,* and *west.*

On the other hand, we <u>do</u> capitalize words that talk about sections of our country. For example, we might write about the swamps in the *South,* or the deserts in the *Southwest.* This is common sense. We capitalize the names of states, and we also capitalize the names of sections of our country.

Exercise 20-7

Number your work paper 1-10. Read the following sentence pairs. Pay attention to the capital letters. Only one sentence in each pair is written correctly. Write the letter of the correctly written sentence on your work paper. Follow the example.

Example: A) *Pete went to the Store.*
             B) *Pete went to the store.*

Answer: B

1. A) We watched the movie at the theater.
   B) We watched the movie at the Theater.
2. A) My Aunt Emma wrote me a letter.
   B) My aunt Emma wrote me a letter.
3. A) James will return Tomorrow.
   B) James will return tomorrow.
4. A) The northeast is well known for its long history.
   B) The Northeast is well known for its long history.
5. A) The Earth revolves around the sun.
   B) The earth revolves around the sun.
6. A) The bus headed south into Texas.
   B) The bus headed South into Texas.
7. A) Everyone knows that the Sun is a star.
   B) Everyone knows that the sun is a star.
8. A) The only continent entirely in a polar region is antarctica.
   B) The only continent entirely in a polar region is Antarctica.
9. A) North Dakota is north of South Dakota.
   B) North Dakota is North of South Dakota.
10.A) The barge chugged up the Mississippi River.
   B) The barge chugged up the Mississippi river.

Always capitalize the names of companies. They are proper nouns. For example, we would write about a *Ford* truck, or *Wrigley's* gum. Do not capitalize the product the company makes, unless you are writing the specific name of the product. The following examples will make this clear.

Examples:

Microsoft software - Microsoft Word
Timex watch - Timex Ironman
Ford truck — Ford Explorer
Clorox bleach — Ultra-Clorox Regular Bleach
Mother's cookies — Mother's Vanilla Crème Cookies
Sony television — Sony Vega

Exercise 20-8

Number your work paper 1-10. All the sentences contain proper nouns. The proper nouns are not capitalized. On your work paper, capitalize the proper nouns. Follow the example. Sentences may have more than one proper noun.

Example: We bought a bottle of pepsi.

Answer: Pepsi

1. The north star is the brightest star in the sky.
2. She won a scholarship to arizona state university.
3. The brooklyn bridge is a fascinating structure.
4. Few mountain climbers have made it to the top of mount everest.
5. Ted's trip to asia brought him to japan and thailand.
6. The hawaiian islands are known for their great beauty.
7. The great communicator, helen keller, was born a healthy baby.
8. Loch Ness is a lake in scotland.
9. Jim bought a nissan frontier pick-up truck.
10. The students worked with compaq computers.

We have learned many conventions of capitalization. Let's summarize. The list tells us what we should capitalize.

1. Proper nouns
2. Heavenly bodies, except *sun, earth, moon*
3. Sections of our country
4. Company names
5. The names of specific products

Exercise 20-9

Number your work paper 1-10. If the sentences follow the rules for capitalization, write the word *Conventional* on your work paper. If the words are not correctly capitalized write *Unconventional*. Be ready to explain your answers.

1. The spacecraft lifted off from the Earth and headed for the stars.
2. The state of Washington is located in the Pacific northwest.
3. Jim's dad bought a new Chevy Suburban.
4. Mary's favorite cereal is made by kellogg's.

5. Everyone stood when general Schwarz entered the room.
6. That popcorn is made by betty crocker, I think.
7. His new panasonic cordless phone didn't work.
8. If you head north, then turn west, you'll find Jaycee Park.
9. Great Britain is divided into scotland, england, and wales.
10. Ancient Egyptians relied on water from the Nile river.

We are learning more and more about the conventions of written English. Of course, it won't help to know the conventions if we don't use them. In the next chapter, we will put our new knowledge to use writing business letters.

Let's make sure we've understood all this.

Review
Answer the questions on your work paper by writing the missing word.

We write to (1)_____ our thoughts and feelings.

We use commas to set off (2)_____ and (3)_____.

Conventions are the rules of (4)_____.

Semicolons are used to join two complete (5)_____.

Proper nouns are always (6)_____.

Nouns which are not usually capitalized are called (7)_____ nouns.

Generally speaking we capitalize the names of companies, but not their (8)_____.

We usually capitalize the names of heavenly bodies. Three words we don't capitalize are (9)_____, (10)_____, and (11)_____.

Quotations may be either direct or (12)_____.

Each group of three words contains a proper noun. The proper noun is not capitalized. Write the proper noun on your work paper. Be sure to capitalize it.

13.	city	denver	state
14.	we	i	they
15.	earth	saturn	sun

Chapter 21

Writing a Business Letter

<u>Correspondence</u>

Communication by mail is called *correspondence.* When we write a letter to someone, we correspond with them. A student might take correspondence classes. In correspondence classes, a teacher mails assignments to students, and students mail completed assignments back to the teacher. If we e-mail someone a note or a letter, we are sending them correspondence.

Business letters are a special form of correspondence. Business letters are not like the friendly type of correspondence we write to friends and family. Business letters must follow a special form. We can always tell a business letter just by looking at it. Business correspondence must look like business correspondence.

We follow conventions, rules, when we write. Businesses follow conventions, too. One of the rules of business is that business letters must look like business letters.

Imagine if people wrote to businesses the same way they write notes to themselves. Business people would waste much time trying to figure out what was written. The correct form of the business letter helps to save business people time.

Below is a typical business letter. Look at the parts. How many parts does it have?

Return Address	Carl Smith 123 Elm St. Palm Springs, Ca 92262 (760) 555-5555
Date	September 3, 2006
Inside Address	Hal Fisher Computer Resources P.O. Box A-124 Los Angeles, CA 90210
Salutation	Dear Mr. Fisher:
Body	I read your advertisement in the <u>Daily Sun</u> and I am interested in buying your company's new wireless keyboard. I am a little worried that it might not work with my current computer system. Please send me information about system requirements. Thank you four your time.
Closing *Signature*	Sincerely, Carl Smith

A business letter has seven parts.

We must always remember our audience when we are writing. When we are writing a business letter, we must remember that we are writing to business people. Business people are very busy. If they cannot understand our writing the first time, they may not give us a second chance. Our letter might end up in the trash!

Look again at the sample business letter. Pay attention to the two parts that deal with addresses.

Addresses

A business letter has two address parts. The two address parts are called the *return address* and the *inside address.*

The *return address* is our own address. In the example letter, the return address is Carl Smith's own address. Carl lives at 123 Elm Street, Palm Springs, California.

The *inside address* is the address of the business to which we are writing. In the example letter, the inside address is the address for a company called Computer Resources. When it comes time to mail our letters, we will use the inside address to help us address our envelopes.

Knowing how to write an address properly is one of the keys to writing a good business letter. Basically, address information is simply a list. You should always list address information this way:

Name
Street Address
City, State   ZIP

Abbreviations

When writing address information, we often use *abbreviations.* Abbreviations are shortened forms of words. One meaning of the word *abbreviate* is *to shorten.* For example, we can shorten the word *Street* to the common abbreviation *St.*

We must take care when abbreviating words. Abbreviated words usually require a period at the end. The period indicates that there are some missing letters in the abbreviation. The abbreviation for *Avenue*, for example, is this:

Ave.

The period at the end of *Ave.* indicates that the abbreviated word is missing some letters. The period is just as important to the abbreviation as the letters themselves.

Abbreviations are often used in letters. Abbreviations are not only used in addresses. Look at the salutation of the example letter. The word *Mister* is abbreviated into this:

Mr.

The period indicates that there are missing letters.

Here is a list of abbreviations used when writing addresses.

Address Abbreviations

Apartment - Apt.	Parkway - Pkwy.
Avenue - Ave.	Place - Pl.
Boulevard - Blvd.	Post Office Box - P.O. Box
Department - Dept.	Road - Rd.
Highway - Hwy.	Street - St.
	Suite - Ste.

Notice how all the words on the list are capitalized. Generally speaking, addresses are considered proper nouns. In the preceding chapter we learned that proper nouns must always be capitalized. When we write addresses we must pay attention to capitalization.

Now let's look at some specific words. Basically, the words *Avenue, Boulevard, Parkway, Street, Place,* and *Highway* all mean the same thing. In general, they all mean *Road.*

One meaning of the word *Suite* (pronounce *sweet*) is *Office.* Some businesses use the word *Suite* because it sounds fancier than *Office.* Let's practice writing some abbreviations.

Exercise 21-1
Number your work paper 1-10. Write abbreviations for the listed words.

1. Avenue
2. Post Office Box
3. Department
4. Road
5. Boulevard
6. Suite
7. Apartment
8. Parkway
9. Place
10. Highway

Exercise 21-2
Number your work paper 1-10. Imagine you are writing a business letter. Rewrite the addresses below. Use abbreviations whenever possible. Include any commas you see.

1. 123 Roosevelt Parkway, Suite 4B
2. 5110 Jupiter Street, Apartment 234
3. Post Office Box 710
4. 32 Wild Rose Avenue
5. 1754 E. First Place, Suite 3
6. 4 Golden State Parkway
7. Post Office Box 65-Q

8. 1122 Salt Road, Box 18-L
9. Highway 35, Department Q
10. 8548 First Avenue, Suite 54W

Here's an interesting fact. The Post Office *wants* letter writers to use abbreviations. The machinery used at the Post Office scans addresses on envelopes and looks for abbreviations. Therefore, the Post Office has established rules, conventions, for the proper use of abbreviations.

State names should be abbreviated according to Post Office conventions. The list below shows how to abbreviate state names. Note that the abbreviations are only 2 letters long. Also note that both letters are capitalized and that there are no periods.

Careful! This method of abbreviation is only proper when writing letters!

State abbreviations

Alabama AL	Georgia GA	Maryland MD	New Mexico NM	South Dakota SD
Alaska AK	Hawaii HI	Massachusetts MA	New York NY	Tennessee TN
Arizona AZ	Idaho ID	Michigan MI	North Carolina NC	Texas TX
Arkansas AR	Illinois IL	Minnesota MN	North Dakota ND	Utah UT
California CA	Indiana IN	Mississippi MS	Ohio OH	Vermont VT
Colorado CO	Iowa IA	Missouri MO	Oklahoma OK	Virginia VA
Connecticut CT	Kansas KS	Montana MT	Oregon OR	Washington WA
Delaware DE	Kentucky KY	Nevada NV	Pennsylvania PA	West Virginia WV
District of Columbia DC	Louisiana LA	New Hampshire NH	Rhode Island RI	Wisconsin WI
Florida FL	Maine ME	New Jersey NJ	South Carolina SC	Wyoming WY

Before we continue, we should take a closer look at the list. Notice the words *District of Columbia*. The District of Columbia is the Capital of the United States, but it is not a state. It is called a *District.*

The District of Columbia is divided into sections. One section of the District of Columbia is called Washington. Washington, in the District of Columbia, is the Capital of the United States. It is on the east coast near the Atlantic Ocean. The White House is there. So is the Washington Monument. It is where our government meets.

If we want to send a letter to the President, we must send it to the area called Washington in the District of Columbia. The Post Office abbreviation for the District of Columbia is DC. Therefore, we address our letters this way:

Washington, DC

On the other hand, there is a state in the United States called Washington. It is on the west coast. One city in Washington is Seattle. If we wanted to write a letter to a business in the city of Seattle in the state of Washington, we would look at the list of Post Office Abbreviations and address our letter this way:

Seattle, WA

One more thing. Sometimes, cities have the same name as the state in which they are located. The best known example of this is the city of New York in the state of New York. Again, we check the list of Post Office abbreviations. We find the abbreviation for the state of New York. We address our letter like this:

New York, NY

Exercise 21-3
Number your work paper 1-10. Rewrite each city and state combination using abbreviations wherever possible. Keep all commas where you see them.

1. Salem, Oregon
2. Denver, Colorado
3. Billings, Montana
4. Sacramento, California
5. Dallas, Texas
6. Las Vegas, Nevada
7. Baltimore, Maryland
8. Portland, Maine
9. Provo, Utah
10. New York, New York

We list address information this way:

Name
Street Address
City, State ZIP

Suppose you see an advertisement for a job in the newspaper. The ad tells you to write to this address:

Tim Smith, 35 Elm St., Provo, UT 55555

When you write your letter, you will write the address this way:

Tim Smith
35 Elm Street
Provo, UT 55555
By the way, what state is this letter going to?
The letter is going to Utah.

Exercise 21-4

Number your work paper 1-5. Answer the questions about this address..
Fred Jones
25 First Ave. Apt. 3
Cleveland, OH 99999

1. How many lines are in the address?
2. What does the abbreviation "Ave." mean?
3. To what state is the letter being sent?
4. What is an abbreviation?
5. Why is there a period after the abbreviation "Apt."?

ZIP codes

Look again at the address for Fred Jones. Look at the last line, and put your fingers on the numbers 99999. You probably know that this is the ZIP code. ZIP stands for Zone Improvement Program. By convention, the word ZIP is written with all letters capitalized and no periods. You must always use a ZIP code in an address. Businesses almost always include their ZIP code when listing their addresses.

Notice one more thing about the address. There is a comma between the city "Cleveland" and the state abbreviation OH. This comma is required. We *always* separate the city from the state with a comma. On the other hand, we *never* use a comma between a state abbreviation and a zip code.

Exercise 21-5

Number your work paper 1-5. Leave several lines between each number. Rewrite each of the addresses below as a list. Follow the example.
Example: Mrs. Karen Jones, 156 Seventh Ave., Boston, MA 89576

Answer: *Mrs. Karen Jones*
                    156 Seventh Ave.
                    Boston, MA 89576

1. Don Simms, 25 Main St., Los Angeles, CA 90222
2. Dr. Earl Jones, 6789 West Ave., Ste. B, New York, NY 60609
3. Jane White, 4 Oak Pl., Washington, DC 78490
4. Dr. Frank Reading, 8902 Atom Ave. Apt. 3A, Alamogordo, NM 45992
5. Mary L. Green, 33 N. Eastern, Phoenix, AZ 85282

We are almost ready to write a business letter. Let's take another look at Carl's letter.

Carl Smith
123 Elm St.
Palm Springs, Ca 92262
(760) 555-5555

September 3, 2006

Hal Fisher
Computer Resources
P.O. Box A-124
Los Angeles, CA 90210

Dear Mr. Fisher:

I read your advertisement in the Daily Sun and I am interested in buying your company's new wireless keyboard.
I am a little worried that it might not work with my current computer system.
Please send me information about system requirements.
Thank you four your time.

Sincerely,
Carl Smith

Begin your business letter by centering your name, address and telephone number at the top of the page. Your phone number is important. Remember, you are writing to business people. It may be more convenient for them to call than write to you.

After you write your name, address, and phone number, skip two lines. Then, on the margin line, write the date. Do *not* abbreviate.

Now, skip two more lines and write the inside address. Look at the example letter. The inside address is longer than the addresses we have been practicing. This is because the new address contains more information.

Sometimes, addresses in advertisements are listed this way:

John Smith, Manager, State Industry, 3 Elm St., Dallas, TX 33453

When we write our letters, we must write the addresses correctly. Often, an address has three lines, like this:

Name

Street Address

City, State ZIP

In our example, we see that John Smith is a Manager. His job position is *Manager*. We simply add the job position to the name line. Include job positions when possible. We separate the name *John Smith* from the position *Manager* with a comma. Like this:

John Smith, Manager

It is always a good idea to include a person's job position when you are able to. Why? Because people work hard to earn their titles! They will appreciate your consideration. Remember - you always write for an audience. Keep them happy!

Organization names

We also know the name of John Smith's company. The company name is called the *organization name.* An *organization name* is the name of an organization to which someone belongs. John Smith belongs to an organization named State Industry.

Organization names are proper nouns. They are always capitalized.

We add the organization name beneath the name John Smith. Like this:

John Smith, Manager
State Industry

A complete inside address should have the information listed this way:

> Name, job position
> Organization
> Street Address
> City, State ZIP

Exercise 21-6

Number your work paper 1-5. Rewrite the addresses using the form required for business letters.

1. Jerry Thomas, Vice President, Aero Inc., 35 Technology Pl., San Jose, CA 90987
2. Dr. Carol Wooster, President, Wooster Corp., 45 Newberry St., Phoenix, AZ 85558
3. Jan O'Toole, 879 E. Fifth Ave., Dallas, TX 77777
4. Bob Hanson, Director of Personnel, Three Diamonds Cement, Inc., 786 Savannah Ave., Rochester, NY 92345
5. Olivia Tate, Editor, Financial News, 35 North St., Ste. 98, New York, NY 34509

Writing a business letter

Sometimes when you read an ad, you do not get all the information you think you should have. For example, you may not know the job position of the person to whom you are writing. You may not even have a name. Perhaps you only know the name of the company and its address.

Don't worry. An advertisement will always include enough information to allow you to get in touch. Just be sure to include all the information that you *do* have.

Now, let's get a business letter started. Suppose you see this advertisement in *School* magazine. You want to write for more information.

> *DIPLOMAS BY MAIL*
> *Litmus Learning, Inc.*
> *Get a high school diploma – FREE!*
> *Let us send you an information pack!*
> *Dr. Wayne Smith, President*
> *P.O. Box 12, Denver, CO 67444*

Exercise 21-7

Number your work paper 1-5. Answer the questions about the ad.
1. Who will you be writing your letter to?
2. What is his title?
3. What is the name of his organization?
4. What is the street address?
5. Write the city, state and ZIP code.

Let's begin our business letter. We will use the example letter below to help us write our own letters.

Exercise 21-8

On a clean sheet of paper, begin writing a business letter to Litmus Learning. Follow these steps:
1. Center your name, address and phone number at the top of your paper.
2. Skip two lines. On the margin line, write today's date. Do not use abbreviations.
3. Skip two lines. Write the inside address for Litmus Learning.
4. Skip two lines. Write the salutation to Dr. Wayne Smith, President. Use a colon (:) at the end of the salutation.

Carl Smith is writing his business letter. We can use his letter as a model for our own. He begins by writing his return address, date, inside address, and salutation. Let's take a look.

Carl Smith

1122 Vista St.

Palm Springs, CA 92262

(555) 555-1111

December 15, 2002

Dr. Wayne Smith, President

Litmus Learning

P.O. Box 12

Denver CO 67444

Dear Dr. Smith:

Now, we are ready to write the body of the letter. The body of the letter contains the information we want to communicate. We want information about Litmus Learning. It is important to remember that we are writing a business letter. We are writing to business people. We must get to the point immediately.

Exercise 21-9
Add a body to your letter. Feel free to use Carl's letter as a model for your own. Here is the body of Carl's letter.

> I read your advertisement for diplomas by mail in <u>School</u> magazine. Please send information to the address listed above.
>
> Thank you for your time.

Notice that Carl indented his paragraph. He kept the body of his letter short and to the point. He understands that business people are busy. Also, he mentioned where he had seen the advertisement. This is the mark of a good letter writer.

Magazine titles are proper nouns. They are always capitalized. Remember this: when writing a letter by hand, the title of a magazine, book, or newspaper must be underlined. When typing, these words can be set in italics, like this :
School

The final line of the body of any letter should be a thank you. It is polite to thank business people for their time. Again, don't be overly long.

A simple "Thank you for your time" should be enough.

Add the closing and your signature, and you are done! Generally speaking, the word *Sincerely* is used. Be sure to spell it properly. Also, be sure to center the closing and your signature. This will make them stand out more clearly.

Exercise 21-10
Start on a new line. Write this:
Sincerely,

Center the word, spell it correctly. Add a comma after the word.

Exercise 21-11
Under the word *Sincerely* sign your name. Write in cursive.

Congratulations! You have finished your business letter. Compare your work to Carl's letter.

Carl Smith
1122 Vista St.
Palm Springs, CA 92262
(555) 555-1111

December 15, 2002

Dr. Wayne Smith, President
Litmus Learning
P.O. Box 12
Denver CO 67444

Dear Dr. Smith:

    I read your advertisement for diplomas by mail in <u>School</u> magazine. Please send information to the address listed above.
    Thank you for your time.

Sincerely,
Carl Smith

Let's talk about salutations. A *salutation* is a kind of greeting. Look at the salutation in the above letter. The salutation ends with a colon (:).

Dear Dr. Smith:

A salutation always includes a person's title. For example, a judge named Jones would be given this salutation:

Dear Judge Jones:

The word *Judge* is a title. When writing a salutation it is important to remember that *everyone* has a title. The title is capitalized.

Often, titles are abbreviated. That is, titles are often shortened, and a period is added at the end to indicate that there are letters missing.

The most common title when writing to a man is *Mr*.

When writing a salutation for a woman, however, take care. Three common titles are used. The title you choose will depend on whether or not the woman is married. It also depends on what the woman prefers. Use titles for a woman this way:

Mrs. - for a married woman

Miss - for a woman who has never been married

Ms. - when you are unsure

Generally speaking, it is better to be safe than sorry. When you are unsure what a woman prefers, or whether she is married or not, simply use *Ms*.

Here is a list of the most commonly used titles. All but the word *Miss* are abbreviations. That is, they are missing letters. Therefore, they require a period.

Doctor - Dr.

Junior - Jr.

Mister - Mr.

Miss - Miss

Missus - Mrs.

Ms. - Ms.

Reverend - Rev.

Father - Fr.

Usually, one title is enough. For example, if Mary Smith is a Reverend, we simply write this:

Dear Rev. Smith

Do not use more than one title. Look.

Incorrect: Dear Rev. Ms. Smith:

Correct: Dear Rev. Smith:

It is also incorrect to use a person's first name with a title.
Incorrect: Dear Mr. Bill Smith:
Correct: Dear Mr. Smith:
Here is one more important point about the salutation line. The salutation line must always end with a colon (:).

If you do not know who will be reading your letter, use these words. Be sure to capitalize them.
To Whom It May Concern:

Exercise 21-12
Number your work paper 1-10. Imagine you are writing a business letter. Write salutations using abbreviations wherever possible. Be sure to include the colon at the end of the salutation.
Example: Doctor Carl Smith
Answer: Dear Dr. Smith:
1. Doctor Simms
2. Doctor Simms, Junior
3. Jane Jones (married)
4. Doctor Jane Jones
5. Jane Jones (never married)
6. Mary Smith (unsure)
7. Reverend Mary Smith
8. Reverend John Hall, Junior
9. Doctor Orville Reed
10. Father Orville Reed

Exercise 21-13
Number your work paper 1-2. Look at each advertisement. Imagine you are writing business letters. Write an inside address, a date, and a salutation for each advertisement. The example will help you.
Example

FREE CANDY SAMPLES!!!
Candy Corp.
Post Office Box 12-4
Ocean, CA 91111

(Check your answer below.)

Candy Corp.
P.O. Box 12-4
Ocean, CA 91111

May 16, 2006

To Whom It May Concern:

1.   Best Counseling , Inc.
        Send for a free brochure!
        Dr. Phil Simms, PhD.
        35 W. 7th St.
        Phoenix, AZ 85282

2.   TIME KEEPERS, INC.
        Get our new catalogue of watches!
        P.O. Box 3456, Salem, Oregon, 88812

Summary
- ✓ Correspondence is communication by mail.
- ✓ Business correspondence must look like business correspon-dence.
- ✓ Business letters have seven parts.
- ✓ Use Post Office abbreviations when writing letters.
- ✓ Always use titles when writing business letters.

Chapter 22

Employment Letters

We can use business letters to apply for employment. One meaning of *employment* is *work*. A person looking for employment is looking for work. *Employers* are the people who hire workers. When we are job hunting, we are asking employers for employment. We are asking for jobs from those who hire. One way to ask an employer for a job is with a business letter.

We have learned that business correspondence must look like business correspondence. We have learned how the seven parts of a business letter should fit onto a page. We have also learned how to abbreviate addresses and titles.

Now we will write employment letters. We will use the TIGER method to help us get organized.

Even though most business letters are short, they require careful planning. The TIGER method can help us write excellent business letters. Our writing will make us look extremely intelligent.

We often write business letters when applying for a job. A job might be advertised in the newspaper. Many times, these advertisements do not include a phone number. You must write a business letter to show you are interested in the job. The employer looks at your business letter carefully. A good letter can help you get the job!

Let's imagine we have read this ad in a newspaper called the <u>Arizona Republic.</u>

> WANTED: *Part-time sales clerk to work afternoons in local store. No experience necessary. Contact Jim Simmons, P.O. Box 349, Phoenix, AZ 85282*

Remember the steps in the TIGER method.

T = Topic sentence
I = Ideas
G = Group
E = Enumerate
R = wRite

Since business letters are so short, the topic sentence will be your most important sentence. Look at the following topic sentence. It gets right to the point.

I am writing in response to your ad in the Arizona Republic for a part-time clerk.

This sentence tells the employer that you are interested in the job; it also tells the employer where you read about the job. The sentence shows that you read newspapers. You make a good impression with this sentence.

Now you must get your ideas together. As always, it is wise to jot your ideas on a sheet of note paper. Your ideas should deal with your ability to work. You should only include information which you feel would make you look like a good person for the job.

Of course, you will put your ideas into logical groups before you write your letter. Then you will enumerate them. Finally, you will write. With careful planning you will end up with an excellent letter.

When possible, it is always best to type a business letter. Do not use unusual fonts; Times New Roman is best. If you are unable to type your letter, you may write by hand. Be sure to use only blue or black ink. Most importantly, be neat.

You will want to make sure that your letter looks like a business letter.

The following checklist will help you write a good letter.

Checklist
_____ *Looks like a business letter*
_____ *Return address*
_____ *Date*
_____ *Inside address*
_____ *Salutation*
_____ *Clear topic sentence & related details*
_____ *Closing*
_____ *Signature*
_____ *Proper mechanics*
    (abbreviations, capitalizations, etc.)
_____ *Typed or neatly hand written (blue or*
    black ink)

Let's look at a letter that Carl wrote.

Carl Smith
1122 Vista St.
Phoenix, AZ 85287
(555) 555-1212

December 15, 2005

Jim Simmons
P.O. Box 349
Phoenix, AZ 85282

Dear Mr. Simmons:
    I am writing in response to your ad in the *Arizona Republic* for a part-time clerk. I am a freshman at Tempe High School; I maintain good grades. I like to meet people, and I am good at math. As a matter of fact, I think I would be a great employee.

    I look forward to an interview.

    Thank you for your time.

Sincerely,
Carl Smith

Good for Carl! He typed his letter! It looks good, and it sounds good, too. He introduced his topic sentence, and his details talked about his topic.

Just for fun, he included a sentence with a semi-colon. Semi-colons are rarely used. When you use a semi-colon correctly, you show others that you are well educated.

Carl also managed to include an interrupter, and look how well he sold himself. He wouldn't just be a good employee - he would be a *great* one.

Bosses take notice of letters like Carl's. Good business letters are written by people who will make good employees. Carl always works hard and works smart. He is exactly what bosses are looking for.

Exercise 22-1
Here is the ad placed by Mr. Simmons. Write a business letter like Carl's. Use his letter as your model. Pay attention to all 7 parts of the letter. Tell Mr. Simmons why you believe you are qualified for the job. Work hard and work smart. Pay attention to details.

(from the <u>Arizona Republic</u>)

> *WANTED: Part-time sales clerk to work afternoons in local store. No experience necessary. Contact Jim Simmons, P.O. Box 349, Phoenix, AZ 85282*

Exercise 22-2
Grade your completed letter against the checklist. Correct your work until you are sure that is perfect.

Exercise 22-3
Read the following ad. Write a business letter telling why you are qualified for the job.   (from the <u>Dallas News</u>)

> *WANTED: Part-time cashier for afternoons and evenings at local movie theater. Some weekend work required.*
> *Mary Jones, P.O. Box 4-A, Dallas, Texas 99999*

Chapter 23

Apostrophes

We have learned some conventions of correct capitalization. We have learned that there are two types of nouns: proper nouns and common nouns. Proper nouns must be capitalized.

We also know that nouns may be either singular or plural. To sum everything up, we can say that nouns may be either singular or plural, and they may be either common or proper.

Possessive nouns

This chapter discusses a new type of noun. The new type of noun is called a *possessive noun*. Possessive nouns show ownership.

Possess means own. A person may possess, own, a skateboard. A family may possess a boat. The word *possessive* comes from the word *possess*. A possessive noun is a noun that shows ownership.

There are different types of possessive nouns. In this book, we will call all possessive nouns *possessives*. We use possessives every day. Look at the following two sentences. The one that sounds correct is the one with the possessive.

> *John ate he lunch.*
> *John ate his lunch.*

In the sentence, *John ate his lunch,* the word *his* is a possessive. The word *his* tells us that John ate his own lunch. We could have been even clearer and written the sentence this way:

John ate his own lunch.

Read this sentence:

John ate Mary's lunch.

Whose lunch did John eat?

He ate Mary's lunch. The word *Mary's* is a possessive. We know that Mary owned the lunch.

Let's look for possessives in sentences.

Exercise 23-1:

Number your work paper 1-10. Each sentence contains a possessive. Write the possessive on your work paper.

1. That book is mine.
2. Mary decided to give her dog a bath.
3. I think those shoes are hers.
4. His father used to work in a gold mine.
5. Those kittens are theirs.
6. The bird feathered its nest.
7. Their garbage can is still on the curb.
8. Our neighbor called the police.
9. Her broken arm healed nicely.
10. Those are my pencils.

We use possessives to show ownership. Some commonly used possessives are listed below.

my, mine	our, ours
her, hers	their, theirs
his	
its	
your, yours	

We all know how to use these words. We all know how to use possessives. If we want to write about things we own, we might write this way:

That is <u>my</u> pencil.

or

That pencil is <u>mine</u>.

We may, however, need to write about a pencil that Ken owns, or we may need to write about some books that Mary owns. What do we do?

We make possessives by adding an apostrophe and an *s*. An apostrophe is a mark of punctuation. It looks like this:

,

Look at the examples of possessives formed by adding *'s*.

That is Ke<u>n's</u> pencil.

Those are Mar<u>y's</u> books.

Singular possessives

Adding *'s* only works when we are dealing with singular nouns. Remember, singular nouns are nouns which name only <u>one</u> person, place, thing, or idea.

Adding *'s* (apostrophe "s") to a singular noun makes the noun a singular possessive. Use this formula to change singular nouns into possessives:

SINGULAR NOUN	+	*'s*	=	*POSSESSIVE NOUN*
John	+	's	=	John's
Kate	+	's	=	Kate's
Sammy	+	's	=	Sammy's
Everybody	+	's	=	Everybody's

Interestingly, the word *everybody* is considered a singular noun. Because *everybody* is a singular noun, we can add *'s* to it and make it a possessive.

Make a singular noun into a possessive by adding *'s*.

Exercise 23-2

Number your work paper 1-10. Turn each of the expressions into a shorter expression by changing the singular noun into a possessive. Follow the example.

Example: The car of Dave
Answer: Dave's car

1. The house of Mary
2. The pencils of Bob
3. The ring of Angela
4. The picture of Tom
5. The money of Mark
6. The car of Dan
7. The volleyball of Nancy
8. The bowling ball of Andrew
9. The truck of Mr. Porter
10. The scissors of Miss Smith

Actually we can add *'s* to almost any singular noun and make a possessive noun. For example, if we want to write about the windows in the classroom, we simply make the word *classroom* a possessive.

The classroom's windows let in a lot of light.

We make a singular noun into a possessive noun by adding *'s*.

SINGULAR NOUN	+	*'s*	=	*POSSESSIVE NOUN*
classroom	+	's	=	classroom's
Michigan	+	's	=	Michigan's
desk	+	's	=	desk's

Exercise 23-3

Number your work paper 1-10. Turn each of the expressions into a shorter expression by changing the singular noun into a possessive. Follow the example.

Example: The color of the desk
Answer: The desk's color

1. The capital of Nevada
2. The population of Japan
3. The height of the mountain
4. The frame of the picture
5. The glow of the light bulb
6. The color of the ink
7. The size of the shirt
8. The tires of the car
9. The blades of the propeller
10. The action of the game

Look again at your answers to the previous exercises. All your answers required apostrophes. We add *'s* to singular nouns to form singular possessives. We show ownership by adding *'s* to singular nouns.

Be careful, though. Not all possessives require an *'s*. Which words do not need *'s* ?

Words like *his*, *hers*, *theirs*, and *ours* do not need apostrophes. These words are already possessives. Review the list of common possessives on page 214. In fact, it is wrong to add *'s* to any of these possessives.

Exercise 23-4
Number your work paper 1-10. Look at each group of three words. Only one word in each group requires an *'s* to make it possessive. Write the word on your work paper. Add *'s* to the word to create the possessive. Follow the example.
Example: my   Tom   our
Answer: Tom's

1. his   her   Jan
2. our   their   family
3. chair   yours   theirs
4. book   mine   its
5. its   ours   teacher
6. hers   pen   ours
7. your   yours   Jim

8. Nevada mine my
9. car their theirs
10. its yours house

Exercise 23-5

Number your work paper 1-10. Each sentence contains only one word which requires an apostrophe. The apostrophe is missing. On your work paper, write the word that requires the apostrophe. Be sure to include the apostrophe. Follow the example.

Example: Their son is at Johns house.
Answer: John's

1. That birds feathers are all over its nest.
2. Janes pencils are not yours.
3. That schools teams are better than ours.
4. Mr. Johnsons house is next to theirs.
5. Marys hair is longer than hers.
6. The books which are ours are not the librarys.
7. Yours are in the locker, but Jims are in the classroom.
8. That houses windows shattered all over its floors.
9. We mixed Toms money with ours.
10. Japans language is different than ours.

Exercise 23-6

Number your work paper 1-10. Change each of the singular nouns into a possessive by adding *'s* . After each possessive, add a word to complete the expression. Follow the examples.

Example: mom
Answer: mom's shoes
Example: bottle
Answer: bottle's shape

1. Jane
2. pen
3. lamp
4. chair
5. teacher
6. dog
7. sailboat
8. picture
9. ice cream
10. gold

Exercise 23-7

Number your work paper 1-10. Rewrite each sentence so that it contains a possessive. Follow the example.

Example: The population of Japan is growing slowly.
Answer: Japan's population is growing slowly.

1. The color of the ink is red.
2. The door of the car is dented.
3. Put the books that Mr. Thompson owns on the table.
4. The ring of the telephone was loud.
5. Be sure to clean the bristles of the toothbrush.
6. We should change the oil that is in the engine.
7. The borders of Canada are long and cold.
8. The dog that family owns is a German shepherd.
9. The direction of the wind is east.
10. The picture on that digital TV is extremely clear.

The correct use of possessives is a convention of written English. We often use possessives when we write.

Knowing the conventions of written English allows us to communicate our thoughts clearly. Our audience will know exactly what we are trying to say. Using possessives correctly is an important skill. When we are able to use possessives correctly, our audience will always know who owns what.

Plural or possessive

One common mistake writers make is confusing plural nouns with possessives. Remember, plural nouns are nouns which represent more than one object. We usually add an *s* to a word to make the word plural. We might talk about *three pencils* or *ten eggs*.

Look at the following sentence. What is the problem?
Mary bought five apple's.

In this sentence the word *apples* should be a plural, not a possessive. We add *'s* to a singular noun to make a possessive. The writer of the above sentence wanted to write this:
Mary bought five apples.

Exercise 23-8

Number your work paper 1-10. If the underlined word is a plural, write *Plural*. If it is a possessive, write *Possessive*.

1. They eat <u>grapes</u>.
2. A <u>grape's</u> color might be green.
3. The <u>airplane's</u> engine roared.
4. Tom bought six <u>donuts</u>.
5. The <u>fans</u> screamed loudly.
6. <u>Winds</u> blew in from the Northwest.
7. Someone ripped the <u>magazine's</u> cover.
8. It seems that <u>Sue's</u> dog is sick.
9. The <u>shoes</u> smelled.
10. Billy ate <u>Jane's</u> cake.

Exercise 23-9

Number your work paper 1-10. Each sentence contains a mistake with either a plural, a possessive, or both. Rewrite the sentences correctly on your work paper.

1. Johns parent's told him to get home early.
2. Those are Marys pens and pencils.
3. According to this mornings weather report, we are in for storms.
4. Jane lost her friends scissors.
5. That bakerys cake's are the best.
6. Mr. Thompsons tie's are very bright.
7. The computers disc drives didn't work.
8. Everyones watches were wrong.
9. The bow's in the girls hair were yellow.
10. Jims books are on that shelf.

Exercise 23-10

Number your work paper 1-5. Change the singular nouns into possessives, and use them in a sentence. Follow the example.
Example: Jim
Answer: That cat is Jim's.

1. Kim
2. car
3. dog

4. book
5. pencil

Plural Possessives

What if we need to write about several people who possess something? Suppose we want to write about five boys who each own some books. We could do this:

The books of the boys

This is an awkward sentences. It would sound much better with a possessive. Look.

The boys' books.

The rule that concerns forming plural possessives is one of the easiest writing conventions to remember. Here it is:

Make a possessive of any noun ending with "s" by placing the apostrophe at the end of the word.

Look at the examples.

PLURAL NOUN	*PLURAL POSSESSIVE*
cars	*cars'*
desks	*desks'*
papers	*papers'*

Now look at the possessives in sentences.
(Think of five cars)   The five cars' windshields were broken.
(Think of three desks) The three desks' tops were polished.
(Think of ten papers)   The papers' titles were very clear.

Exercise 23-11

Number your work paper 1-5. Change the plural words into plural possessives by adding an apostrophe.

1. girls
2. computers
3. radios
4. lamps
5. pork chops

In general, we can make a possessive of <u>any</u> noun that ends in "s" by adding an apostrophe to the end of the word. Look.

pants	*pants'*
scissors	*scissors'*
glasses	*glasses'*

This often happens with names. Look.

Chris	*Chris'*	*(pronounce: CHRIS-es)*
Bess	*Bess'*	*(pronounce: BESS-es)*
Tess	*Tess'*	*(pronounce: TESS-es)*
Mars	*Mars'*	*(pronounce: MARS-es)*

Exercise 23-12
Number your work paper 1-5. Write the word that requires an apostrophe. Be sure to include the apostrophe.
1. Mars color is red.
2. The pants pockets were torn.
3. The scissors blades were sharp.
4. I think that those are Chris notebooks.
5. Bess scissors are in the drawer.

<u>Summary</u>
✓ Possessive nouns show ownership.
✓ Apostrophes are the mark of punctuation used when making possessives.
✓ The possessive of <u>any</u> noun that ends with "s" can be formed by adding an apostrophe to the end of the word.

Chapter 24

Fact and Opinion Review

Let's review facts and opinions.

Read these two sentences. One states a fact, the other states an opinion. Which one states an opinion?

A) Many students want part-time jobs.
B) Students should be allowed to have part-time jobs.

Sentence *B* states an opinion. It would be an excellent thesis statement for a persuasive composition.

Sentence *A* states a fact. It would make an ideal topic sentence.

Be careful! When stating the opinions of others, you are actually stating a fact. Look.

(FACT) Don thinks that ghosts are real.

This is Don's opinion, it is not the writer's opinion. When a writer reports someone else's opinion, the writer is reporting a fact. The fact is, Don believes in ghosts. When stating an opinion, a writer must state a personal feeling. Look.

(OPINION) I don't believe in ghosts.

-or maybe-

(OPINION) I think that Don is crazy for believing in ghosts.

When stating an opinion, be certain that you really *are* stating an opinion. Remember, only opinion sentences may begin a persuasive composition. A thesis statement is an opinion.

Exercise 24-1

Number your work paper 1-10. The following sentence pairs contain one fact, and one opinion. Decide which sentence is the opinion sentence, and write the letter of the sentence on your paper. Follow the example.

Example: A) Many people believe that students should wear uniforms.

          B) Students should wear uniforms.

Answer: B

1. A) Hard work can lead to great success.
   B) Hard work should be its own reward.
2. A) There are too many TV stations.
   B) The number of TV stations keeps growing larger.
3. A) Large numbers of students use calculators in math class.
   B) Students should be allowed to use calculators in math class.
4. A) All handguns should be registered.
   B) Many believe that all handguns should be registered.
5. A) Some scientists believe we are in a period of global warming.
   B) I believe we are in a period of global warming.
6. A) School uniforms should be blue and white.
   B) Most school uniforms are blue and white.
7. A) Many think that oil prices will rise.
   B) Oil prices will probably rise, I think.
8. A) John believes in the Loch Ness Monster.
   B) I can't believe that John believes in the Loch Ness Monster.
9. A) Movies are getting longer and longer.
   B) Movies are getting too long.
10. A) The color red is the most beautiful color.
    B) The color red can be seen in many hues.

Chapter 25

Paragraph Review

TIGER

We have learned much about writing paragraphs. Most importantly, we have learned the TIGER method of writing. TIGER works well for letters, stories, paragraphs of fact, and paragraphs of opinion.

We have also learned a number of conventions to follow when we write. We've learned about semicolons, and we've learned about appositives and interrupters. We've learned about subject/verb agreement, and we've also learned one way of writing quotations.

In this lesson, we will put everything together to write two paragraphs about Samuel Morse, the inventor of the telegraph and of Morse code. One paragraph will be a paragraph of fact. The other will be a paragraph of opinion. As good writers, we need to be able to change from one style to another without difficulty. The TIGER writing method will help us accomplish this.

The first paragraph we will write, the paragraph of fact, will require a topic sentence and a list of facts hat help explain the topic.

Our second paragraph will be a paragraph of opinion.

What will we call the first sentence of our paragraph of opinion?

We'll call it a thesis statement. It is a statement of opinion. When we write our paragraph of opinion, we will construct a fact and opinion sandwich. We will use TIGER to help us with this paragraph, too.

Before we begin, let's remember other famous people we've written about. First, we wrote about Helen Keller; after that, we wrote about Alexander Graham Bell.

Soon, we will be writing five paragraph compositions. We'll want to remember everything we've done when it comes time to write five paragraph compositions.

For now, let's read about Samuel Morse, the inventor of the telegraph and Morse code.

Samuel Morse

Samuel F. B. Morse, the inventor of the telegraph and Morse code, was born in 1791, in Charlestown, Massachusetts. He was a bright student and began attending Yale University at the age of only fourteen. Although he was interested in the sciences, Morse wanted to become an artist.

To help fulfill his dreams, he went to England and became a painter. After that, he returned to the United States and set up an art studio in New York City.

Morse began teaching art at New York University. At the same time, he began attending science lectures there. He was fascinated by electromagnets, and his job at the university gave him many opportunities to learnabout electromagnetism.

In 1825, a tragedy occurred in Morse's life. His wife died; however, because he was out of the city at the time, he did not receive the news of her death until several days after she was buried. At this time in history, before electricity became common, communication was very slow.

Several years passed, and Morse returned to Europe for a time. It was while he was on board a ship returning to the United Sates that Morse suddenly hit upon the idea of communication using electro-magnets. He believed that by using wires, magnets, and batteries, he could develop a system for communication that would be so fast that it could transmit messages over long distances in an instant.

After returning to New York City, Morse began working on his new invention, the telegraph. Not only did Morse have to solve the problems of electro-magnets and electrical current, he also had to develop a way to send messages over wires. This led to the development of Morse code, a system of letters represented by dots and dashes.

Finally, in May, 1844, Morse was ready to test his telegraph system. He wired two telegraphs together over a distance of more than thirty-five miles. One was in Washington D.C., and the other was in Baltimore, Maryland. He sent the first message ever sent by telegraph: "What hath God wrought!"

Morse's invention was a huge success. Messages could be sent quickly over long distances. Morse had never forgotten the long delay in learning of his wife's death. He received world-wide fame and honors for his telegraph.

Morse eventually remarried and had four more children. He died on April 2, 1872.

Now it's time to write. Complete Exercise 25-1 and 25-2. Reread the models on pages 51 and 80 to help get started.

Exercise 25-1
Using TIGER, arrange your ideas for a paragraph of facts about Samuel Morse. On a clean sheet of paper, write your paragraph. It should be at least eight sentences long.

Exercise 25-2
Using TIGER, arrange your idea for a paragraph of opinion about Samuel Morse. Include facts and opinions. On a clean sheet of paper, write your paragraph. It should be at least eight sentences long.

Chapter 26

Compound Sentences with Commas

We know that when we talk about English conventions we are talking about the rules of written English. One convention of written English, for example, is that interrupters must be set off with commas. Another convention of written English is this common rule: sentences must begin with a capital letter.

Here is an interesting convention we learned in an earlier chapter: we usually capitalize the names of heavenly bodies like Mercury and Venus, but the names of three heavenly bodies in particular are never capitalized. Do you remember which ones?

The words *sun*, *earth*, and *moon* are never capitalized.

There are many conventions in the English language that are not well known. In this chapter we will study some of these conventions. Knowing the rules of written English will help us become better communicators.

By the way, have you ever stopped to ask yourself what makes a person smart? We often think people are smart when they know something we don't know. For example, you may think that a person is smart if he can take an engine apart and put it back together. You'll think he's even smarter if the engine still runs!

Once you learn the conventions of English writing, you will be able to spot mistakes in newspapers and magazines. Not only will you be able to spot them, but you will know why the mistakes *are* mistakes, and you will be able to fix them. You will be a mechanic of the English language. People will think you are smart because you can explain something that surrounds them every day - the English language!

Let's begin.

We know that a semicolon is used to join two complete sentences into a compound sentence. Here is some advanced information.

There is another way to join two sentences.

Comma + joining word

Two sentences may be joined by a *comma + joining word.* The two most common joining words are listed below.

> *and*
> *but*

Read the example sentences. Notice how two sentences can be made into a compound sentence using either a *semicolon,* or a *comma + joining word.*

> *John runs. His dog walks.*
> *John runs; his dog walks.*
> *John runs,* **but** *his dog walks.*

It's very simple. Be sure to remember one very important detail. The comma comes *before* the joining word.

Also, notice the word after the joining word. This word should not be capitalized unless it is a proper noun. Study the example sentence.

We studied about history, and we learned some science.

Let's practice writing some compound sentences using the new construction of *comma + joining word.*

Exercise 26-1

Number your work paper 1-5. The following compound sentences are written with semicolons. Change each using a *comma + joining word*. The joining word you should use is in parentheses at the end of each sentence. Follow the example.

Example: Jane baked the cake; her brother ate it. (but)
Answer: Jane baked the cake, but her brother ate it.

1. Pharaohs were kings in Ancient Egypt; the pyramids were their tombs. (and)
2. Polar regions are cold; tropical regions are hot. (but)
3. Pens use ink; pencils use lead. (but)
4. John has a job after school; he plays football, too. (and)
5. We went on a field trip to the museum; it was boring. (but)

Notice that when we use the *comma + joining word* construction, the word *and* is used to help add information or to show how things are the same. The word *but* is used to show how things are different.

Tom went to the car show, and he looked at the cars.
(The word *but* would sound awkward here.)

Tom went to the car show, but he decided to go home early.
(The word *but* is the best choice here.)

Here is another word that is often used as a joining word:
so

*We were late, **so** we hurried.*

Let's make a few more compound sentences. This time you will be given two complete sentences. Use the joining word which you feel best fits the situation.

Exercise 26-2
Number your work paper 1-5. Combine the two sentences using the *comma + joining word* method. Use the joining word you feel best fits the situation. Be sure to put the comma *before* the joining word.

1. The boys played football. The girls played soccer.
2. Helen Keller was born healthy. She became very ill.
3. A dime isn't much. It's better than nothing.

4. Ron is a mechanic. He knows about electronics, too.
5. The computer was broken. A repairman fixed it.

We can write compound sentences using the *comma* + *joining word* method. We must always be certain, however, that we are actually dealing with two <u>complete</u> sentences.

The compound sentence below is incorrect. It is not made from two complete sentences. It is made from a sentence and a fragment. The fragment is underlined.

John sawed the wood all morning, and <u>sanded it all afternoon.</u>

This is a common mistake. Because we are mechanics of the English language, however, we can easily fix the problem. We will simply add a subject to the underlined fragment. Now we have a compound sentence.

*John sawed the wood all morning, and **he** sanded it all afternoon.*

No matter what word you use as a joining word, remember this rule:

Compound sentences require two complete sentences.

Exercise 26-3

Number your work paper 1-10. If the compound sentence is formed correctly from two complete sentences write *Correct*. If it is not formed correctly write *Incorrect*.

1. They walked up the road, and picked flowers as they went.
2. Josh decided he wanted to go out for track, so he began jogging everyday.
3. Tina wanted to get home early, but her car broke down.
4. Tina wanted to be on time, so she left early.
5. A thunderstorm moved in, and filled the sky with gray clouds.
6. Jim played the piano, and his sister played the drums.
7. The Nile, a river in Egypt, runs northwards, and provides water to farmers.
8. The video player was broken, and Jim couldn't fix it.
9. The movers carried the boxes downstairs, and used a cart to haul them to the truck.

10. John wanted to play basketball, but he never learned to shoot.

We are learning the conventions of written English in order to find mistakes in our own writing before our audience reads it. The most important member of our audience is our teacher. We can be sure that our teachers will find our mistakes, so we must be certain to correct our writing before we hand it in.

Exercise 26-4

Number your work paper 1-5. Read the following story. Look for mistakes in compound sentences. You will find five mistakes. Remember all compound sentences require two complete sentences. Make a note of the mistakes you find by writing the first two words of the sentences that contain mistakes. Follow the example.

Example: *John runs; Jane walks. They like to exercise, but not on Fridays.*

Answer: *They like*

Taxi Ride

It was a hot morning. The sun was shining, and birds were singing. John woke up early, and decided to head to the swimming pool. The swimming pool was close, so he walked. On the way he met his friend Jim, and another friend named Tim. The boys thought it would be a good idea to stop at the drugstore, and buy some candy and soda to take to the pool. They bought what they wanted; they left the store.

A taxi pulled up, and honked its horn. The driver leaned out, and he asked the boys if they wanted a ride. They decided that was a good idea, too, so they climbed inside. The driver drove them around the block three times. Finally, he pulled up at the pool.

He said, "That will be ten dollars."

The boys barely had enough money to pay the driver. After paying, they didn't have enough money to get into the pool.

John asked, "Why did you drive us around the block three times?"

The driver said, "I just remembered that today is my

anniversary, and I need money to buy my wife a present." He floored the gas, and drove off.

In addition to our new method for constructing compound sentences, we must also look at a pair of common interrupters.

Too

One common interrupter is the word *too*. We have been introduced to this word in a previous chapter.

When the word *too* is used as a synonym for *also* it must be set off from the rest of the sentence with commas. The examples make this clear.

> *Jane was invited to the party, **too**.*
> *Jane, **too**, was invited to the party.*

In both of the above sentences, the word *too* has the meaning of the word *also*. When the word *too* is used as a synonym for *also*, it must be set off from the sentence with commas.

Direct address

Another common interrupter is called *direct address*. The word *address* can mean *speak to*. When we speak to someone, we address them. Read the sample sentences.

> *The teacher **spoke to** the class.*
> *The teacher **addressed** the class.*

When we use direct address, we speak directly to someone. We speak their name. Look at the example.

> *Sara, listen to me.*
> *Listen, Sarah, to me.*
> *Listen to me, Sara.*

When we call a person by name, we must set off their name with commas. In the above sentences, we must set off Sara's name with commas because we are speaking directly to her.

We often write notes to people in exactly this way. People speak to each other through their writing. For example, John came home from school and found this note waiting for him on the kitchen table:

John, take out the trash.

John's mom was speaking to him through her writing. John found the note when he got home from school.

Before he left for baseball practice, John left a note for his mother. Good for John! He used direct address.

Mom, I took out the trash. It's in the backyard.

When deciding whether or not you are dealing with direct address, pay attention to the meaning of the sentence. Common sense will always be your best friend. The only time a name needs to be set off with commas is when the name is being directly spoken. The examples make this clear.

Direct Address: *Did you remember to clean your room, Mary?*
Not Direct Address: *Did Mary remember to clean her room?*
Direct Address: *Bill, I saw you at the store.*
Not Direct Address: *I saw Bill at the store.*

Exercise 26-5

Number your work paper 1-5. Rewrite the sentences correctly.

1. We watched a movie too.
2. Jane did you do your homework?
3. Bill did you do your homework too?
4. The price of oil Phil seems to be getting higher.
5. I think Mr. Jones that you are correct.

Exercise 26-6

Number your work paper 1-10. This is a mixed practice. You will find all types of interrupters in these sentences. Rewrite the sentences on your work paper and insert commas. When you are finished count the commas. The number in parentheses at the end of each sentence tells how many commas the sentence requires. You should find a total of 26 commas.

1. Tom did you ask your doctor Dr. Smith? (2)
2. The car a Volkswagen swerved to the left too. (3)
3. Dr. Simon the famous brain surgeon studied in France by the way. (3)

4. As a matter of fact my brother a truck driver knows that road. (3)
5. The airliner a 747 went into a steep dive. (2)
6. Class please open your books. (1)
7. Mary too wanted to visit the museum it seems. (3)
8. By the way did you want to go too Jim? (3)
9. Seal the envelope Jane and put a stamp on it too. (3)
10. Remember Phil to stay away from spinning propellers too. (3)

Compound sentences with interrupters

We can create long, complicated-looking sentences by combining comma + joining word compound sentences with several interrupters. We call this "sentence building." Read the examples.

Compound sentence: Jim went to school, but he forgot his books.

Added interrupter: <u>*As a matter of fact*</u>*, Jim went to school, but he forgot his books.*

Another interrupter: As a matter of fact, <u>Mary</u>, Jim went to school, but he forgot his books.

Final interrupter: As a matter of fact, Mary, Jim went to school, but he forgot his books, <u>too</u>.

Exercise 26-7
Sentence building

Number your work paper 1-5. Next to the number 1, write this compound sentence:

> *Don went to the store, but he didn't buy anything.*

Now, next to the number 2, rewrite the sentence, but add this interrupter to the beginning:

> *By the way,*

Now, next to the number 3, you will rewrite your answer to number 2. After the words *By the way,* add this direct address:

> *Tony*

Now, next to the number 4, you will rewrite you answer to number 3. This time, add this appositive after the word *Don.*

> *, my older brother,*

Last of all, next to the number 5 you will rewrite your answer to number 4. This time, add this interrupter after the word *store*:

> *,too*

Check your answer carefully in the back of the book. Did you include all necessary commas?

Exercise 26-8
Sentence building
Number your paper 1-5. Next to the number 1, write this compound sentence.

> *Jim laughs; Mary cries.*

Copy sentence number 1 next to the number 2, but add this appositive after the name *Jim*:

> *,my cousin,*

Copy sentence number 2 next to the number 3. Add this appositive after the name *Mary*:

> *,his sister,*

Copy sentence number 3 next to the number 4. Add this interrupter after the appositive *his sister*:

> *,however,*

Copy sentence number 4 next to the number 5. Add this interrupter after the appositive *my cousin*:

> *by the way*

Compare your final answer carefully against the answer in the back of the book. Did you include all the necessary commas?

Sentence building is important because it shows us a simple fact:

> *We can always make sentences longer by making compound sentences, using appositives, and inserting interrupters.*

Exercise 26-9
Mixed review. Number your work paper 1-10. Read each sentence. If

the sentence is written correctly, write *Correct*. If it is written incorrectly, write *Incorrect*.

1. Jim's dog, Shep, runs like the wind.
2. The class studied a chapter about the Earth and Mars.
3. Chocolate is everybody's favorite.
4. Wendell ran home from school, but he forgot why.
5. Have you heard about the new teacher, Jill.
6. My sister, too, wants to go, but my parents won't let her.
7. After we got home; we ate dinner.
8. Dad said, "Take a look at that, Billy."
9. The coach asked, "who threw that ball?"
10. That teacher, by the way, lives here.

Let's take a quick quiz to make sure we are progressing.

Quiz

Number your work paper 1-5. Copy the sentences onto your paper. Underline your answers.

1. One common interrupter is called direct _____.
2. Compound sentences can be constructed using a comma and a _____ word.
3. _____ are the rules for written English.
4. The names of these three heavenly bodies should never be capitalized: _____, _____, and _____.
5. We can construct compound sentences without using a comma + joining word if we use a _____.

If the underlined word is direct address, write *DA*. If it is not direct address write *N*.

6. Tell the umpire, <u>Jim</u>, that the ball was foul.
7. Jim will tell the <u>umpire</u> that the ball was foul.
8. <u>Everyone</u> will stand when the President enters.
9. <u>Everyone</u>, please stand when the President enters.
10. <u>Mary</u> told her mom about the prom.

Summary

- ✓ We can create compound sentences using the *"comma + joining word"* method.
- ✓ Three common joining words are: *and, but, so*
- ✓ When creating compound sentences, always be sure to join <u>two complete</u> sentences.
- ✓ When the word *too* means *also*, it must be set off with commas.
- ✓ We can create long sentences by making compound sentences and adding interrupters and appositives.
- ✓ Direct address is a form of interrupter. Separate direct address from a sentence using a comma.

Chapter 27

Five Paragraph Compositions

So far, we have learned many rules for writing, and we have written a variety of compositions. We've written paragraphs of fact and paragraphs of opinion. We've also written narratives, descriptions and letters.

All of our writing assignments have been relatively short. We have been concentrating on writing excellent paragraphs. That is because if you can write one excellent paragraph, you can write one thousand excellent paragraphs.

In this lesson, we will write five paragraphs. They will all fit together into a five paragraph composition.

Three topics

A five paragraph composition requires three topics. From three topics, we can write excellent five paragraph compositions.

Let's make an analogy. An *analogy* is a *comparison*.

Imagine that someone hands you a shoe box, and you look inside and see three things: a stapler, a ruler, and a pair of scissors. You explain what you see this way:

(Introduction)
I see a stapler, a ruler, and a pair of scissors.

(Topic 1)
The stapler is kind of long. It is black. It looks old because the paint is chipped.

(Topic 2)
The ruler is made of wood. It has pencil marks on it. There are some teeth marks on it, too.

(Topic 3)
The scissors have red handles. The blades are long. They look sharp.

(Conclusion)
I see a stapler, a ruler and a pair of scissors in the box.

We have just read the basic beginnings of a five paragraph composition. A five paragraph composition discusses three topics (in this case the stapler, the ruler and the scissors).

The first paragraph, called the *introduction*, quickly de-scribes the three items we see when we first look in the box (the stapler, the ruler, and the scissors). The introduction plays a special role. The introduction tells our audience what they will be reading about. This introductory paragraph makes a promise to our audience: we will write about only three items.

After the introduction, we describe the three objects in the box. We write one paragraph to describe the stapler. We write another paragraph to describe the ruler, and we write one more paragraph to describe the scissors.

After we have written one paragraph about each of the items, it is time to conclude the composition.

We write a concluding paragraph. The conclusion has a simple purpose. The conclusion sums things up. We remind our audience of what they have just read. We do not add any new information to the conclusion. In fact, the conclusion is much like the introduction.

Let's look at how the introduction, the three topics, and the conclusion go together to form a five paragraph composition.

Building a five paragraph composition

Paragraph 1:

Look into the box. Quickly mention the three things that you see inside (stapler, ruler, scissors).

Paragraph 2:

Write a paragraph about the first item, the stapler. Describe it as well as you can in one paragraph.

Paragraph 3:

Write a paragraph about the ruler. Describe it as well as possible.

Paragraph 4:

Write a paragraph about the scissors. Be sure you describe only the scissors.

Paragraph 5:

Write a quick conclusion. Mention the stapler, ruler, and scissors. Then end your composition.

Now that we have a clear picture of what we are doing, let's put everything into words.

We will be writing five paragraph compositions. First, we will pick three topics. With three topics we can write a five paragraph composition. We will always prewrite before actually writing any of our paragraphs. TIGER is one method we might use to help us organize our thoughts.

Before we begin our own five paragraph compositions, let's take a look at a completed model.

The paragraphs in this model composition are labeled. When writing our own compositions, we will not label the paragraphs. The paragraphs in this text are labeled to help show the organization in the composition. Each paragraph has a purpose.

Introduction:

This box contains a stapler, a ruler and a pair of scissors. The stapler looks a little old, the ruler looks like it has been used, too. The scissors, on the other hand, look almost new.

Topic 1(the stapler):

The stapler is the kind that teachers keep on their desks. It is kind of long, about five or six inches, and it is black. It looks a little worn; the paint is scratched and chipped. I wouldn't be surprised to learn that this stapler has been on a teacher's desk for years and years.

Topic 2 (the ruler):

The ruler is just an ordinary wooden ruler. It has been used quite a bit, judging from the pencil marks all over it. There are even some teeth marks where someone chewed on it once. Maybe they were trying to solve a math problem; maybe they were just hungry. Can anybody ever be that hungry? Suddenly, I'm thinking about lunch.

Topic 3 (the scissors):

The scissors are the final item in the box. They look new. The handles are red plastic, and the blades are dull silver. They look sharp, and there is a name stamped on them.

Conclusion:

In conclusion, the box holds three items: a stapler, a ruler, and a pair of scissors. If there is anything else in there, I don't see it.

We're done!

Of course, this is a simplified example. We used it to study the structure of a five paragraph composition.

Here is the main point:

Our first paragraph promises our audience that we will talk about three items only. The best way to write a five paragraph composition is to limit the composition to three topics.

Look at the introduction paragraph of the example composition. Only three items were mentioned. By mentioning these three items (the stapler, the ruler, and the pair of scissors) the writer promised to discuss these things and nothing else in the composition's remaining paragraphs. Now, maybe you can see why we have spent so much time focusing on paragraphs.

Five excellent paragraphs make an excellent five paragraph composition. If you can write one excellent paragraph you can certainly write five.

We have written paragraphs about Helen Keller, Alexander Graham Bell, and Samuel Morse. Let's put what we know about these famous Americans into a five paragraph composition of fact.

To do this, we will return to our analogy about the box. Someone has just handed us a box, and inside the box we have found three short encyclopedia articles: one about Helen Keller, one about Alexander Graham Bell, and one about Samuel Morse.

Our job is to write a five paragraph composition of fact about what we find in the box. In other words, we will write a five paragraph composition dealing with these three topics: Helen Keller, Alexander Graham Bell, and Samuel Morse.

Exercise 27-1

Draw five boxes on your work paper. Imagine that each box symbolizes a paragraph in a five paragraph composition about Helen Keller, Alexander Graham Bell, and Samuel Morse. Write a few words inside each box describing what the paragraphs will discuss.

Remember that your fist paragraph is simply a promise you make to your audience. You will name the three topics you intend to write about. The next three paragraphs are used to list your topics one at a time.

The final paragraph, the conclusion, simply sums up what you have written. Do not include any new information in the conclusion.

Each paragraph serves a purpose. Look.

Paragraph 1 (Introduction):

Mention Helen Keller, Alexander Graham Bell, and Samuel Morse.

Paragraph 2 (Helen Keller):

Discuss only Helen Keller.

Paragraph 3 (Alexander Graham Bell):

Discuss only Alexander Graham Bell

Paragraph 4 (Samuel Morse):

Discuss only Samuel Morse.

Paragraph 5 (Conclusion):

Quickly sum up a little about Helen Keller, Alexander Graham Bell, and Samuel Morse. Do not add any new information.

We know what we must do, now we have to get there. Let's look at the checklist.

Checklist
_____ *5 indented paragraphs*
_____ *topic sentence for each paragraph*
_____ *detail sentences that support each topic*
_____ *clear writing that is unambiguous*
_____ *a variety of sentence types*
_____ *no fragments*
_____ *interrupters*
_____ *appositives*
_____ *compound sentence using a semicolon*
_____ *compound sentence with joining word*
_____ *correct use of conventions*

To get us started, we must write the first paragraph. We will call the first paragraph the introduction. We use it to introduce the three topics we will discuss in our composition. The introduction is our promise to our audience that we will discuss only three topics.

Since we will be writing five paragraphs of fact, this introduction paragraph must begin with a topic sentence. Our job is to invent a topic sentence that will lead into our entire five paragraph composition. The first sentence of a five paragraph composition tells the audience exactly what they will be reading.

Here is an example of a good topic sentence for this composition: *Three people who changed America are Helen Keller, Alexander Graham Bell, and Samuel Morse.*

Exercise 27-2
Write a topic sentence for your introduction. Study the model sentence above if you need help.

Now we will simply gather a little information into the introduction. Let's list our ideas. Remember, we only have to make mention of a fact or two about each of the individuals we will be writing about. We simply want to let our audience know our topic, that's all. We will go into greater detail later. For right now, let's generate a few quick ideas for our introduction paragraph.

List the word *IDEAS* at the top of your paper.

Now, simply write an idea or two about Helen Keller, Alexander

Graham Bell, and Samuel Morse. Use the example below as a model.

IDEAS

Helen Keller was deaf and blind
She overcame great obstacles to become a write and a speaker.
Alexander Graham Bell invented the telephone.
Samuel Morse invented the telegraph.

There isn't very much to an introduction, is there? These ideas are good enough, however, to get us started. Remember, we are only writing an introduction. We will write full paragraphs about each of these individuals later.

Write out your own list of ideas. Check them to make sure that they are in the order you like, and also check to make sure that they are gouped logically.

Is everything grouped the way it should be? Is everything listed in the proper order?

At this point, we are ready to write our introduction. Of course, we will want to use as many writing tricks as possible in this first paragraph to capture the interest of our audience. Remember, we always write for an audience.

Read the example introduction paragraph.

Three people who changed America are Helen Keller, Alexander Graham Bell, and Samuel Morse. Are you familiar with these names? Helen Keller overcame serious handicaps to become a great writer and speaker. Alexander Graham Bell invented the telephone; Samuel Morse developed the telegraph. What changes they created! The names of these three individuals will live forever in history.

That's it! It's just that easy! We have peeked into the box, and we have quickly described what was inside. One sentence for each item is good enough. A concluding sentence rounds out the first paragraph.

Exercise 27-3
Write your own introduction. Use the example above as your guide.

Now, of course, we have to write a paragraph about each of the individuals: Helen Keller, Alexander Graham Bell, and Samuel Morse.

This should not be difficult, though, because we have already written about these people.

Remember, use TIGER to organize your thoughts about each person before writing the paragraph.

Exercise 27-4
Write a topic sentence about Helen Keller. Make sure that it is a sentence of fact, not opinion.

Exercise 27-5
Use TIGER to organize details about the life of Helen Keller.

Exercise 27-6
Add a paragraph about Helen Keller to your composition.
Follow the example.

Three people who changed America are Helen Keller, Alexander Graham Bell, and Samuel Morse. Are you familiar with these names? Helen Keller overcame serious handicaps to become a great writer and speaker. Alexander Graham Bell invented the telephone; Samuel Morse developed the telegraph. What changes they created! The names of these three individuals will live forever in history.

Helen Keller was born a healthy baby, but as a child she suffered an illness that left her deaf and blind. Luckily, Helen's father knew Alexander Graham Bell. Bell suggested a teacher for Helen; the teacher's name was Annie Sullivan. Sullivan taught Helen a special way of communicating by using a sign language that she pressed into the little girl's hand. Slowly Helen learned to communicate. Eventually, she learned to speak; however, she never heard the sound of her own voice. Helen graduated from Radcliffe, a famous college and wrote her autobiography, The Story of My Life. Helen Keller was an inspiration to millions.

Exercise 27-7
Follow the same steps to add paragraphs of fact about Alexander Graham Bell and Samuel Morse to your composition. Remember to use TIGER before writing each paragraph. We always want to collect our thoughts before we begin writing.

We are practically finished with our five paragraph compositions. All we need to do now is add the conclusion. Remember, the purpose of the conclusion is to sum things up. We want to remind our audience of what they have just read.

Does this sound strange? Could anybody's memory really be so short?

Actually, when people are reading, their minds often wander. How many times have you read an entire page from a book, only to realize that you have no idea what you were just reading?

A good writer understands that people are people. Their minds will wander as they read. This is common sense. If we want our audience to remember what we have written, we must give them a gentle reminder. Therefore, we write a concluding paragraph.

The concluding paragraph never introduces new information. It simply helps our readers remember the basic facts of what they have just read.

One way to write a good conclusion is to look back at the introduction paragraph. By simply changing a few words, and changing a few sentences, we can create a concluding paragraph.

In conclusion

It is a good idea to let your audience know that you are concluding by adding this simple interrupter to the beginning of your paragraph:

In conclusion,

Read the example concluding paragraph.

In conclusion, America was changed by three historic Americans. Helen Keller overcame physical handicaps to become a great communicator. Alexander Graham Bell invented the telephone, and Samuel Morse invented the telegraph and Morse code. They helped make the world a better place.

Exercise 27-8

Use TIGER to quickly arrange a concluding paragraph. Get ideas for your concluding paragraph from your introduction paragraph.

Exercise 27-9

Complete your essay by adding the concluding paragraph.

Exercise 27-10
Check your complete composition against the checklist. How well did you do?

Exercise 27-11
Add anything you may have overlooked. Check everything one more time. Now, neatly rewrite your paper. Don't try to be the first one done. Try to be the best one done!

Exercise 27-12
We have completed a five paragraph composition of fact.
Now we will write a new five paragraph composition. We will write five paragraphs of opinion. We will use the five paragraphs we just completed to help us.
By adding sentences of opinion to our fact paragraphs we will create sandwich writing. We will convert paragraphs of fact into paragraphs of opinion.
The checklist for this assignment is nearly the same as the checklist for our five paragraphs of fact. One requirement is changed (Topic sentences become Thesis statements), and one requirement has been added: sandwich writing.
Look at the checklist.

Checklist

_____ *5 indented paragraphs*
_____ *Thesis statement for each paragraph*
_____ *detail sentences that support each thesis*
_____ *sandwich writing*
_____ *concluding sentence for each paragraph*
_____ *clear writing that is unambiguous*
_____ *a variety of sentence types*
_____ *no fragments*
_____ *interrupters*
_____ *appositives*
_____ *compound sentence using a semicolon*
_____ *compound sentence with joining word*
_____ *correct use of conventions*

Chapter 28

More Conventions

Conventions are the rules which govern written English. We have learned many conventions in this text. Now it is time to learn some advanced conventions. We want to be able to write without mistakes. When we make mistakes in our writing, our audience sees gaps in our education. We always want to show our audience what we know, not what we don't know.

Subject-verb agreement

Earlier we studied subject-verb agreement. We learned that nouns may be either singular or plural. We also learned that verbs may be either singular or plural. We studied these facts because we always want to write correctly. The example sentences will help refresh our memories.

(Correct)   *John eats breakfast.*
(Incorrect)   *John eat breakfast.*

(Correct)   *Mary and Ellen study French.*
(Incorrect)   *Mary and Ellen studies French.*

We can often tell if a subject agrees with a verb by speaking the sentence aloud. If the sentence sounds fine, then we can be pretty sure the subjects and verbs agree.

Problems can occur, however, if we have learned to speak in an unconventional way. For example, what if a person learned to speak this way:

He don't got no money.

If a person has learned to speak in an unconventional way, that person will also write in an unconventional way. You cannot correct a problem if you do not know you have a problem.

As we work through some of the rules of advanced conventions, you may think that our new sentences sound strange. This is because the conventions are new to you. Rest assured that the rules in this book are correct. You should make a habit of practicing all new rules. Your English skills will increase, and people will respect what you say and write.

Before continuing further, let's remember the basic idea of subject-verb agreement. Here it is:

Singular subject + Singular verb = Agreement
Plural subject + Plural verb = Agreement

Exercise 28-1

Number your work paper 1-10. Write the subject and the verb of each sentence. Follow the example.
Example: The boys ride skateboards.
Answer: boys ride

1. We go to the movies on Friday night.
2. Airplanes fly over the airport.
3. Those pencils are sharp.
4. Tim's pen is dry.
5. The vase holds flowers.
6. Dad's favorite chair is old.
7. All those people think they are right.
8. At the end of the race, Jane was tired.
9. We were happy with the results.
10. Tim always burns his toast.

If we can find the subject of a sentence, we can always tell if it is singular or plural. Knowing if a subject is singular or plural tells us whether the verb should be singular or plural.

Let's remember the general rule for making words plural.

NOUN (add s)	VERB (subtract s)
boys	run
girls	jump
cowboys	ride

Generally speaking, plural nouns end with an *s*, but plural verbs do not end with an *s*.

Exercise 28-2

Plural noun practice. Number your work paper 1-10. Read the groups of words. Each group contains one plural noun. Write the plural noun.

1. eggs   egg   chicken
2. ropes   roper   roping
3. class   classy   classes
4. beast   beasts   beastly
5. tubs   tube   tuber
6. loop   loops   looping
7. base   based   bases
8. bass   bosses   brass
9. leads   leader   lead
10. cases   case   cased

Remember, in general, to make a plural verb, we do the opposite of what we do to make a plural noun. To make a plural verb, we often subtract the letter *s*.

Exercise 28-3

Plural verb practice. Number your work paper 1-10. Each group of words contains only one plural verb. Write the plural verb on your paper. (Hint: use the word *They* as a subject)

1. goes   go   going
2. jumping   jumps   jump
3. eat   eats   eaten

4. playing	play	plays
5. write	written	writes
6. reading	read	reads
7. counts	counting	count
8. figure	figures	figuring
9. breaking	breaks	break
10. want	wanting	wants

Exercise 28-4

Singular or plural? Number your work paper 1-10. Read the following subject/verb pairs. If the word pair is singular, write *S* on your paper. If it is plural write *P*.

1. John reads
2. they think
3. we enjoy
4. girl bakes
5. book falls
6. books fall
7. propellers spin
8. people clap
9. everyone thinks
10. Tim pays

Exercise 28-5

Singular or plural? Number your work paper 1-10. Read the following sentences. If the sentences contain a singular subject and verb write *S* on your paper. If the subject and verb are plural write *P*.

1. Tim buys bread.
2. Tim and Pete play catch.
3. We all think private thoughts.
4. Sometimes Mary and her friend make cookies.
5. Sometimes Jim eats fish.
6. At Cape Canaveral, rockets often blast into space.
7. Standing on the mountain, they will watch the sunrise.
8. By the way, that girl is crying.
9. Everyone buys milk.

10. Mary is considered a great cook.

We know that, in general, nouns can be made plural by adding an *s*. We also know that we can make verbs plural by subtracting an *s*. Some words, however, do not fit our pattern. Let's look at them.

Always plural

Four words are always considered plural. Here they are:

> *both*
>
> *few*
>
> *many*
>
> *several*

These words are often the subjects of sentences. When they are the subjects of sentences, the sentences require a plural verb. Read the examples. The subjects and plural verbs are underlined.

> <u>Both</u> of the boys <u>run</u> quickly.   (both run)
>
> <u>Few</u> in the crowd <u>smile</u>.   (few smile)
>
> <u>Many</u> around the President <u>shake</u> hands   (many shake)
>
> <u>Several</u> in the group <u>are</u> sick.   (several are)

Using logic

Here is an exercise in simple logic. Suppose we have red shirts and white shirts in a dresser drawer. We only have red shirts and white shirts. If we pull out a shirt and it is not white, what color must it be?

Of course, it must be red.

Let's try another exercise.

Suppose that we have a cookie jar, and inside that cookie jar we have chocolate chip and oatmeal cookies. Remember, we have *only* chocolate chip and oatmeal cookies. We reach into the jar and pull out a cookie that is not a chocolate chip. What kind of cookie must we be holding?

We must be holding an oatmeal cookie.

Answering these questions was easy because we only had two possible answers. Here's one last problem. A word may be either singular or plural. Suppose we know that the word is not plural. What must the word be?

It must be singular.

There are many words in the English language that are singular. These words are sometimes words which describe groups. For example, the word *bunch* is considered a singular word when it is used this way:

A <u>bunch</u> of bananas is not expensive.

At first glance, we might not realize that a singular word really *is* a singular word. An example of a singular word that might not seem singular is this one:

everybody

The word *everybody* is a singular word.

Here are several more singular words:
one everyone no one someone either neither nobody

We may use words like *everybody* while writing. We want to know if they are singular or plural. We must make sure that our subjects and our verbs agree. How can we make a decision?

We can remember that these words are always considered plural:
>*both*
>*few*
>*many*
>*several*

Read the examples:
>*Both are happy.*
>*Few are happy.*
>*Many are happy.*
>*Several are happy.*

Let's use common sense. Any word that is not plural is singular. Therefore, any word describing a group that is not *both*, *few*, *many*, or *several* should be treated as a singular word.

When in doubt, use this simple test. This test will tell you if a noun is plural or not. Insert the noun you are not sure of into this simple test sentence:

Plural Test
_____ *are there.*

Say the sentence out loud. If it sounds correct to you, the noun is probably a plural. Try the test sentence with the word *mice*.
Mice are there.

This sentence sounds correct because the word *mice* is a plural word. The verb *are* is also a plural. The subject agrees with the verb. Both are plural.
Now try the word *mouse* in the test sentence.
Mouse are there.

This sentence does not sound correct. Why?
The sentence does not sound correct because the singular subject *mouse* does not agree with the plural verb *are*. Remember, a singular subject requires a singular verb.
If the test sentence does not sound correct, we know that the noun we are testing is *not* a plural word. A noun that is not plural is singular. In other words, by inserting the word *mouse* in this test sentence, we can be pretty sure that the word *mouse* is not a plural. Therefore, it must be a singular.

Exercise 28-6
Singular or plural?
Number your work paper 1-10. Read the groups of words. Each group contains only one plural. Remember there are only four words that are always considered plural (see page 255)! Write the plural on your paper.

1.	one	both	anybody
2.	few	each	no one
3.	neither	many	everybody
4.	anyone	several	everyone
5.	few	each	anybody
6.	somebody	no one	few
7.	several	neither	either
8.	anyone	both	one

9. everyone   no one   many
10. each   both   neither

Before we continue, let's review. We often form plural verbs by subtracting *s*. In other words, it is fairly safe to say that a verb that does not end in an *s* is a plural verb.

Look at the verb pairs. The second verb in each pair does not end with an s. The second verb in each pair is a plural verb.

(runs, run)

(asks, ask)

(explores, explore)

In this book we will use a simple convention when listing verb pairs. The first verb in a verb pair will be singular. The second will be plural.

(singular, plural)

Remember, these four words are always considered plural:
both, few, many, several

Exercise 28-7

Verb practice

Number your work paper 1-10. Choose the verb that agrees with the subject word. Write the verb on your work paper. Follow the example.

Example: many (sees, see)

Answer: see

1. both   (runs, run)
2. anybody   (eats, eat)
3. one   (reads, read)
4. several   (thinks, think)
5. few   (believes, believe)
6. no one   (expects, expect)
7. neither   (tells, tell)
8. several   (argues, argue)
9. everybody   (plays, play)
10. many   (tolerates, tolerate)

We know that the words *both, few, many,* and *several* are always considered plural words. Knowing this, we can guess that many other words, which might be confusing, are actually singular words.

Sometimes, though, we have trouble locating the true subject of a sentence. We can follow two rules. Here is the first:

The subject rarely follows words like:

of

around

in

by

Read these sentences. Notice that they contain the words listed above. The subject does not follow these words.

Each *of* the matches *in* the box is wet.

singular subject ↗   ↖ singular verb

Several *of* the books *by* that man are interesting.

plural subject ↗   ↖ plural verb

The second rule for locating the subject of a sentence is this:
The subject never appears in an interrupter or an appositive.

Read these sentences, notice that the subject is never in an interrupter or an appositive.

In the lake, we swim.

interrupter ↗   ↖subject

That man, advisor to presidents, is well respected.

subject ↗   ↖appositive

Actually, the best way to locate the subject in any sentence is to use common sense. Ask yourself who or what the sentence is mainly talking about - that word will be the subject.

Strange subjects

Sometimes the subject of a sentence is one of the words we studied earlier. Read the example sentences. The subjects are underlined.

Everyone wants to be successful.
Many think oil prices will rise.
Few understand analytic geometry.

Exercise 28-8

Number your work paper 1-10. Write the subject of each sentence.
1. One of those boys plays football.
2. Few of the pages in the book are ripped.
3. From the shore, most can see the oil rig.
4. Many of the people in the crowd around the garden are smiling.
5. Of all the boys, Tim is the best reader.
6. John, an insurance agent, watches TV every night.
7. Neither of them watches TV.
8. Everyone believes that she will be on time.
9. Both of the pieces of bread taste stale.
10. Few in the crowd write every day.

Exercise 28-9

Number your work paper 1-10. Read each sentence and choose the verb that agrees with the subject. Remember, singular verbs are listed first, plural verbs are listed second. Write the verb on your work paper.
1. Many on the two crews (collects, collect) bottles.
2. On the bus, few in the aisle (speaks, speak).
3. After dinner, Tom, one of my older brothers, (reads, read) books.
4. In the afternoon, many (gathers, gather) at the hotel.
5. We, every one of us, (thinks, think) we are right.
6. The suit, hidden in one of the closets, (is, are) old.
7. No one in the audience (hears, hear) the speaker.
8. An airplane in the clouds (flies, fly) by instruments.
9. Every one of the airplanes (is, are) late.
10. Each of the balloons (flies, fly) away.

Exercise 28-10

Number your work paper 1-10. Read each of the sentences. If the subject agrees with the verb write *A* on your paper. If the subject and

the verb do not agree write *NA*.
1. Each of the soldiers march every day.
2. Many in the crowd cheer for the home team.
3. After a few weeks, the weather improves.
4. Every one of the kids plays with toys.
5. Neither of the cars run well.
6. Several in the group of baseball players practices every day.
7. Around the corner, both of them, Mary and Helen, run.
8. Those flowers in the vase is pretty.
9. One of the electrical cords upstairs are dangerous.
10. With the end in sight, both of the runners races to the finish line.

You may remember this sentence from a previous lesson:
> *Correct: The earrings or the bracelet is gold.*
> *Incorrect: The earrings or the bracelet are gold.*

We are ready to discover why we must use the word *is* in this sentence.

As usual, we will need a little background.

Let's begin by remembering one way in which words and sentences are alike. Both words and sentences can form compounds. Look.
> *Compound word :   football*
> *Compound sentence: Jim likes football; Ted likes baseball.*

The idea of compounds is important. Remember, a compound is formed by joining two or more things together. To form a compound word, we join two words together. To form a compound sentence, we join two sentences together.

Compound subjects

Now we'll look at a compound that can be formed inside a sentence. It is called a compound subject. Look at how a compound subject is made. The compound subject is underlined.
> *Sentence 1:   Tom likes football.*
> *Sentence 2:   Jim likes football.*

New sentence: <u>Tom and Jim</u> like football.

Notice the verb in Sentence 1 and Sentence 2. The verb *likes* is a singular verb. In Sentence 1, the singular verb *likes* agrees with the singular subject *Tom*. Likewise, in Sentence 2, the singular verb *likes* agrees with the singular subject *Jim*.

In the compound subject sentence, though, the verb changes to the plural form *like*. This is because the compound subject *Tom and Jim* is talking about two people. The compound subject is plural.

Generally speaking, compound subjects that are formed with the word *and* are considered plural. Look.

<u>The cat</u> and <u>the dog</u> play in the yard.
(the cat and the dog make a plural)

<u>A pen</u> and <u>a pencil</u> are required in this class.
(a pen and a pencil combine to make a plural)

Compound subjects are often formed by the word *and*.

The word *or* on the other hand, does not form a compound subject. Look.

Sentence 1: *Tom likes football.*
Sentence 2: *Jim likes football*
New Sentence: *Tom or Jim likes football.*

Subjects with "or"

Notice that the singular verb *likes* is used in all three of the above sentences. This is because, by convention, the word *or* does not form a compound. The word *or* joins two separate things.

Now, let's look at our original sentence.

The earrings or the bracelet is gold.

The subject of this sentence is not a compound. The word *or* is used to combine two separate things, the earrings and the bracelet. If these objects were laying on a table we would see 2 earrings (plural) and 1 bracelet (singular).

The subject of this sentence is the <u>earrings</u> *or* the <u>bracelet</u>. We will call this type of subject an "or subject."

When looking at an "or subject" we can easily decide which form of the verb to use by looking at the subject word which is closest to the verb.

If the subject word closest to the verb is singular, we use the singular form of the verb.

If the subject word closest to the verb is plural, we use the plural form of the verb.

> *The earrings or the <u>bracelet is</u> gold. (singular)*
> *The bracelet or the <u>earrings are</u> gold. (plural)*

Exercise 28-11

Number your work paper 1-10. Write the noun closest to the verb and the verb form that agrees with the noun. Follow the example.
Example: The cats or the dog (chases, chase) the mouse.
Answer: dog chases

1. The dog or some cats (chases, chase) the mouse.
2. Some cats or the dog (chases, chase) the mouse.
3. The nickel or the pennies (is, are) on the desk.
4. A dozen eggs or a pound of ham (costs, cost) more than a dollar.
5. The picture on the wall or the drawings in the book (is, are) worth a lot of money.
6. The drawings in the book or the picture on the wall (is, are) worth a lot of money.
7. Trophies or cash (makes, make) good prizes.
8. One page or ten pages (prints, print) off that single machine.
9. One man or two boys (lifts, lift) that box.
10. The books or the backpack (weighs, weigh) too much.

Exercise 28-12

Number your work paper 1-10. The sentences contain either compound subjects or "or subjects." Write the correct form of the verb.
1. Tim and Mark (runs, run) the mile every day.
2. The girls or the boys (plays, play) volleyball.

3. The coach or the girls (is, are) making plans for the game.
4. Mary or her sisters (bakes, bake) cookies.
5. His brothers or his dad (helps, help) Jim do his math homework.
6. Magazines or a book (helps, help) pass time.
7. A bus and a train (runs, run) from here to Bay City.
8. A bus or a train (runs, run) from here to Bay City.
9. Bats or a snake (lives, live) in that cave.
10. Cars and boats (is, are) used for transportation.

Summary

✓ Singular subjects agree with singular verbs; plural subjects agree with plural verbs.
✓ Four words are always considered plural: both, few, many, several.
✓ Use this simple test sentence to determine if a noun is singular or plural: _____ are there.
✓ Subjects rarely follow words like *of*, *around*, *in*, or *by*.
✓ Compound subjects joined with the word *and* are plural.
✓ "Or subjects" may be either singular or plural.

Chapter 29

Apostrophes in Contractions

We have learned about apostrophes. We know that *apostrophe + s* signals ownership. It tells our audience that someone possesses something. We know that when we add *apostrophe + s* to a noun we form a possessive.

There is another common use of the apostrophe. We can use an apostrophe to help us combine and shorten words. Look at the examples.

he will = *he'll*
does not = *doesn't*

Contractions

When we combine and shorten words we say we have made a contraction. A contraction is a pair of words which have been joined and shortened by removing letters. Contraction comes from the word *contract*. One meaning of *contract* is *make smaller*, so a contraction is a word which is made smaller. We use an apostrophe to make contractions. *The apostrophe takes the place of letters that we remove.*

By the way, you might wonder what the difference is between a contraction and an abbreviation. Remember, we used abbreviations when we wrote business letters. Contractions and abbreviations are both shortened forms of words. The difference is this: abbreviations are made from one word (Doctor becomes Dr.), but contractions are made from two words (he will becomes he'll).

Apostrophes and missing letters

When making a contraction with an apostrophe, follow this simple rule:

The apostrophe takes the place of missing letters.

Read the example. What letter is missing from the contraction?

are not = aren't

The letter *o* is missing from the contraction. We use an apostrophe to show that a letter is missing.

Sometimes an apostrophe takes the place of more than one letter. Look at the example.

we will = we'll

We have made a contraction by combining two words and leaving the letters *wi* out of the new word. We show that we have left these letters out by using an apostrophe.

Contraction equations

Making contractions is like doing a simple math problem. The first step is adding. The second step is subtracting. The third step is contracting. Look.

Step 1: add   they + are = theyare

We'll subtract a letter from *theyare*

Step 2: subtract   theyare

$$- \quad a$$

they re

Now, we'll shorten *they re*

Step 3: contract   they're

265

The final word is shorter than the original two words. That is why we call the word a contraction.

they're *is shorter than* **they are**

Let's do one more. We will make the word *we'll* from the two words *we will*.

Step 1: add   we + will = wewill

Step 2: subtract   wewill
                          -      wi

                          _____

                              we   ll

Step 3: contract   we'll

we'll *is shorter than* **we will**

In contractions, notice how the apostrophe always takes the place of the missing letters

We cannot simply invent contractions. For example, the two words *baseball* and *bat* cannot be combined and contracted to make this new word *baseb't.* If you tried to use this word in a report or other piece of writing, no one would understand your meaning.

Our audience will only understand what we write if we follow conventions. When contracting a word, be sure you are writing a word you have heard or seen before. Be sure that your audience will understand what you are writing.

If you are unsure whether a contraction is conventional or not, do not use the contraction. It is always safe to use two words.

Let's add some words together. When we add words together the new word looks like a nonsense word. Look.

Iam

We will call this an "added word."

Exercise 29-1

Number your work paper 1-10. Add the words. Your answer will be

an added word. Follow the example.
Example: we + are =
Answer: weare

1. They + will =
2. I + am =
3. Stan + is =
4. You + are =
5. Should + have =
6. Might + have =
7. We + will =
8. You + have =
9. Mary + is =
10. Ron + will =

Exercise 29-2

Number your work paper 1-10. Subtract unnecessary letters from the added words. Leave a blank to show where you subtracted the letters. Follow the example.
Example: youhave
Answer: you ve

1. weare
2. theyhave
3. carwill
4. shouldhave
5. Maryis
6. Iam
7. mighthave
8. Tomwill
9. theyare
10. Stanis

We have practiced making added words, and we have practiced subtracting unnecessary letters from added words. Now let's contract some words.

We know that contractions are formed by joining two words. We shorten them and add an apostrophe to indicate that letters are

missing. Here is the important point:
Put the apostrophe where the missing letters are supposed to go.

A common mistake is to put the apostrophe in the wrong place.

(correct)	*don't*	*(correct)*	*we're*
(incorrect)	*do'nt*	*(incorrect)*	*wer'e*

Exercise 29-3

Number your work paper 1-10. Contract the added words. Follow the example.

Example: hewill
Answer: he'll

1. shewill
2. theyare
3. whois
4. wouldhave
5. Tomwill
6. shouldhave
7. weare
8. Maryis
9. theywill
10. Iam

Exercise 29-4

Number your work paper 1-10. The following words are all missing apostrophes. Rewrite the words on your work paper. Be sure to include apostrophes in the correct place.

1. havent
2. couldnt
3. shell
4. hes
5. were
6. shouldve
7. everyonell
8. Im

9. well

10. Ill

When making contractions, apostrophes are extremely impor-tant. If you leave out an apostrophe, you might end up with a word you did not intend to write. Look.

WITH APOSTROPHE	*WITHOUT APOSTROPHE*
she'll	*shell*
we'll	*well*
I'll	*Ill*

Possessive, plural, or contraction?
Words with apostrophes may sometimes be confusing. Look.

Jane's

This word is ambiguous. Why?

We don't know if this word is a contraction or a possessive. Remember, possessives are words that show ownership. One way to form possessives is by adding *'s* to a singular noun.

Let's look at the way the word *Jane's* might be used in two different sentences. The first sentence shows the possessive use of the word. The second sentence shows the word used as a contraction.

(Possessive)   That is Jane's purse.   (The purse belongs to Jane.)
(Contraction) Jane's reading a book.   (Jane is reading a book.)

An *'s* might signal either a possessive or a contraction. The only way to know for sure is to look at the meaning of the word in a sentence. That is, we must use the context of the sentence to help us understand the meaning of the word. *Context* means *within the text*. When we use *context* to help us understand the meaning of a word, *we look into the sentence, to all the words, for clues.*

Exercise 29-5
Number your work paper 1-10. Read each sentence. Use context. If

the underlined word is a possessive write *Possessive* on your paper. If it is a contraction write *Contraction*.

1. That car is <u>Jim's</u>.
2. <u>Mary's</u> planning a trip to Spain.
3. My brother said <u>he's</u> too busy.
4. The <u>car's</u> exhaust system was rusted.
5. The <u>pen's</u> on the desk.
6. The <u>plane's</u> jets ignited.
7. Those are the <u>truck's</u> mud flaps.
8. It was <u>Jenny's</u> turn to read.
9. The <u>telephone's</u> answering machine picked up.
10. <u>Ted's</u> thinking about getting a job.

When writing, we have to make decisions about using apostrophes. Apostrophes should only be used in contractions and possessives. A common mistake is to put an apostrophe into a plural. Look.

> *(Correct)*   *Mary has two purses.*
> *(Incorrect)*   *Mary has two purse's.*

When making a plural noun, we normally do not add apostrophes.

Exercise 29-6

Number your work paper 1-10. Each sentence has an underlined word. The word might be a plural, a contraction, or a possessive. On your paper, write whether the word is a *Plural*, *Contraction*, or *Possessive*.

1. The <u>dime's</u> under the table.
2. Those are Mary's <u>dimes</u>.
3. That <u>dime's</u> face is scratched.
4. We bought two <u>televisions</u>.
5. The <u>television's</u> picture is crystal clear.
6. That <u>television's</u> too expensive.
7. John reads <u>books</u>.
8. That <u>book's</u> expensive.
9. That <u>book's</u> cover looks interesting.
10. John's books are television <u>manuals</u>.

Here is an advanced convention. There are times when we must add an *'s* to make a plural. This is an exception to the normal rule; however, it is also a standard convention. We use an *'s* when forming the plurals of numbers and letters. Look.

> *Ron got five <u>A's</u> on his report card.*
> *There are three <u>5's</u> in that phone number.*
> *How many <u>e's</u> are there in "permanent"?*
> *Your <u>three's</u> look like <u>eight's</u>.*

We also add *'s* to form a plural when we actually write a word that we are talking about. The examples will make this clear.

> *Jane used too many <u>and's</u> in her report.*
> *Some people use too many <u>like's</u> when they speak.*
> *I don't want to hear any <u>if's</u>, <u>and's</u>, or <u>but's</u>.*

Exercise 29-7

Number your work paper 1-10. Write whether the underlined word is a *Plural*, *Possessive*, or a *Contraction*.

1. His advice didn't do a <u>nickel's</u> worth of good.
2. There are too many <u>however's</u> in this report.
3. <u>That's</u> the answer we need.
4. Five <u>Shohr's</u> were listed in the phone book.
5. They say <u>Ed's</u> coming home next week.
6. The <u>car's</u> color is faded.
7. There are five <u>seven's</u> on the license plate.
8. When did you last see <u>Mr. Thompson's</u> pen?
9. We have three <u>Mr. Thompson's</u> at this school.
10. I heard that <u>Mr. Thompson's</u> a good teacher.

Some words are possessives, but they do not have apostrophes. These are common words.

> *its   his   hers   theirs   yours*

The most commonly mistaken word is *its*. Students often add an apostrophe because they do not know the proper conventions for this word.

The word *it's* with an apostrophe is a contraction, it means *it is*.

Contraction: <u>*It's*</u> *getting cold.* (<u>*It is*</u> *getting cold.*)

Possessive: *The wolf returned to its den. (the wolf's den)*

If you are confused about whether or not to put an apostrophe into the word *its*, do this:

> *Substitute the words **it is** into the sentence.*

If the sentence makes sense ***add*** an apostrophe. Look.

> *It is going to be hot today.*
> *It's going to be hot today.*

Here's a way to remember that *it's* means *it is*.
First, imagine that *it is* is an added word.

> *itis*

Now, watch as the second *i* in the added word grows smaller until it becomes an apostrophe.

> *itis*   *it's*   *it's*

Think of the apostrophe in the word *it's* as a tiny letter *i*. Now, every time you read the word *it's*, you'll think *it is*.

Exercise 29-8

Number your work paper 1-10. If the underlined words need apostrophes write them correctly on your paper. If they do not need apostrophes, write *NA*. Follow the examples.

Example: <u>*Janes*</u> *mom said she could go.*

Answer: *Jane's*

Example: *The* <u>*birds*</u> *sang in the trees.*

Answer: *NA*

1. That book is <u>Carls</u>.
2. There are three <u>Carls</u> in this class.
3. The bird feathered <u>its</u> nest.
4. <u>Cars</u> raced around the track.
5. Jet <u>engines</u> produce thrust.

6. The <u>engines</u> oil line was cut.
7. The <u>colors</u> ran together when wet.
8. Bill said that the <u>tapes</u> in the drawer.
9. <u>Its</u> going to be expensive to fix that pump.
10. How many <u>nines</u> are in your answer?

The word *won't* is a contraction that is a completely different form of the two words from which it is made: *will not*

I <u>will not</u> be there until later.

I <u>won't</u> be there until later.

Exercise 29-9

Number your work paper 1-10. Each sentence contains one word which needs an apostrophe. Write the word correctly on your work paper. Be sure to include the apostrophe. Follow the example.
Example: Jims cousins own three cars.
Answer: Jim's

1. The skateboards wheels fell off.
2. Dad said hed be early.
3. Those are Bobs stamps but not his coins.
4. Its not every day that trains collide.
5. Were planning to leave in three weeks.
6. The desks held everybodys work.
7. The paints drying on the walls.
8. No ones going to leave until all the rulers are returned.
9. Hes not as old as he looks.
10. We wont know unless we try.

Short notes

One place we often use apostrophes is in messages that we leave for others to read. In cases like these, we want to communicate as much information as possible using as few words as necessary. Look.

Mom,

Dad called. He'll be late.

Tim

Notice the comma after *Mom*. This note was written directly to "mom." *Mom* is a form of direct address. Direct address is always set off with commas.

Of course, the apostrophe in *he'll* takes the place of the letters *wi*. The word *he'll* is a contraction of the two words *he will*.

Exercise 29-10

Number your work paper 1-5. Write short notes that sum up the information. Try to abbreviate as much as possible. Remember to sign your name at the bottom. Follow the example:

Information: Mr. Smith called for dad. Mr. Smith will be arriving on
         Saturday.

Note:

        Dad,

        Mr. Smith called; he'll be arriving Saturday.

        Tim

1. Information: Mr. Parks, your English teacher, called to speak to your mom. He is free for a meeting.
2. Information: The department store called for your parents. They will deliver the couch Saturday.
3. Information: Mr. Weaver called for your boss Mr. Smith. Mr. Weaver has a car with an oil leak. He will not be able to make it to the meeting today.
4. Information: Tell your mom you got an A in every class – five, all together. You will show her your report card when you get home from work.
5. Information: Tell your mom you went to the mall. You will be back in time for dinner.

Summary

✓ Contractions are word pairs that have been joined and shortened.

✓ Apostrophes take the place of missing letters in contractions.

✓ Some special plurals require an apostrophe.

✓ Notes should be short and to the point.

Chapter 30

A Final Challenge

This final chapter isn't really a chapter, at all. It is a final challenge.

We have learned much about writing in this course. We have learned that we write for an audience, and we have learned that we must follow conventions in order to make ourselves understood.

We have also learned how to write about a variety of different subjects. We have studied paragraphs of fact, opinion, description and narrative.

Putting everything together, we wrote five paragraph compositions of fact and opinion.

Your final challenge is to write a five paragraph composition of opinion. Pick three topics from this text that you feel helped you become a better writer. Write a five paragraph composition of opinion explaining how these topics helped you.

Remember the form of a five paragraph composition. First, you will write an introduction that mentions the three topics you intend to discuss. Then you will write one paragraph about each of the topics. Finally, you will sum things up with a concluding paragraph.

Since you are writing opinion, you will want to remember to cook up some fact and opinion sandwiches in each of your paragraphs. Use TIGER to help you organize your thoughts and get writing.

Then, keep writing, and writing, and writing.

Your reward will be constant improvement and the knowledge that you are doing your best.

Answers

Chapter 1

1-1

1. The exchange of thoughts or information
2. Verbal
3. Verbal uses words, nonverbal doesn't
4. It doesn't use words
5. Verbal

1-2

1. It's
2. its
3. Its
4. Its
5. it's
6. its
7. its
8. It's it's
9. It's it's
10. its

1-3

1. its
2. Its
3. It's
4. it's
5. it's
6. its
7. It's
8. It's its
9. it's
10. Its

Chapter 2

2-1

1. Symbol
2. Verbal and nonverbal
3. symbol
4. thinks
5. clearly

2-2

1. the exchange of thoughts or information
2. Verbal and nonverbal
3. symbols
4. Our audience
5. teacher

2-3

1. There
2. Their
3. There
4. their
5. Their
6. there
7. their

8. There
9. there
10. their

2-4

1. too
2. blew
3. passed
4. scene
5. meet

Chapter 3

3-2 (possible answers)

1. The gray sky turned blue.
2. The Pirates beat the cubs.
3. John stood in front of Diane.
4. The tour guide ate the cannibals.
5. The rock fell on the paper.
6. The cats dreamed about chasing dogs.
7. People can fly planes.
8. Insects eat spiders.
9. The kittens played with the cat.
10. A can is not a bottle.

3-4

1. Sentence form
2. Not sentence form
3. Not sentence form
4. Sentence form
5. Not sentence form
6. Not sentence form
7. Sentence form
8. Not sentence form
9. Sentence form
10. Not sentence form

3-5

1. Fragment
2. Fragment
3. Fragment
4. Sentence
5. Fragment
6. Sentence
7. Fragment
8. Sentence
9. Fragment
10. Sentence

3-6

1. F
2. F
3. S
4. F
5. F
6. F
7. S
8. S
9. F
10. F

3-8

1. 2
2. 1

3. 1
4. 2
5. 1
6. NF
7. 1
8. 2
9. 1
10. 1

3-9
1. Although she as just a tiny child
2. When Helen was five years old
3. In Boston, Massachusetts
4. While pressing her fingers into Helen's hand
5. And even read in Braille, a special alphabet for the blind
6. Because she could not hear
7. When they are learning to speak
8. Including The Story of My Life
9. During World War II
10. A world of shared thoughts and dreams

3-10
1. I was born in Los Angeles, California.
2. Jean collects coins.
3. Marty tried to staple his papers.
4. Mary was sure that she could make the jump.
5. I know a lot of people

3-11
1. there
2. There
3. Their there
4. There there
5. Their there
6. Their their
7. There there
8. There
9. Their their
10. There there

3-12
1. Their their
2. It's there
3. There Their
4. There their
5. Its
6. Their their
7. Its
8. It's there
9. There there
10. There there

Chapter 4

4-1
1. Foot ball
2. News paper
3. Sand storm
4. Butter fly
5. Gold fish

4-2
1. Outside

2. Overlook
3. Nevertheless
4. Likewise
5. Bookkeeper

4-3
1. I
2. C
3. C
4. C
5. I
6. C
7. C
8. C
9. C
10. I

4-4
1. I
2. C
3. C
4. I
5. C

4-5
1. I
2. I
3. C
4. I
5. C

4-6
1. I
2. C
3. I
4. C
5. C

4-7
1. Doug is a lawyer; he handles bankruptcy cases.
2. Rain was falling; it pattered on the roof.
3. My friend's name is Maria; she is a student.
4. John Steinbeck is a famous author; he wrote The Pearl.
5. Felix yawned; he was tired.
6. They made their travel plans; Hawaii was going to be great!
7. That old book is boring; it's much too long.
8. Some people love the Super Bowl; others prefer the World Series.
9. The crowd roared; Dave won the race.
10. Smoke filled the air; a fire was burning in the mountains.

4-8
1. I
2. C
3. I
4. C
5. C
6. C
7. C
8. C

9. C
10. I

Chapter 5
5-1
1. 2
2. 2 indentations
3. Bats are mammals.
4. There are many kinds of bats.
5-2
1. Topic sentence
2. Detail sentences
3. (Any sentence that is not the topic sentence)
   (Any sentence that is not the topic sentence)
5-3
1. 3
2. 3
3. I
4. Ghdkle
5. 3
6. 7
5-4
1. B
2. F
3. I
5-5
1. Fish breathe using gills.
5-6
(Topic Sentence + one possible answer)Thomas Edison was one of the world's greatest inventors. He is known as the king of inventors because of the many useful devices he invented. For example, he invented the phonograph and the electric light bulb. He also invented the motion picture camera. Millions of people the world over have benefited from his inventive mind.
5-7
        Fingerprints serve many purposes. They help police identify crime suspects. They are also used to check the backgrounds of people applying for jobs in the military. Finally, they aid in the identification of disaster victims. In conclusion, fingerprints have many uses.
5-9
1. Their their
2. their
3. there
4. There
5. There their
5-10
1. to
2. aunt
3. cedar
4. colonel
5. fur
5-11
1. They're
2. There

3. There
4. They're
5. They're

Chapter 7
7-1
1. Fragment
2. No end point
3. Not capitalized
4. No mistakes
5. Incorrect semicolon
6. No mistakes
7. Question mark
8. No mistakes
9. Fragment
10. Misspelled word
7-2
1. Mechanical mistake
2. No mistakes
3. Mechanical mistake
4. No mistakes
5. No mistakes
6. Mechanical mistake
7. Mechanical mistake
8. No mistakes
9. Mechanical mistake
10. Mechanical mistake
7-3
1. ,my best friend,
2. , the process by which green plants create their own food using sunlight,
3. ,words that mean nearly the same thing,
4. , a form of Japanese writing,
5. , a security guard at the airport,
6. , the most feared kind of bats,
7. ,the inventor of the telephone,
8. ,digital video discs,
9. ,a stealth bomber,
10. , an enormous stone discovered in Egypt,
7-4
1. Mr. Jones drives a Viper.
2. Ernest Hemingway was an outdoorsman.
3. Ice forms at thirty-two degrees.
4. Hydrogen is very light.
5. George Washington commanded forces during the Revolutionary War.
6. The telephone changed the world.
7. Mechanics will be graded in this class.
8. Appositives are easy to use.
9. Physics is a fascinating science.
10. Tim writes well.
7-5
1. Ron, my cousin, drives a four wheel drive.
2. That man, Mr. Jones, likes ice cream.
3. The knife, a cleaver, dropped to the floor and stuck.
4. Tsunamis, tidal waves, are common after

earthquakes.
5. Ernest Hemingway, the famous author, wrote "A Day's Wait."
6. Lasers, concentrated beams of light, perform many important functions.
7. Louis Braille, the inventor of the Braille system, gave millions of blind people the ability to read.
8. Braille, a system which uses raised dots to represent printed letters, allows the blind to read using the sense of touch.
9. Two famous inventors, Alexander Graham Bell and Louis Braille, helped make the world a better place for millions of people.
10. One famous writer and speaker , Helen Keller, devoted her life to helping others.

7-6
1. Joan, a senior, works after school.
2. Appositives, sentence interrupters, can be tricky.
3. John Steinbeck, a famous American author, wrote The Pearl.
4. Cannery Row, another of John Steinbeck's books, was made into a movie.
5. The history of the people of Japan, the Japanese, goes back thousands of years.
6. Kanji, one form of Japanese writing, can be difficult to learn.
7. The aorta, the main artery leading from the heart, carries an enormous amount of blood.
8. The femur, sometimes called the thigh bone, is one of the heaviest bones in the body.
9. Paintings by Fredrick Remington, a cowboy artist, are worth thousands of dollars.
10. Emeralds, valuable gemstones, are green.

7-7
1. , her autobiography.
2. , the king of inventors.
3. , liquid crystal display.
4. , the longest river in the United States.
5. , a great story by John Steinbeck.
6. , a Ford.
7. , Dr. Samuels.
8. , the plane that dropped the atomic bomb on Hiroshima.
9. , lizards and snakes.
10. , the exchange of thoughts or information.

7-8
1. Jack never misses a chance to play basketball, his favorite sport.
2. Carol gave her new dog a name, Shep.
3. The library subscribes to Time, a weekly news magazine.
4. Andrew bought a new painting, a watercolor.
5. Special equipment can be used to examine the aorta, the largest blood vessel leading from the heart.

6. Paul Tibbits piloted the Enola Gay, a B-29 bomber.
7. Margaret loved to wear her favorite piece of jewelry, a string of pearls.
8. The students appreciate Mr. Thompson, their science teacher.
9. The house had a terrible design flaw, a wooden chimney.
10. That truck has a V-12, a type of engine.

7-9
1. Jerry, a dentist, graduated from college in two years.
2. My dad spends every Saturday morning doing what he loves most, mowing the lawn.
3. Jane, the school's top student, wrote a report about photosynthesis, the process which plants use to convert sunlight into food.
4. Nelly enjoyed her favorite morning drink, hot chocolate.
5. The Enola Gay, a B-29 bomber, was piloted by a famous American, Paul Tibbits.
6. Kanji, a form of Japanese writing, uses pictures to represent words.
7. Sewers, people who sew for a living, make bows, ribbons for girls to wear in their hair.
8. We have learned how to use the semicolon, a mark of punctuation.
9. A compound sentence, two sentences joined to form one, may be made using a semicolon.
10. Our English teacher, a graduate of Harvard, says that John Steinbeck, the author of The Pearl ,was one of America's greatest writers.

7-10
1. Mrs. Ames, our science teacher, collects butterflies; she has been adding to her collection since she was five years old.
2. Thomas Edison, the king of inventors, invented the electric light bulb; he also invented another common tool, the motion picture camera.
3. One common metal, steel, is used in the production of automobiles; another metal, titanium, is used for building aircraft.
4. Hurricanes, swirling storms that begin over warm water, always travel toward the earth's poles; they are called typhoons in Japan.
5. Tim, my younger brother, plays quarterback on the junior varsity football team; next year, his sophomore year, he expects to start on the varsity squad.

7-11
1. John didn't like the heat. However, he hated the cold.
2. John didn't like the heat. In fact, he hated it.
3. Mary wanted to get an "A." However, she got a "B."
4. Mary hoped for an "A." In fact, she got an

"A+."

5. Tim was hungry. In fact, he was very hungry. However, he didn't have enough money for lunch.

7-12
1. In fact,
2. However,
3. However,
4. In fact,
5. However,

Chapter 7 Review
1. semicolon
2. compound
3. Appositives
4. ,my neighbor,
5. ,an award for bravery,
6. , the famous physicist.
7. The TV, an old one, finally stopped working.
8. Mr. Smith's classroom, the last one in the corridor, is usually loud.

Chapter 8
8-1
1. Topic sentence – sentence of fact
2. Thesis statement – sentence of opinion
8-2
1. F
2. O
3. F
4. O
5. F
6. O
7. F
8. F
9. O
10. F
8-3/8-10 (answers will vary)
8-11 (wording may very)
1. Everyone has heard of Benjamin Franklin.
2. They should sell something we could actually use.
3. Good manners have disappeared.
4. We shouldn't have to stand here and wait.
5. Peanut butter and jelly is the best.
8-12 (wording may vary)
1. Could they make us wait any longer?
2. Hasn't everyone heard of Amelia Earhart?
3. Doesn't everyone have a TV?
4. Who wouldn't want to see less crime?
5. Who doesn't like to get presents?
8-15
1. It's
2. Their
3. However,
4. There
5. In fact,
Chapter 9
9-1
1. Declarative

2. Interrogative
3. Exclamatory
4. Declarative
5. Imperative
6. Declarative
7. Interrogative
8. Imperative
9. Declarative
10. Exclamatory
9-2
1. .
2. !
3. ?
4. .
5. ?
6. .
7. !
8. .
9. ?
10. .
9-3 (wording may vary)
1. How cold the classroom is!
2. You are very tall.
3. How tall are you?
4. Will we leave soon?
5. What a delicious dinner!
6. Did we see Bill at the movies?
7. Wash your hands.
8. Will you open your book?
9. What an interesting composition!
10. Please, remember to buy bread.
9-4
1. Be on time.
2. Be prepared to take a test tomorrow.
3. Please take a seat.
4. Tell me who said that.
5. Don't chew gum in the classroom.
9-6
1. C
2. C
3. I
4. C
5. C
6. I
7. C
8. I
9. C
10. C
Chapter 10
10-1
1. First of all, we got up early to go to the park.
2. Secondly, we ate a good breakfast.
3. Next, we loaded up the car.
4. After that, we headed out onto the highway.
5. Then, dad said that he saw the exit sign.
6. Finally, we got off the freeway.
7. At last, the day was ours to enjoy.

8. Later, we played volleyball.
9. In the middle of the game, the dog ran away.
10. After we found him, we drove back home.

10-2
1. When I was walking to school this morning, a strange thing happened.
2. First of all, a man wearing a mask and carrying a burlap sack ran down the street.
3. After that, a barking police dog passed me.
4. Next, a policeman ran by blowing his whistle.
5. Just then, I realized that a movie crew was trying to make a movie.

10-3
1. game,
2. questions,
3. First,
4. cover,
5. Next,
6. math,
7. school,
8. dance,
9. Later,
10. that,

10-4
1. Last week, we went to Lake Smith.
2. When we got there, we picked out a camping spot.
3. After that, we unloaded the car.
4. While we were busy, our dog, Rex, ran away.
5. For three hours, we searched for him.
6. Finally, we found him.
7. After getting back to the camp site, we were ready to set up camp.
8. First, dad set up the tent.
9. Then, we all moved our sleeping bags inside.
10. At last, we were set up and ready to camp.

10-6
Set 1:
1. Last year
2. First,
3. After that,
4. Next,
5. At first,
6. then,
Set 2: Who would have thought there was so much to read?
Set 3: What a great idea!
Set 4: After that I had to narrow my topic; in fact, I decided to concentrate on using solar energy to boil water.
At first, nothing seemed to happen, but then, the water began to boil.

Chapter 11
11-1
1. , thunderheads,
2. ,all of us,
3. , a German shepherd,

4. , stainless steel,
5. , the largest state,

11-2
1. John lives in Las Vegas.
2. Cathy works every day.
3. That woman loves to read.
4. Dreadnaughts were fierce weapons in World War II.
5. Jumbo jets are getting larger and larger.

11-3
1. Jane likes truffles, chocolates with soft centers.
2. The photograph, a black and white one, was fuzzy.
3. That woman, the one in the red dress, dances well.
4. Helen Keller, the famous writer, was deaf and blind.
5. The way words and punctuation work together is known by a simple word, mechanics.
6. Semicolons, marks of punctuation used to join two sentences into one compound sentence, make sentences interesting.
7. Sewers, pipes that carry waste water, are buried deep in the ground.
8. Sewers, people who operate sewing machines, work hard.
9. The pen, old and dry, could barely write.
10. Thomas Edison, the king of inventors, was born over 100 years ago.

11-4
1. To tell the truth,
2. , however
3. , for example,
4. By the way,
5. , I believe,
6. , I believe
7. Nevertheless,
8. On the contrary,
9. , on the other hand,
10. , in my opinion,

11-5
1. Frank gets straight A's in math.
2. Helen Keller was born a healthy baby.
3. Football is the greatest sport.
4. A bad dinner is better than no dinner.
5. We must consider opposing views.
6. John will be arriving late.
7. We weren't happy.
8. It rained.
9. Helen Keller learned to speak.
10. Philosophers study knowledge.

11-6
1. F
2. M

3.   L

4.   M

5.   M

6.   F

7.   F

8.   F (it begins a new sentence)

9.   L

10.   M

11-7

1.   To tell the truth, she is an excellent cook.

2.   For example, a red light signals stop.

3.   However, I don't want to.

4.   In my opinion, baseball is better than football.

5.   In fact, tadpoles become frogs.

11-8 (answers may vary)

1.   She is, to tell the truth, an excellent cook.

2.   A red light, for example, signals stop.

3.   I, however, don't want to.

4.   Baseball, in my opinion, is better than football.

5.   Tadpoles, in fact, become frogs.

11-9

1.   She is an excellent cook, to tell the truth.

2.   A red light signals stop, for example.

3.   I don't want to, however.

4.   Baseball is better than football, in my opinion.

5.   Tadpoles become frogs, in fact.

Chapter 12

12-1

1.   The Viper is parked in the driveway.

2.   The TV with the thirty-seven inch screen is in the corner.

3.   John drinks black coffee in a blue mug.

4.   A window on the side of the house is broken.

5.   The clock that runs fast is on the desk.

6.   The spoiled milk is in the refrigerator.

7.   Mary, a soccer player, bought a turtle.

8.   The painting on the wall was admired by a man.

9.   Janice, a good student, always carries a note-book.

10.   A man with long hair was working on the truck.

12-3

1.   <u>John</u>   reads the newspaper every day.

2.   <u>He</u>   turns to the sports section.

3.   <u>Football</u>   is his favorite sport.

4.   <u>Baseball and hockey</u>   interest him, too.

5.   <u>That young man</u>   played high school football.

12-4

1.   The pictures in hieroglyphics

2.   Ancient Egyptians

3.   Hieroglyphics

4.   People called scribes

5.   The meaning of Egyptian hieroglyphics

6.   A French soldier

7.   The stone

8.   It

9.   This famous stone

10.   The Rosetta Stone

12-5

1.   represent

2.   used

3.   can

4.   wrote

5.   remained

6.   discovered

7.   was

8.   was

9.   came

10.   helped

12-6

1.   F

2.   S

3.   S

4.   F

5.   F

6.   S

7.   S

8.   F

9.   S

10.   S

12-7

1.   The engine

2.   Mary

3.   You

4.   John

5.   Joanne

6.   She

Chapter 13

13-1

1)   ?

2)   .

3)   .

4)   !

5)   .

6)   .

7)   ?

8)   .

9)   .

10)   .

13-2

1.   <u>You</u> are going where.

2.   <u>Mary</u> did see Phil.

3.   <u>The teacher</u> is saying what about English.

4.   <u>The newspaper</u> did arrive when.

5.   <u>The fan</u> is on the table.

6. John and Mary were at school.
7. Birds do find worms how.
8. Bats are mammals or birds.
9. Boiling water is how hot.
10. Mary and Jane were at the mall when.

13-3
1. Interrogative
2. Fragment
3. Interrogative
4. Imperative
5. Declarative
6. Interrogative
7. Declarative
8. Declarative
9. Imperative
10. Interrogative

13-4
1. Interrogative
2. Fragment
3. Declarative
4. Interrogative
5. Exclamatory

13-6
1. The jetliner
2. All members of the team
3. John's dad
4. That old computer
5. the cat

13-7
1. jetliner
2. members
3. dad
4. computer
5. cat

13-8
1. chapter
2. school
3. students
4. museums
5. boy
6. cars
7. motel
8. box
9. paper
10. We

13-9
1. We | never expected to find you here.
2. The object of the game | is to win.
3. Many people | have visited Washington D.C.
4. The pencil lead | broke.
5. Ron | cut his hand while doing yard work.
6. That newspaper | is one of the country's largest.

7. Dogs | are social animals.
8. A very large truck | passed us on the highway.
9. The smoke | made us cough.
10. Basketball players | are often very tall.

13-10
1. Subject
2. Declarative
3. Question mark
4. .
5. .
6. ?

Chapter 14

14-1
1. The old man
2. John
3. The well-dressed gentleman
4. Pete
5. A class of students

14-2
1. Cats and dogs play together.
2. The girls jumped rope.
3. The light bulb burned out.
4. A little boy is running up the street.
5. Tom became team captain.

14-3
1. Tim and his brother + share the same books.
2. A sharp pair of scissors + cuts through thick paper.
3. The silver vase + reflected light.
4. Bill + listens to loud music.
5. The pad of paper + was written on.

14-4
1. CS
2. CP
3. CS
4. CS
5. CP
6. CP
7. CS
8. CS
9. CP
10. CP

14-5
1. Fragment
2. Sentence
3. Sentence
4. Fragment
5. Sentence

14-6
1. Helen Keller | was born in 1880.
2. Young Helen | suffered a serious illness.
3. The little girl | became deaf and blind.

283

4. Helens father | met with Alexander Graham Bell.
5. The science of sound | fascinated Mr. Bell.
6. Alexander Graham Bell | invented the telephone.
7. He | suggested that Mr. Keller contact the Perkins Institute.
8. The Kellers | were visited by Annie Sullivan.
9. Annie Sullivan | had great patience.
10. She | taught Helen a special sign language.

14-7
1. Words are symbols.
2. We use words to communicate our thoughts.
3. Nonverbal communication may signal our feelings.
4. Nearly everyone can communicate in some way.
5. Deaf football players face a special problem.
6. They can't hear the quarterback's calls.
7. One school found a solution to this problem.
8. A big bass drum is used.
9. The coach pounds the drum.
10. Deaf players feel the vibrations of the pounding drum.

Chapter 15

15-1
1. A group of boys from that school started their own football team.
2. The box of books fell from the shelf.
3. The girls missed the bus.
4. Nebraska is one of the fifty states.
5. That baseball bat was used by Babe Ruth.
6. Paul bought a phone with two lines.
7. Happiness can be shared.
8. Mary divided her stamp collection into two halves.
9. The room at the end of the hall was locked.
10. Freedom of thought is the greatest freedom.

15-2
1. thing
2. thing
3. person
4. place
5. thing
6. person
7. idea
8. person
9. place
10. idea

15-3
1. repairman, months, computer
2. scissors, weapons

3. Hank, shoes
4. speakers, bass
5. shelf, wood, pounds
6. jet, trails, sky
7. Anger, emotion
8. smell, onions, kitchen
9. people, patience, virtue
10. Writing, skill, anyone

15-4
1. apples – things
2. spider – thing
3. members – people
4. TV – thing
5. shoes – things
6. blades – things
7. push ups – things
8. Dan- person
9. attic – place
10. doubt - idea

15-5
1. eggs
2. boys
3. invitations
4. coats
5. static
6. money
7. noise
8. clouds
9. people
10. umbrellas

15-6
1. Location, we
2. Location, he
3. Expletive, winds
4. Location, we
5. Expletive, something
6. Expletive, coins
7. Location, we
8. Expletive, ants
9. Location, keys
10. Expletive, time

15-7
1. is
2. are
3. are
4. are
5. is
6. is
7. is
8. are
9. are
10. is

15-8
1. There is
2. There are

3. There are
4. There is
5. There are
Chapter 17
17-1
1. Direct
2. Direct
3. Indirect
4. Indirect
5. Indirect
6. Direct
7. Indirect
8. Direct
9. Direct
10. Indirect
17-2 (answers may vary)
1. The teacher said that it was time for a test.
2. Mary said that she was hungry.
3. The teacher asked if anyone was absent.
4. The mechanic said that the job would cost two hundred dollars.
5. Mary asked me if I liked ice cream.
6. I said that I had ten dollars.
7. I told Phil that he would have to wait a few minutes.
8. Bob shouted that the water was cold.
9. Tim said that he would like some French fries.
10. Dad asked if Liz was home.
17-3
1. The policeman said, "Clear the area."
2. That girl asked, "How much is the gold necklace?"
3. Tom said, "I'm a mechanic."
4. The golfer shouted, "My club is bent."
5. Maria wondered, "How will I pay for that?"
17-4
1. Our English teacher said, "My best friend is a doctor."
2. Mr. McGee asked, "Will anyone donate to this charity?"
3. The judge told the convict, "You are guilty."
4. The newsman reported, "Stocks took a fall today."
5. Jim said, "Everyone should be as lucky as me."
17-5
1. The repairman said, "It will cost ten dollars for me to look at it."
2. The attorney said, "This man is innocent."
3. Everyone looked when Mary screeched, "No toothpicks?"
4. Donald said, "English and Latin are related."
5. The sewer said, "The sewers are backed up again."
17-7

1. Indirect
2. Direct   Phil asked, "Are you going to the park?"
3. Direct   The old man said, "Things were different in my day."
4. Indirect
5. Indirect
6. Indirect
7. Indirect
8. Direct   The salesman said, "You look like a man who deserves the best."
9. Direct   Tom told his boss, "I quit."
10. Indirect
17-9
1. Dan asked, "I wonder, does anyone have a nickel?"
2. The student said, "I, uh, don't know."
3. Professor English remarked, "Thomas Edison was a great thinker, in my opinion."
4. Sandy said, "The score was tied, I think."
5. The plumber answered, "However, it's going to cost you."
17-10
1. Mary said, "My brother is rolling in dough." Her friend Sylvia asked, "Is he a banker?" Mary answered, "No, he's a baker."

2. Tom said, "I can't believe my cousin got an 'A' for cutting class." Tim, Tom's friend, said, "Uh, what kind of school gives an 'A' for cutting class?" Tom said, "Barber school."

3. Little Billy told his mother, "Today at school, I was the only one who knew the answer to one of the teacher's questions." His mother asked proudly, "What was the question?" Little Billy said, "Who threw the baseball through the window?"
Chapter 18
18-1
1. coughs
2. sees
3. thinks
4. runs
5. explains
6. dances
7. answers
8. wonders
9. argues
10. believes
18-2
1. runs

285

2. screams
3. believes
4. sees
5. learns

18-3
1. cough
2. see
3. play
4. answer
5. think
6. argue
7. declare
8. spin
9. stare
10. wonder

18-4
1. Verb
2. Subject
3. Verb
4. Subject
5. Verb
6. Verb
7. Subject
8. Subject
9. Verb
10. Subject

18-5
1. They
2. He
3. He
4. They
5. They
6. He
7. They
8. He
9. They
10. They

18-6
1. vase
2. chair
3. girls
4. rain
5. wind
6. lead
7. hammer
8. bow
9. thought
10. idea

18-7
1. Singular
2. Plural
3. Plural

4. Singular
5. Singular
6. Singular
7. Plural
8. Plural
9. Singular
10. Singular
11. Singular
12. Plural
13. Singular
14. Plural
15. Plural
16. Singular
17. Plural
18. Singular
19. Plural
20. Singular

18-8
1. Two cows chew.
2. Two kites soar.
3. Two girls sing.
4. Two bears play.
5. Two groups of boys run.
6. Two teams of girls play.
7. Two birds land.
8. Two boys lead.
9. Two students write.
10. Two cups of milk spill.

18-9
1. likes
2. barks
3. sing
4. throw
5. wonder
6. answer
7. bloom
8. swims
9. fall
10. are

18-10
1. Do not agree
2. Agree
3. Do not agree
4. Do not agree
5. Agree
6. Agree
7. Do not agree
8. Agree
9. Agree
10. Do not agree

18-11
1. is

2. was
3. are
4. were
5. is
6. are
7. were
8. were
9. are
10. is

18-12

1. are
2. was
3. is
4. is
5. were
6. are
7. was
8. were
9. are
10. are

18-13

There are a lot of people in here.

Review

1. Conventions
2. predicate
3. verb
4. noun
5. Singular
6. Plural
7. plural
8. agree
9. Verb
10. Noun
11. Verb
12. Noun
13. Noun
14. Noun
15. Verb
16. Eric buys
17. Birds are
18. Girls look
19. Boy is
20. Dan carved
21. shout
22. buys
23. learns
24. think
25. is
26. A
27. NA
28. NA
29. A

30. NA

Chapter 19

19-1

1. living room   modern times
2. red planet   future
3. auditorium   modern times
4. sailing ship   past
5. field   modern times

19-2

1. phone trouble
2. phaser is dead
3. She is tripping over her own feet.
4. no supply ships
5. first time at bat

Chapter 20

20-1

1. Unconventional
2. Unconventional
3. Conventional
4. Conventional
5. Unconventional
6. Conventional
7. Conventional
8. Unconventional
9. Conventional
10. Unconventional

20-2

1. Unconventional
2. Unconventional
3. Conventional
4. Unconventional
5. Unconventional
6. Conventional
7. Unconventional
8. Conventional
9. Conventional
10. Unconventional

20-4

1. Metropolitan Museum of Art
2. Judge Murphy
3. Elm City Book Days
4. Cinema Six Theater
5. Jim, Bob, Friday

20-5

	Common	Proper
1.	museum	John
2.	We	Fourth of July
	parade	
3.	applications	Tuesday
4.	car	Chevy
5.	boy	Wal-Mart
6.	you	Loch Ness Monster

7. week   Sixty-seventh Street Bridge
            Wednesday
8. band   Catskill High
    field
9. Students   Senator Smith
10. Automobiles
    transportation

20-6
1. Central High School
2. Judge Carpenter
3. Rocky Mountains
4. Snake River, Montana
5. Shep
6. River Street
7. Solomon Islands, Pacific Ocean
8. Grand Canyon
9. Nile, Egypt
10. Mazda

20-7
1. A
2. A
3. B
4. B
5. B
6. A
7. B
8. B
9. A
10. A

20-8
1. North Star
2. Arizona State University
3. Brooklyn Bridge
4. Mount Everest
5. Asia, Japan, Thailand
6. Hawaiian Islands
7. Helen Keller
8. Scotland
9. Nissan Frontier
10. Compaq

20-9
1. Unconventional
2. Unconventional
3. Conventional
4. Unconventional
5. Unconventional
6. Unconventional
7. Unconventional
8. Conventional
9. Unconventional
10. Unconventional

Review
1. communicate
2. appositives
3. interrupters (or speakers)
4. writing and speaking
5. sentences
6. capitalized
7. common
8. products
9. sun
10. moon
11. earth
12. indirect
13. Denver
14. I
15. Saturn

Chapter 21
21-1
1. Ave.
2. P.O. Box
3. Dept.
4. Rd.
5. Blvd.
6. Ste.
7. Apt.
8. Pkwy.
9. Pl.
10. Hwy.

21-2
1. 123 Roosevelt Pkwy., Ste. 4B
2. 5110 Jupiter St., Apt. 234
3. P.O. Box 710
4. 32 Wild Rose Ave.
5. 1754 E. First Pl., Ste. 3
6. 4 Golden State Pkwy.
7. P. O. Box 65-Q
8. 1122 Salt Rd., Box 18-L
9. Hwy. 35, Dept. Q
10. 8548 First Ave., Ste. 54W

21-3
1. Salem, OR
2. Denver, CO
3. Billings, MT
4. Sacramento, CA
5. Dallas, TX
6. Las Vegas, NV
7. Baltimore, MD
8. Portland, ME
9. Provo, UT
10. New York, NY

21-4
1. 3
2. Avenue
3. Ohio

4. Shortened form of a word
5. Indicates missing letters
21-5
1. Don Simms
   25 Main St.
   Los Angeles, CA 90222

2. Dr. Earl Jones
   6789 West Ave., Ste. B
   New York, NY 60609

3. Jane White
   4 Oak Pl.
   Washington, DC 78490

4. Dr. Frank Reading
   8902 Atom Ave. Apt. 3A
   Alamogordo, NM 45992

5. Mary L. Green
   33 N. Eastern
   Phoenix, AZ 85282
21-6
1. Jerry Thomas, Vice President
   Aero Inc.
   35 Technology Pl.
   San Jose, CA 90987

2. Dr. Carol Wooster, President
   Wooster Corp.
   45 Newberry St.
   Phoenix, AZ 85558

3. Jan O'Toole
   879 E. Fifth Ave.
   Dallas, TX 77777

4. Bob Hanson, Director of Personnel
   Three Diamonds Cement, Inc.,
   786 Savannah Ave.
   Rochester, NY 92345

5. Olivia Tate, Editor,
   Financial News
   35 North St., Ste. 98
   New York, NY 34509
21-7
1. Dr. Wayne Smith, President
2. President
3. Litmus Learning, Inc.
4. P.O. Box 12
5. Denver, CO 67444
21-12
1. Dear Dr. Simms:
2. Dear Dr. Simms, Jr.:
3. Dear Mrs. Jones:

4. Dear Dr. Jones:
5. Dear Miss Jones:
6. Dear Ms. Smith:
7. Dear Rev. Smith:
8. Dear Rev. Hall, Jr.:
9. Dear Dr. Reed:
10. Dear Fr. Reed:
21-13
1. Dr. Phil Simms, PhD.
   Best Counseling, Inc.
   35 W. 7th St.
   Phoenix, AZ 85282

   Dear Dr. Simms:

2. Time Keeprs, Inc.
   P.O. Box 3456
   Salem, OR 88812

   To Whom It May Concern:
Chapter 22
(Compare letters to model and checklist)
Chapter 23
23-1
1. mine
2. her
3. hers
4. his
5. theirs
6. its
7. Their
8. Our
9. Her
10. my
23-2
1. Mary's house
2. Bob's pencils
3. Angela's ring
4. Tom's picture
5. Mark's money
6. Dan's car
7. Nancy's volleyball
8. Andrew's bowling ball
9. Mr. Porter's truck
10. Miss Smith's scissors
23-3
1. Nevada's capital
2. Japan's population
3. The mountain's height
4. The picture's frame
5. The light bulb's glow
6. The ink's color
7. The shirt's size
8. The car's tires
9. The propeller's blades
10. The game's action
23-4

1. Jan's
2. family's
3. chair's
4. book's
5. teacher's
6. pen's
7. Jim's
8. Nevada's
9. car's
10. house's

23-5
1. bird's
2. Jane's
3. school's
4. Johnson's
5. Mary's
6. library's
7. Jim's
8. house's
9. Tom's
10. Japan's

23-7
1 The ink's color is red.
2 The car's door is dented.
3 Put Mr. Thompson's books on the table.
4 The telephone's ring was loud.
5 Be sure to clean the toothbrush's bristles.
6 We should change the engine's oil.
7 Canada's borders are long and cold.
8 That family's dog is a German shepherd.
9 The wind's direction is east.
10 That digital TV's picture is extremely clear.

23-8
1. Plural
2. Possessive
3. Possessive
4. Plural
5. Plural
6. Plural
7. Possessive
8. Possessive
9. Plural
10. Possessive

23-9
1. John's parents told him to get home early.
2. Those are Mary's pens and pencils.
3. According to this morning's weather report, we are in for storms.
4. Jane lost her friend's scissors.
5. That bakery's cakes are the best.
6. Mr. Thompson's ties are very bright.
7. The computer's disc drives didn't work.
8. Everyone's watches were wrong.
9. The bows in the girl's hair were yellow.
10. Jim's books are on that shelf.

23-10

(answers will vary)
23-11
1. girls'
2. computers'
3. radios'
4. lamps'
5. pork chops'

23-12
1. Mars'
2. pants'
3. scissors'
4. Chris'
5. Bess'

Chapter 24
24-1
1. B
2. A
3. B
4. A
5. B
6. A
7. B
8. B
9. B
10. A

Chapter 26
26-1
1. Pharaohs were kings in Ancient Egypt, and the pyramids were their tombs.
2. Polar regions are cold, but tropical regions are hot.
3. Pens use ink, but pencils use lead.
4. John has a job after school, and he plays football, too.
5. We went on a field trip to the museum, but it was boring.

26-2 (answers may vary)
1. The boys played football, and the girls played soccer.
2. Helen Keller was born healthy, but she became very ill.
3. A dime isn't much, but it's better than nothing.
4. Ron is a mechanic, and he knows about electronics, too.
5. The computer was broken, so a repairman fixed it.

26-3
1. Incorrect
2. Correct
3. Correct
4. Correct
5. Incorrect
6. Correct
7. Incorrect
8. Correct

9. Incorrect
10. Correct

26-4

1. John woke
2. On the
3. The boys
4. A taxi
5. He floored

26-5

1. We watched a movie, too.
2. Jane, did you do your homework?
3. Bill, did you do your homework, too?
4. The price of oil, Phil, seems to be getting higher.
5. I think, Mr. Jones, that you are correct.

26-6

1. Tom, did you ask your doctor, Dr. Smith?
2. The car, a Volkswagen, swerved to the left, too.
3. Dr. Simon, the famous brain surgeon, studied in France, by the way.
4. As a matter of fact, my brother, a truck driver, knows that road.
5. The airliner, a 747, went into a steep dive.
6. Class, please open your books.
7. Mary, too, wanted to visit the museum, it seems.
8. By the way, did you want to go, too, Jim?
9. Seal the envelope, Jane, and put a stamp on it, too.
10. Remember, Phil, to stay away from spinning propellers, too.

26-7

1. Don went to the store, but he didn't buy anything.
2. By the way, Don went to the store, but he didn't buy anything.
3. By the way, Tony, Don went to the store, but he didn't buy anything.
4. By the way, Tony, Don, my older brother, went to the store, but he didn't buy anything.
5. By the way, Tony, Don, my older brother, went to the store, too, but he didn't buy anything.

26-8

1. Jim laughs; Mary cries.
2. Jim, my cousin, laughs; Mary cries.
3. Jim, my cousin, laughs; Mary, his sister, cries.
4. Jim, my cousin, laughs; Mary, his sister, however, cries.
5. Jim, my cousin, by the way, laughs; Mary, his sister, however, cries.

26-9

1. Correct
2. Incorrect
3. Correct
4. Correct
5. Incorrect
6. Correct
7. Incorrect
8. Correct
9. Incorrect
10. Correct

Quiz

1. address
2. joining
3. conventions

4. earth moon sun
5. semicolon
6. DA
7. N
8. N
9. DA
10. N

Chapter 28

28-1
1. We go
2. Airplanes fly
3. pencils are
4. pen is
5. vase holds
6. chair is
7. people think
8. Jane was
9. We were
10. Tim burns

28-2
1. eggs
2. ropes
3. classes
4. beasts
5. tubs
6. loops
7. bases
8. bosses
9. leads
10. cases

28-3
1. go
2. jump
3. eat
4. play
5. write
6. read
7. count
8. figure
9. break
10. want

28-4
1. S
2. P
3. P
4. S
5. S
6. P
7. P
8. P
9. S
10. S

28-5
1. S
2. P
3. P
4. P

5. S
6. P
7. P
8. S
9. S
10. S

28-6
1. both
2. few
3. many
4. several
5. few
6. few
7. several
8. both
9. many
10. both

28-7
1. run
2. eats
3. reads
4. think
5. believe
6. expects
7. tells
8. argue
9. plays
10. tolerate

28-8
1. One
2. Few
3. most
4. Many
5. Tim
6. John
7. Neither
8. Everyone
9. Both
10. Few

28-9
1. collect
2. speak
3. reads
4. gather
5. think
6. is
7. hears
8. flies
9. is
10. flies

28-10
1. NA
2. A
3. A
4. A
5. NA
6. NA

7. A
8. NA
9. NA
10. NA

28-11
1. cats chase
2. dog chases
3. pennies are
4. pound costs
5. drawings are
6. picture is
7. cash makes
8. pages print
9. boys lift
10. backpack weighs

28-12
1. run
2. play
3. are
4. bake
5. helps
6. helps
7. run
8. runs
9. lives
10. are

Chapter 29
29-1
1. Theywill
2. I am
3. Stanis
4. Youare
5. Shouldhave
6. Mighthave
7. Wewill
8. Youhave
9. Maryis
10. Ronwill

29-2
1. we re
2. they ve
3. car ll
4. should ve
5. Mary s
6. I m
7. might ve
8. Tom ll
9. they re
10. Stan s

29-3
1. she'll
2. they're
3. who's
4. would've

5. Tom'll
6. should've
7. we're
8. Mary's
9. they'll
10. I'm

29-4
1. haven't
2. couldn't
3. she'll
4. he's
5. we're
6. should've
7. everyone'll
8. I'm
9. we'll
10. I'll

29-5
1. Possessive
2. Contraction
3. Contraction
4. Possessive
5. Contraction
6. Possessive
7. Possessive
8. Possessive
9. Possessive
10. Contraction

29-6
1. Contraction
2. Plural
3. Possessive
4. Plural
5. Possessive
6. Contraction
7. Plural
8. Contraction
9. Possessive
10. Plural

29-7
1. Possessive
2. Plural
3. Contraction
4. Plural
5. Contraction
6. Possessive
7. Plural
8. Possessive
9. Plural
10. Contraction

29-8
1. Carl's

2. Carl's
3. NA
4. NA
5. NA
6. engine's
7. NA
8. tape's
9. It's
10. nine's

29-9
1. skateboard's
2. he'd
3. Bob's
4. It's
5. We're
6. everybody's
7. paint's
8. one's
9. He's
10. won't

29-10 (answers will vary)

1. Mom,
 Mr. Parks, my English teacher, called. He's free for a meeting.
 Tim

2. Mom & Dad,
 The dept. store called. They'll deliver the couch on Sat.
 Tim

3. Mr. Smith,
 Mr. Weaver called. He won't be able to make the meeting today. His car has an oil leak.
 Tim

4. Mom,
 I got 5 A's on my report card. I'll show you when I get home from work.
 Tim

5. Mom,
 I'm at the mall. I'll be home for dinner.
 Tim

www.ingramcontent.com/pod-product-compliance
Lightning Source LLC
Chambersburg PA
CBHW032037080426
42733CB00006B/108